SAS® SQL 1: Essentials

Course Notes

SAS® SQL 1: Essentials Course Notes was developed by Davetta Dunlap and Mark Jordan. Additional contributions were made by David Ghan, Marty Hobbs, Alistair Horn, Marya Ilgen-Lieth, Cynthia Johnson, Kathy Kiraly, Natalie McGowan, Linda Mitterling, and Ian Sedgwick. Editing and production support was provided by the Curriculum Development and Support Department.

SAS® SQL 1: Essentials Course Notes

Book code E1500, course code LWSQL1, prepared date 16Jun2009.   LWSQL1_002

ISBN 978-1-60764-242-8

Table of Contents

Course Description

This course teaches you how to process SAS data using Structured Query Language (SQL).

To learn more...

For information on other courses in the curriculum, contact the SAS Education Division at 1-800-333-7660, or send e-mail to training@sas.com. You can also find this information on the Web at support.sas.com/training/ as well as in the Training Course Catalog.

For a list of other SAS books that relate to the topics covered in this Course Notes, USA customers can contact our SAS Publishing Department at 1-800-727-3228 or send e-mail to sasbook@sas.com. Customers outside the USA, please contact your local SAS office.

Also, see the Publications Catalog on the Web at support.sas.com/pubs for a complete list of books and a convenient order form.

Prerequisites

Before attending this class, you should be able to

- submit SAS programs on your operating system
- create and access SAS data sets
- use arithmetic, comparison, and logical operators
- invoke SAS procedures.

You can gain this experience from the SAS® Programming 1: Essentials course. No knowledge of SQL is necessary.

Chapter 1   Getting Started

1.1   Course Logistics

Objectives

- Explain the naming convention that is used for the course files.
- Compare the three levels of exercises that are used in the course.
- Describe at a high level how data is used and stored at Orion Star Sports & Outdoors.
- Navigate to the SAS Help facility.

3

Filename Conventions

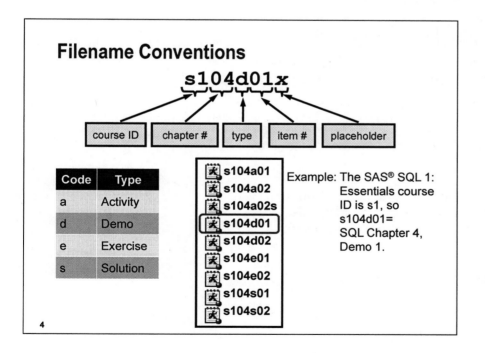

Example: The SAS® SQL 1: Essentials course ID is s1, so s104d01= SQL Chapter 4, Demo 1.

4

Three Levels of Exercises

Level 1	The exercise mimics an example presented in the section.
Level 2	Less information and guidance are provided in the exercise instructions.
Level 3	Only the task you are to perform or the results to be obtained are provided. Typically, you will need to use the Help facility.

✎ You are not expected to complete all of the exercises in the time allotted. Choose the exercise or exercises that are at the level you are most comfortable with.

5

Orion Star Sports & Outdoors

Orion Star Sports & Outdoors is a fictitious global sports and outdoors retailer with traditional stores, an online store, and a large catalog business.

The corporate headquarters is located in the United States with offices and stores in many countries throughout the world.

Orion Star has about 1,000 employees and 90,000 customers, processes approximately 150,000 orders annually, and purchases products from 64 suppliers.

6

Orion Star Data

As is the case with most organizations, Orion Star has a large amount of data about its customers, suppliers, products, and employees. Much of this information is stored in transactional systems in various formats.

Using applications and processes such as SAS Data Integration Studio, this transactional information was extracted, transformed, and loaded into a data warehouse.

Data marts were created to meet the needs of specific departments such as Marketing.

7

The examples and exercises in this course are based on the files of a fictitious retail company. These files include information about the following:

- employees
- customers
- sales

The SAS Help Facility

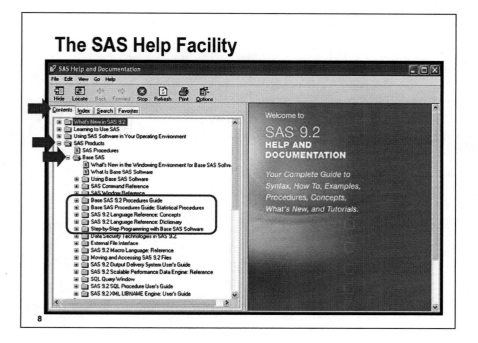

8

The SAS Help Facility

- Invoke the SAS Help facility by doing one of the following actions:
  - Type **Help** on the command line.
  - Select **Help** from the menu.
  - Select the **Help** button on the toolbar.
- Additional help and documentation are available at www.support.sas.com/documentation.

9

The SAS Help Facility

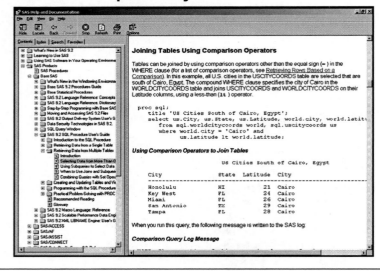

10

Setup for the Poll

- Start your SAS session.
- Open the SAS Help facility.

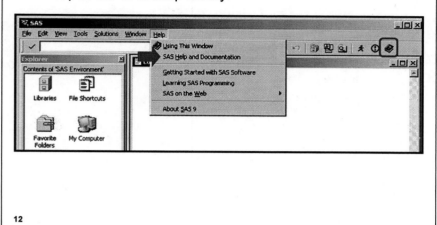

12

1.01 Poll

Were you able to open the Help facility in your SAS session?

○ Yes

○ No

13

1.02 Multiple Choice Poll

Which choice best describes your programming and SQL experience level?

a. I have little or no programming experience.
b. I can write programs in languages other than SQL.
c. I can write database-specific SQL programs.
d. I can write SAS PROC SQL programs.
e. I can program in multiple languages, including SQL.

14

1.03 Multiple Choice Poll

What version of SAS do you use?

a. I do not use SAS.
b. SAS 8.2
c. SAS®9
d. SAS 9.1
e. SAS 9.2
f. Other

15

1.2   Introducing the Structured Query Language

Objectives

- Describe the historical development of Structured Query Language (SQL).
- Explain how SQL is used.

17

Structured Query Language

Structured Query Language (SQL) is a standardized language originally designed as a relational database query tool.

SQL is currently used in many software products to retrieve and update data.

18

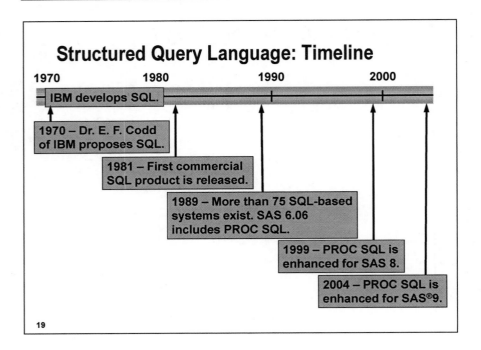

Structured Query Language: Timeline

1970   1980   1990   2000

IBM develops SQL.

1970 – Dr. E. F. Codd of IBM proposes SQL.

1981 – First commercial SQL product is released.

1989 – More than 75 SQL-based systems exist. SAS 6.06 includes PROC SQL.

1999 – PROC SQL is enhanced for SAS 8.

2004 – PROC SQL is enhanced for SAS®9.

19

The SQL Procedure

The SQL procedure has the following characteristics:

- enables the use of SQL in SAS
- is part of Base SAS software
- follows American National Standards Institute (ANSI) standards
- includes enhancements for compatibility with SAS software

20

The SQL Procedure Features

With PROC SQL, you can use SQL language syntax
to do the following:

- query SAS data sets
- generate reports from SAS data sets
- combine SAS data sets in many ways
- create and delete SAS data sets, views, and indexes
- update existing SAS data sets
- sometimes reproduce the results of multiple DATA
  and procedure steps with a single query

21

 After it is invoked, PROC SQL remains active until terminated with a QUIT statement, or subsequent invocation of another SAS procedure or DATA step. Each PROC SQL query (statement) is automatically and immediately executed when it is submitted. A RUN statement is not needed.

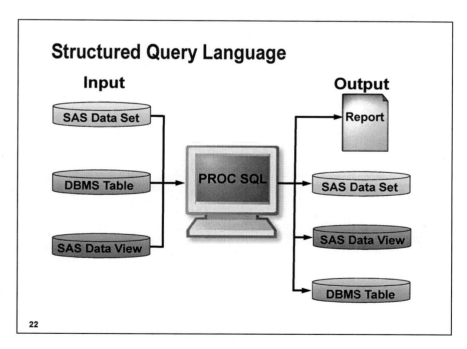

22

 You must have appropriate authority to create objects in your DBMS (database management system).

Setup for the Poll

- Issue a LIBNAME statement for the **orion** library, which contains the course data. You can use the **s101a01** program if you want. Change the data location, if necessary.
- Submit the program **s101a02**.
- Answer the following questions:
  - What is the name of the input SAS data set?
  - Do the column names appear in the SELECT statement?

24   s101a02

1.04 Multiple Choice Poll

What is the name of the input SAS data set?

a. orion.Employee_payroll
b. SQL
c. SELECT
d. None of the above

25

1.05 Poll

Did the names of the columns that appeared in the results appear in the SELECT statement in the code?

○ Yes

○ No

27

The SQL Procedure

The SQL procedure **is**

- a tool for querying data
- a tool for data manipulation and management
- an augmentation to the DATA step.

The SQL procedure is **not**

- a DATA step replacement
- a custom reporting tool.

29

SAS Data Sets

A SAS data set can be any of the following:

- a SAS data file that stores data descriptions and data values together in native SAS format
- a DBMS table accessed via a SAS/ACCESS engine
- a SAS data view, using one of the following technologies:
  - PROC SQL view – a stored SQL query that retrieves data stored in other tables
  - DATA step view – a stored DATA step that retrieves data stored in other files
  - SAS/ACCESS view – a stored ACCESS descriptor containing information required to retrieve data stored in a DBMS (older technology)

30

SAS/ACCESS descriptors are no longer recommended for accessing relational databases. SQL views enable use of the LIBNAME statement, which provides greater control over DBMS operations such as locking, spooling, and data-type conversions, as well as handling long field names. In addition, SQL views are platform independent; SAS/ACCESS descriptors are not.

If you currently use SAS/ACCESS descriptors, the CV2VIEW procedure in SAS 9.1 can convert them to SQL views.

Terminology

Data Processing	SAS	SQL
File	Data Set	Table
Record	Observation	Row
Field	Variable	Column

31

1.3 Introducing the Business Scenario

Objectives

- Describe the data used in this course.
- Explain the relationships between the various tables.

34

The Orion Star Company

Analyze a subset of Orion Star data including the following:

- employees in the United States and Australia
- customers from Australia, Canada, Germany, Israel, South Africa, the United States, and Turkey
- the years 2002 through 2007

The tables and columns are related as shown on the next slide.

35

✎   All tables required to complete the exercises are listed on the following pages. Some of the tables used for demonstrations might not be shown.

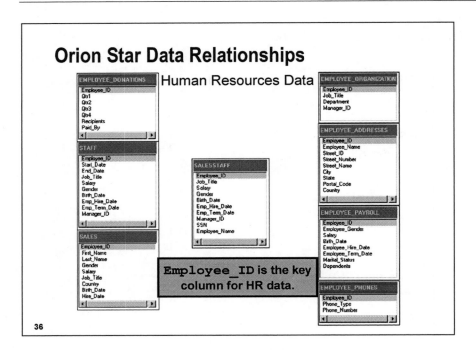

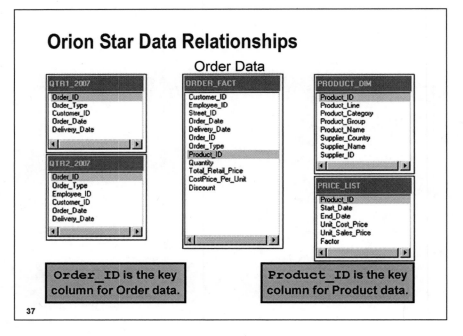

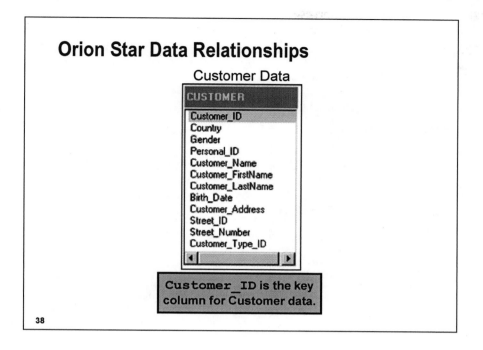

Orion Star Data Relationships

Customer Data

CUSTOMER

- Customer_ID
- Country
- Gender
- Personal_ID
- Customer_Name
- Customer_FirstName
- Customer_LastName
- Birth_Date
- Customer_Address
- Street_ID
- Street_Number
- Customer_Type_ID

Customer_ID is the key column for Customer data.

38

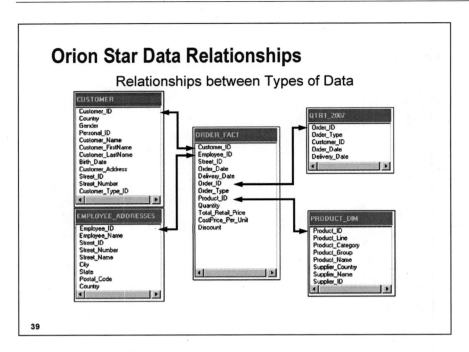

The **orion.Order_Fact** table contains the key identifier columns **Employee_ID**, **Customer_ID**, **Order_ID**, and **Product_ID**, and can be used to relate data from the different groups to each other. For instance, to identify the name of an employee who made any sale to a customer in South Africa in 2007, you need information from three different tables:

- **Employee_Name** from **orion.Employee_Addresses**

- **Order_Date** from **orion.Order_Fact**

- **Country** from **orion.Customer**

You can relate **Employee_Name** to **Order_Date** by finding the rows in **orion.Employee_Addresses** and **orion.Order_Fact** where **Employee_ID** matches.

You can relate **Country** to **Order_Date** by finding the rows in **orion.Customer** and **orion.Order_Fact** where **Customer_ID** matches.

By the end of this class, you will be able to retrieve the employee name (**orion.Employee_addresses**) for employees who sold something with an order date in 2007 (**orion.Order_fact**) to a customer where **Country="ZA"** (**orion.Customer**) using **orion.Order_fact** as the cross-referencing table.

1.06 Multiple Answer Poll

Which of the Order data tables contain the column `Employee_ID`?

a. `orion.QTR1_2007`

b. `orion.QTR2_2007`

c. `orion.Order_Fact`

d. `orion.Price_List`

e. `orion.Product_Dim`

f. All of them

41

Orion Country Codes

Code	Country
AU	Australia
CA	Canada
DE	Germany
IL	Israel
TR	Turkey
US	United States
ZA	South Africa

43

Orion Product ID Codes

Codes are numeric in the form **XXYYZZZZZZZ**.

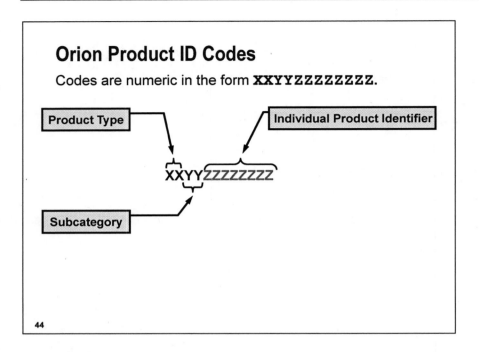

44

Orion Product ID Codes

Code	Product Type
21	Children
22	Clothes and Shoes
23	Outdoors
24	Sports

45

1.07 Quiz

Use the data relationship charts on pages 1-16 through 1-18 to answer the following question:

Which table(s) contains the column **Order_Date**?

47   **s101a03**

Alternatively, if you do not want to use the data relationship charts, you can do one of the following:

- Right-click the table icon in the SAS Explorer window, and select **View Columns** to view the data structure.

- Submit the **s101a03** program code, which generates a report referencing each of the tables in the **orion** library, and review the listing output.

1.4   Solutions

Solutions to Student Activities (Polls/Quizzes)

1.04 Multiple Choice Poll – Correct Answer

What is the name of the input SAS data set?

(a.) orion.Employee_payroll
b. SQL
c. SELECT
d. None of the above

26

1.05 Poll – Correct Answer

Did the names of the columns that appeared in the results appear in the SELECT statement in the code?

○ Yes
(○) No

28

1.06 Multiple Answer Poll – Correct Answer

Which of the Order data tables contain the column
`Employee_ID`?

a. `orion.QTR1_2007`
(b.) `orion.QTR2_2007`
(c.) `orion.Order_Fact`
d. `orion.Price_List`
e. `orion.Product_Dim`
f. All of them

42

1.07 Quiz – Correct Answer

Use the data relationship charts on pages 1-16 through
1-18 to answer the following question:

Which table(s) contains the column `Order_Date`?

1. `orion.Order_Fact`
2. `orion.Qtr1_2007`
3. `orion.Qtr2_2007`

48   s101a03

Chapter 2 Basic Queries

2.1 Overview of the SQL Procedure

Objectives

- List key features of the SQL procedure.
- Identify key syntax of the SQL procedure.

3

The SQL Procedure

The following are features of PROC SQL:

- The PROC SQL statement does not need to be repeated with each query.
- Each statement is processed individually.
- No PROC PRINT step is needed to view query results.
- No PROC SORT step is needed to order query results.
- No RUN statement is needed.
- PROC SQL is terminated with a QUIT statement.

4

SQL is considered a modular language because queries (or statements) are composed of smaller building blocks (or clauses).

You can use the Output Delivery System (ODS) to customize SQL output.

The SELECT Statement

A SELECT statement is used to query one or more
SAS data sets.

```
proc sql;
    select Employee_ID, Employee_Gender,
           Salary
       from orion.Employee_Payroll
       where Employee_Gender = 'F'
       order by Salary desc;
quit;
```

✎ Although it contains multiple clauses, each SELECT
   statement begins with the SELECT keyword and
   ends with a semicolon.

5   s102d01

The SELECT Statement

A SELECT statement contains smaller building blocks
called *clauses*.

```
proc sql;
    select Employee_ID, Employee_Gender,
           Salary
clauses from orion.Employee_Payroll
       where Employee_Gender = 'F'
       order by Salary desc;
quit;
```

6   s102d01

✎ Remember to place a semicolon at the end of the last clause **only**.

SELECT Statement Syntax

General form of the SELECT statement with selected clauses:

```
SELECT column-1<, ...column-n>
    FROM table-1|view-1<, ...table-n|view-n>
    <WHERE expression>
    <GROUP BY column-1<, ...column-n>>
    <HAVING expression>
    <ORDER BY column-1<DESC><, ...column-n>>;
```

7

SELECT   specifies the columns to be selected.

FROM   specifies the table to be queried.

WHERE   subsets the data based on a condition.

GROUP BY   classifies the data into groups.

HAVING   subsets groups of data based on a group condition.

ORDER BY   sorts rows by the values of specific columns. By default, results are sorted in ascending order. Use the DESC keyword to sort in descending order.

The order of the above clauses within the SELECT statement **is** significant. Some programmers find it helpful to use a mnemonic as a memory aid.

table   is a SAS data set (data file or data view).

column   is a column name or expression that can include DATA step functions, summary functions, or character literals.

Features of the SELECT Statement

The SELECT statement has the following features:

- selects data that meets certain conditions
- groups data
- specifies an order for the data
- formats the data
- queries 1 to 256 tables

8

Table names can be 1 to 32 characters in length and are not case sensitive.

Variable names can be 1 to 32 characters in length and are stored in mixed case, but are normalized for lookups and comparisons. However, the first usage of the variable name, when the table is created, determines the capitalization pattern.

Librefs and filerefs are limited to eight characters. Starting in SAS®9, format and informat names can be a maximum of 32 characters in length.

The maximum number of tables in a query increased to 256 in SAS 9.1.3 Service Pack 4. Prior to SAS 9.1.3 Service Pack 4, the maximum number of tables in a query was limited to 32.

Setup for the Poll

- Open and submit the program **s102a01**.
- The program consists of three steps. Consider the output from the first two steps.
  1) Which step generated errors?
  2) What error message was generated?
- Run the third step and review the SAS log.

10

2.01 Multiple Choice Poll

Which step generated errors?

a. Step 1
b. Step 2
c. Step 3

11

2.02 Quiz

What error message was generated in Step 2?

```
  /* Step 2 */
proc sql;
   from orion.Employee_Payroll
   select Employee_ID, Employee_Gender,
          Salary
   where Employee_Gender = 'M'
   order by EmpID;
quit;
```

14   s102a01

The VALIDATE Keyword

Use the VALIDATE keyword to check the SELECT statement syntax.

Partial SAS Log

```
proc sql;
   validate
   select Employee_ID, Employee_Gender,
          Salary
      from orion.Employee_Payroll
      where Employee_Gender = 'F'
      order by Salary desc;
NOTE: PROC SQL statement has valid syntax.
```

16   s102d02

The VALIDATE Keyword

A common syntax error is to include a comma after the last item in a list.

Partial SAS Log

```
proc sql;
   validate
      select Employee_ID, Employee_Gender,
             Salary,
         from orion.Employee_Payroll
         where Employee_Gender = 'F'
         order by Salary desc;
ERROR: Syntax error, expecting one of the following: !, !!, &,
       (, *, . . .
```

17   s102d03

In SQL, use commas to separate items in a list, such as a list of column or table names.

Features of the VALIDATE Keyword

The VALIDATE keyword has the following features:

- tests the syntax of a query without executing the query
- checks column name validity
- prints error messages for invalid queries
- is used only for SELECT statements

18

The NOEXEC Option

Use the NOEXEC procedure option to check the syntax of the entire procedure without executing the statements.

Partial SAS Log

```
proc sql noexec;
   select Employee_ID, Employee_Gender,
          Salary
      from orion.Employee_Payroll
      where Employee_Gender = ' F'
      order by Salary desc;
NOTE: Statement not executed due to NOEXEC option.
```

19   s102d04

The NOEXEC option checks for invalid syntax in all types of SQL statements. The VALIDATE keyword applies only to the SELECT statement.

Resetting Options

You can use the RESET statement to add or change PROC SQL options without re-invoking the procedure.

General form of the RESET statement:

RESET *option(s)*;

> After the EXEC option is reset, the query can be executed.

For example:

```
reset exec;
    select Employee_ID, Employee_Gender,
           Salary
       from orion.Employee_Payroll
       where Employee_Gender = 'F'
       order by Salary desc;
quit;
```

20   s102d04

Additional PROC SQL Statements

PROC SQL supports many statements in addition to the SELECT statement.

PROC SQL *<option <option>...>*;

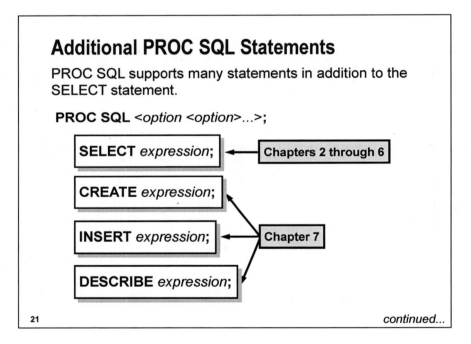

SELECT *expression*;   ← Chapters 2 through 6

CREATE *expression*;

INSERT *expression*;   ← Chapter 7

DESCRIBE *expression*;

21   *continued...*

SELECT	specifies columns to be printed.
CREATE	builds new tables.
INSERT	adds rows of data to tables.
DESCRIBE	displays table attributes or view definitions.

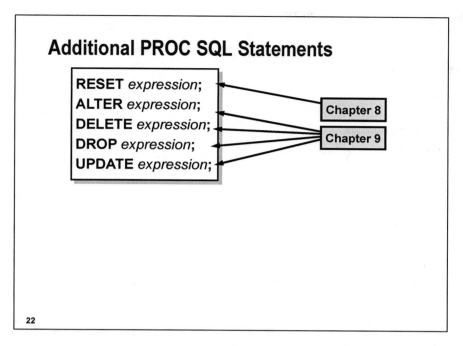

RESET	adds to or changes PROC SQL options without re-invoking the procedure.
ALTER	adds, drops, and modifies columns in a table.
DELETE	eliminates unwanted rows from a table or view.
DROP	eliminates entire tables, views, or indexes.
UPDATE	modifies data values in existing rows of a table or view.

2.2 Specifying Columns

Objectives

- Display columns directly from a table.
- Display columns calculated from other columns in a query.
- Calculate columns conditionally using the CASE expression.

25

Business Scenario

Produce a report that contains the employee identifier, gender, and salary for all Orion Star employees. The data is contained in the `orion.Employee_Payroll` table, a table with which you are not familiar.

26

Retrieving Data from a Table

You can use an asterisk in a SELECT statement to print all of a table's columns in the order that they were stored.

```
proc sql;
select *
    from orion.Employee_Payroll;
quit;
```

Partial PROC SQL Output

```
                        The SAS System

           Employee_           Birth_  Employee_  Employee_  Marital_
Employee_ID Gender   Salary      Date  Hire_Date  Term_Date  Status  Dependents

   120101    M       163040     6074    15887        .       S          0
   120102    M       108255     3510    10744        .       O          2
   120103    M        87975    -3996     5114        .       M          1
   120104    F        46230    -2061     7671        .       M          1
   120105    F        27110     5468    14365        .       S          0
   120106    M        26960    -5487     5114        .       M          2
```

27   s102d05

The FEEDBACK Option

When using an asterisk for the select list, you can specify the FEEDBACK option to write the expanded SELECT statement to the SAS log.

General form of the PROC SQL FEEDBACK option:

```
PROC SQL FEEDBACK;
    SELECT *
        FROM table-1|view-1<, ...table-n|view-n>
        <WHERE expression>
        <GROUP BY column-1<, ...column-n>>
        <HAVING expression>
        <ORDER BY column-1<DESC><, ...column-n>>;
QUIT;
```

28

Setup for the Poll

Submit the program **s102a02** and review the SAS log to answer the following question:

- How are the column names represented in the expanded log?

30

2.03 Multiple Choice Poll

How are the column names represented in the expanded log?

a. The column names are preceded by the table name (**EMPLOYEE_PAYROLL**).

b. The column names are preceded by the library reference (**ORION**).

c. The column names are preceded by **Work**.

31

The FEEDBACK Option

The column names are preceded by the table name.

Partial SAS Log

```
proc sql feedback;
   select *
      from orion.Employee_Payroll;
NOTE: Statement transforms to
      select EMPLOYEE_PAYROLL.Employee_ID,
EMPLOYEE_PAYROLL.Employee_Gender,EMPLOYEE_PAYROLL.Salary,
EMPLOYEE_PAYROLL.Birth_Date,EMPLOYEE_PAYROLL.Employee_Hire_Date,
EMPLOYEE_PAYROLL.Employee_Term_Date,
EMPLOYEE_PAYROLL.Marital_Status,EMPLOYEE_PAYROLL.Dependents
         from ORION.EMPLOYEE_PAYROLL;
quit;
```

33   s102d06

Retrieving Data from a Table

You can also familiarize yourself with the columns in
a table using the DESCRIBE statement.

```
proc sql;
   describe table orion.Employee_Payroll;
quit;
```

Partial SAS Log

```
Employee_ID num format=12.,
Employee_Gender char(1),
Salary num,
Birth_Date num,
Employee_Term_Date num,
Marital_Status char(1)
Dependents num
```

34   s102d07

Retrieving Data from a Table

After familiarizing yourself with the columns in a table, you can specify the columns to be printed in the order that you want them displayed by using a column list in the SELECT statement.

```
proc sql;
    select Employee_ID, Employee_Gender,
          Salary
       from orion.Employee_Payroll;
quit;
```

s102d08

35

Remember to use commas to separate items in a list, such as a list of column or table names.

Employee IDs, Genders, and Salaries

Partial PROC SQL Output

```
               The SAS System

                     Employee_
    Employee_ID  Gender            Salary

        120101   M                 163040
        120102   M                 108255
        120103   M                  87975
        120104   F                  46230
        120105   F                  27110
        120106   M                  26960
        120107   F                  30475
        120108   F                  27660
        120109   F                  26495
```

36

Business Scenario

You need to modify your previous report to drop the **Employee_Gender** column, and add a new column named **Bonus**. The new column should contain an amount equal to 10% of the employee's salary.

37

Calculated Columns

Calculate the new column's value using the data in an existing column, and name the new columns using the AS keyword.

```
proc sql;
   select Employee_ID, Salary,
          Salary * .10 as Bonus
      from orion.Employee_Payroll;
quit;
```

38   s102d09

🖉   The new column name (**Bonus**) is called an *alias*. Assigning an alias to a calculated column is optional, but if an alias **is** assigned, the AS keyword is required. Omission of the alias causes the column heading to be blank.

Employee Bonuses

Partial PROC SQL Output

```
                    The SAS System

Employee_ID          Salary           Bonus
──────────────────────────────────────────────
     120101          163040           16304
     120102          108255         10825.5
     120103           87975          8797.5
     120104           46230            4623
     120105           27110            2711
     120106           26960            2696
     120107           30475          3047.5
     120108           27660            2766
     120109           26495          2649.5
```

39

Business Scenario

You need to modify the previous bonus report to conditionally calculate bonuses based on the employee's job title.

- Level I employees receive a 5% bonus.
- Level II employees receive a 7% bonus.
- Level III employees receive a 10% bonus.
- Level IV employees receive a 12% bonus.
- All others receive an 8% bonus.

The **Staff** table contains all of the information that you need to create this report.

40

Computing Columns Conditionally

Read data from the `orion.Staff` table, and base your bonus calculations on the job title and salary.

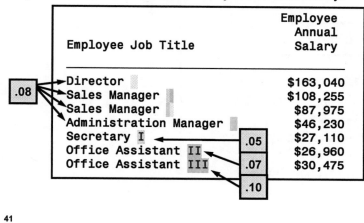

Employee Job Title	Employee Annual Salary
Director	$163,040
Sales Manager	$108,255
Sales Manager	$87,975
Administration Manager	$46,230
Secretary I	$27,110
Office Assistant II	$26,960
Office Assistant III	$30,475

.08

.05

.07

.10

41

2.04 Multiple Choice Poll

Which of these SAS character functions will be the most useful for identifying the level value for conditional processing?

a. CHAR( )

b. FIND( )

c. SCAN( )

d. SUBSTR( )

43

The SCAN Function

The SCAN function returns the *n*th word or segment from a character string after breaking it up by the delimiters.

General form of the SCAN function:

SCAN(*string,n<,charlist><,modifier(s)>*)

string   a character constant, variable, or expression

n   an integer specifying the number of the word or segment that you want SCAN to select

charlist   characters used as delimiters to separate words

modifier   a character that modifies the action of the SCAN function

45

If the third argument (*charlist*) is omitted, the default delimiters are as shown below:

ASCII (PC, UNIX)	blank . < (+ | & ! $ *) ; - / , % ^
EBCDIC (z/0s)	blank . < (+ | & ! $ *) ; - / , % ¢ ¬

Extracting the Level from `Job_Title`

Example: Return the third word from `Job_Title` and use a blank space as the delimiter.

```
scan(Job_Title,3,' ')
```

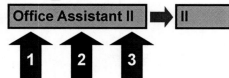

46   ...

Extracting the Level from `Job_Title`

Some `Job_Title` values have fewer than three words. If the value of *n* is greater than the number of words in the character string, the SCAN function returns a missing value.

```
scan(Job_Title,3,' ')
```

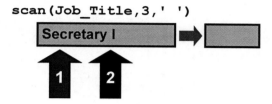

47

Extracting the Level from `Job_Title`

If the value of *n* is negative, the SCAN function selects the word in the character string starting from the end of the string.

```
scan(Job_Title,-1,' ')
```

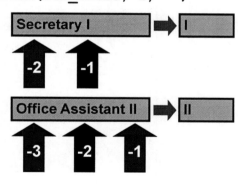

48

The CASE Expression

You can use a CASE expression in a SELECT statement to create new columns.

General form of the CASE expression in the SELECT statement:

```
SELECT column-1<, ...column-n>
    CASE <case-operand>
        WHEN when-condition THEN result-expression
        <WHEN when-condition THEN result-expression>
        <ELSE result-expression>
    END <as column>
FROM table;
```

49

Calculating the Bonus

The CASE expression creates employee bonuses based on job titles. Two methods are available.

Method 1:

```
proc sql;
    select Job_Title, Salary,
            case scan(Job_Title,-1,' ')
                when 'I' then Salary*.05
                when 'II' then Salary*.07
                when 'III' then Salary*.10
                when 'IV' then Salary*.12
                else Salary*.08
            end as Bonus
        from orion.Staff;
quit;
```

50   s102d09a

A CASE expression returns a single value. The CASE expression is evaluated for each row of a table or view. The WHEN clauses select the value returned, based on the conditions that you specify. The first WHEN clause that evaluates as true determines which value is returned by the CASE expression. Subsequent WHEN clauses are not evaluated, which is similar to a series of IF-THEN/ELSE statements in conventional SAS programming. The optional ELSE expression provides an alternate action if none of the WHEN expressions is true. If no ELSE expression is present and every WHEN condition is false, the CASE expression returns a missing value.

Calculating the Bonus

Method 2:

```
proc sql;
   select Job_Title, Salary,
          case
             when scan(Job_Title,-1,' ')='I'
                  then Salary*.05
             when scan(Job_Title,-1,' ')='II'
                  then Salary*.07
             when scan(Job_Title,-1,' ')='III'
                  then Salary*.10
             when scan(Job_Title,-1,' ')='IV'
                  then Salary*.12
             else Salary*.08
          end as Bonus
      from orion.Staff;
quit;
```

51   s102d09a

Method 1 is more efficient because the SCAN function is evaluated only once. This method also assumes an EQUAL comparison operator, which means that if you need another operator, you must use Method 2.

Calculating the Bonus

Partial PROC SQL Output

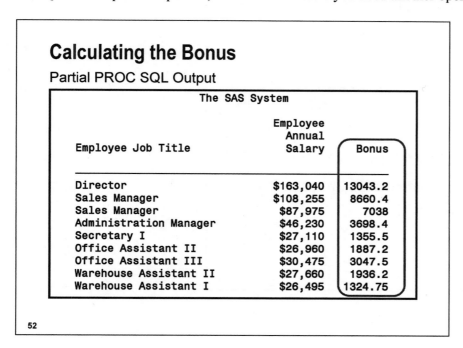

Employee Job Title	Employee Annual Salary	Bonus
Director	$163,040	13043.2
Sales Manager	$108,255	8660.4
Sales Manager	$87,975	7038
Administration Manager	$46,230	3698.4
Secretary I	$27,110	1355.5
Office Assistant II	$26,960	1887.2
Office Assistant III	$30,475	3047.5
Warehouse Assistant II	$27,660	1936.2
Warehouse Assistant I	$26,495	1324.75

52

Business Scenario

Management needs a report that includes the employee identifier, gender, and age for an upcoming audit.

Here is a sketch of the desired report:

Employee_ID	Employee_Gender	Age
120101	M	31
120102	M	38

53

SAS Date Values (Review)

A SAS date is stored as the number of whole days between January 1, 1960, and the date specified.

Stored Values

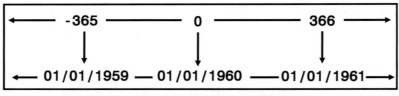

Display Values (formatted MMDDYY10.)

54

Selected SAS Numeric Functions

The following SAS numeric functions are frequently used when you work with SAS dates.

Function	Used To Return	Example
TODAY()	today's date in SAS date form	`today() as date`
MONTH(*arg*)	the month portion of a SAS date variable as an integer between 1-12	`month(Birth_Date) as Birth_Month`
INT(*arg*)	the integer portion of a numeric value	`int(fullage) as age`

55

Additionally, SAS date constants are used throughout this course.

Syntax	Used to	Example
'*ddMONyyyy*'d	convert a calendar date into a SAS date	`date='15JUN2008'd`

Most SAS DATA step functions are supported. However, some are not supported, for example, the LAG and DIF functions. For a complete list of functions that are not supported in SQL, see the most recent documentation.

Calculated Columns Using SAS Dates

Calculating the age of each employee.

```
proc sql;
   select Employee_ID, Employee_Gender,
          int((today()-Birth_Date)/365.25)
          as Age
      from orion.Employee_Payroll;
quit;
```

56

s102d10
...

Using SAS Dates in Calculations

Calculate **Age** based on today's date being 14NOV2007 and a **Birth_Date** value of 18AUG1976.

`17484`   `6074`

```
proc sql;
   select Employee_ID, Employee_Gender,
          int((today()-Birth_Date)/365.25)
          as Age
      from orion.Employee_Payroll;
quit;
```

57   s102d10
                                                                ...

Using SAS Dates in Calculations

Calculate **Age** based on today's date being 14NOV2007 and a **Birth_Date** value of 18AUG1976.

```
proc sql;
   select Employee_ID, Employee_Gender,
          int((today()-Birth_Date)/365.25)
          as Age
      from orion.Employee_Payroll;
quit;
```
`31.23887748`

58   s102d10
                                                                ...

Using SAS Dates in Calculations

Calculate **Age** based on today's date being 14NOV2007 and a **Birth_Date** value of 18AUG1976.

```
proc sql;
   select Employee_ID, Employee_Gender,
   31 ──▶ int((today()-Birth_Date)/365.25)
          as Age
      from orion.Employee_Payroll;
quit;
```

s102d10

59

Employee Ages

Partial PROC SQL Output

```
                    The SAS System

                 Employee_
Employee_ID      Gender                Age


     120101      M                      31
     120102      M                      38
     120103      M                      58
     120104      F                      53
     120105      F                      32
     120106      M                      62
     120107      F                      58
     120108      F                      23
     120109      F                      20
```

60

2.05 Quiz

What numeric function would you use to create the **Birth_Month** column for the following rows from the **Employee_Payroll** table?

```
                        The SAS System

                                           Employee_
 Employee_ID   Birth_Date   Birth_Month    Gender

    120101          6074             8      M
    120102          3510             8      M
    120103         -3996             1      M
    120104         -2061             5      F
    120105          5468            12      F
```

62

2.06 Poll

Would you like to create a table from the results of your queries?

○ Yes
○ No

65

Creating a Table

To create and populate a table with the rows from an SQL query, use the CREATE TABLE statement.

General form of the CREATE TABLE statement:

```
CREATE TABLE table-name AS
    query-expression;
```

66

Create and Populate a Table with an SQL Query

The SELECT list defines the structure of the `work.birth_months` table, and the rows are populated with the data returned by the query.

```
proc sql;            Define table columns.
   create table work.birth_months as
      select Employee_ID, Birth_Date,
             month(Birth_Date) as
             Birth_Month,
             Employee_gender
      from orion.Employee_Payroll;
   describe table work.birth_months;
   select * from work.birth_months;
quit;
```

67   s102d10b

If a new column is computed and contains an alias (for example, **Birth_Month**), the column name in the new table is the name of the alias. Assigning an alias to a calculated column is optional. If an alias is not assigned and a table is created, the omission of the AS keyword causes the new column name to be **_TEMA001**. If other new columns are created without the AS keyword, the new names would be **_TEMA002**, **_TEMA003**, and so on.

Create and Populate a Table with an SQL Query

Partial SAS Log

```
NOTE: Table WORK.BIRTH_MONTHS created, with 424
rows and 4 columns.
```

```
create table WORK.BIRTH_MONTHS
  (Employee_ID num format=12.,
   Birth_Date num,
   Birth_Month num,
   Employee_Gender char(1))
```

68

Create and Populate a Table with an SQL Query

Partial SAS Output (5 out of 424)

Employee_ID	Employee_Birth_Date	Birth_Month	Gender
120101	6074	8	M
120102	3510	8	M
120103	-3996	1	M
120104	-2061	5	F
120105	5468	12	F

69

 **Exercises**

Submit a LIBNAME statement to assign the libref **orion** to the SAS data library for this course.

```
libname orion '_____';
```

Level 1

1. **Querying a Table**

    a. Write a query that displays all rows and all columns from the **orion.Employee_Payroll** table.

    Partial PROC SQL Output

Employee_ID	Employee_ Gender	Salary	Birth_ Date	Employee_ Hire_Date	Employee_ Term_Date	Marital_ Status	Dependents
120101	M	163040	6074	15887	.	S	0
120102	M	108255	3510	10744	.	O	2
120103	M	87975	-3996	5114	.	M	1
120104	F	46230	-2061	7671	.	M	1
120105	F	27110	5468	14365	.	S	0

    b. Recall the previous query and alter it so that only the columns for **Employee_ID**, **Employee_Gender**, **Marital_Status**, and **Salary** are displayed.

    Partial PROC SQL Output

		The SAS System		
	Employee_ID	Employee_ Gender	Marital_ Status	Salary
	120101	M	S	163040
	120102	M	O	108255
	120103	M	M	87975
	120104	F	M	46230
	120105	F	S	27110

Level 2

2. Calculating a Column

Write a query that generates the report below. The report should do the following:

- display **Employee_ID**, **Employee_Gender**, **Marital_Status**, **Salary**, and a new column (**Tax**) that is one-third of the employee's salary
- use the **orion.Employee_Payroll** table

Partial PROC SQL Output

	The SAS System			
Employee_ID	Employee_ Gender	Marital_ Status	Salary	Tax
120101	M	S	163040	54346.67
120102	M	O	108255	36085
120103	M	M	87975	29325
120104	F	M	46230	15410
120105	F	S	27110	9036.667
120106	M	M	26960	8986.667
120107	F	M	30475	10158.33
120108	F	S	27660	9220
120109	F	M	26495	8831.667
120110	M	M	28615	9538.333
120111	M	M	26895	8965
120112	F	M	26550	8850
120113	F	S	26870	8956.667
120114	F	M	31285	10428.33
120115	M	M	26500	8833.333
120116	M	S	29250	9750
120117	M	O	31670	10556.67
120118	M	M	28090	9363.333
120119	M	M	30255	10085
120120	F	M	27645	9215

Level 3

3. Conditional Processing

Create a report that displays **Employee_ID**, **Level**, **Salary**, and **Salary_Range** using the **orion.Staff** table. **Level** and **Salary_Range** are two new columns in the report. The report should also only contain salary information for the Orion Star executives. Conditionally assign values to the two new columns as follows:

Job_Title (Last Word)	Level	Salary Ranges		
		Low	Medium	High
Manager	Manager	< 52,000	52,000-72,000	> 72,000
Director	Director	<108,000	108,000-135,000	> 135,000
Officer, President	Executive	<240,000	240,000-300,000	> 300,000
Other	N/A	DO NOT INCLUDE IN THE REPORT.		

Partial PROC SQL Output

```
            Salary Ranges For Orion Star Management

                               Employee
                                 Annual
          Employee ID  Level     Salary  Salary_Range
          ─────────────────────────────────────────────
               120101  Director  $163,040  High
               120659  Director  $161,290  High
               121142  Director  $156,065  High
               120800  Director  $80,210   Low
               120270  Director  $48,435   Low
               120259  Executive $433,800  High
               120262  Executive $268,455  Medium
               120261  Executive $243,190  Medium
               120260  Executive $207,885  Low
               121141  Executive $194,885  Low
               120102  Manager   $108,255  High
               121143  Manager   $95,090   High
               120103  Manager   $87,975   High
```

2.3 Specifying Rows

Objectives

- Select a subset of rows in a query.
- Eliminate duplicate rows in a query.

73

Specifying Rows in a Table

Example: Display the names of the Orion Star departments
using the **orion.Employee_Organization**
table.

```
proc sql;
   select Department
      from orion.Employee_Organization;
quit;
```

74   s102d11

All Rows in a Table

Partial PROC SQL Output

```
                  The SAS System
Department
_____

Sales Management
Sales Management
Sales Management
Administration
Administration
Administration
Administration
Administration
Administration
Administration
Administration
Administration
Administration
Administration
Administration
Administration
Engineering
Engineering
```

75

Eliminating Duplicate Rows

Use the DISTINCT keyword to eliminate duplicate rows
in query results.

Example: Determine the distinct departments in the
         Orion Star organization.

```
proc sql;
   select distinct Department
      from orion.Employee_Organization;
quit;
```

76   s102d11

✎   The DISTINCT keyword applies to all columns in the SELECT list. One row is displayed for
     each unique combination of values.

Eliminating Duplicate Rows

Partial PROC SQL Output

```
                    The SAS System

Department
_____

Accounts
Accounts Management
Administration
Concession Management
Engineering
Executives
Group Financials
Group HR Management
IS
Logistics Management
Marketing
Purchasing
Sales
```

77

2.07 Multiple Answer Poll

Which SELECT clauses select only the unique combinations of **Employee_Gender** and **Job_Title**?

a. `select distinct Employee_Gender, distinct Job_Title...`

b. `select unique Employee_Gender, Job_Title...`

c. `select distinct Employee_Gender, Job_Title...`

d. `select distinct Employee_Gender Job_Title...`

79

Business Scenario

Create a list of personnel with salaries above $112,000.
Include the employee identifier, job title, and salary.

81

Subsetting with the WHERE Clause

Use a WHERE clause to specify a condition that the
data must satisfy before being selected.

Example: Display all employees who earn more than
        $112,000.

```
proc sql;
   select Employee_ID, Job_Title, Salary
      from orion.Staff
      where Salary > 112000;
quit;
```

82   s102d12

Subsetting with the WHERE Clause

Partial PROC SQL Output

```
                     The SAS System
                                          Employee
                                            Annual
     Employee ID  Employee Job Title         Salary

         120101  Director                  $163,040
         120259  Chief Executive Officer   $433,800
         120260  Chief Marketing Officer   $207,885
         120261  Chief Sales Officer       $243,190
         120262  Chief Financial Officer   $268,455
         120659  Director                  $161,290
         121141  Vice President            $194,885
         121142  Director                  $156,065
```

83

Subsetting with the WHERE Clause

You can use all common comparison operators in
a WHERE clause.

Mnemonic	Symbol	Definition
LT †	<	Less than
GT †	>	Greater than
EQ †	=	Equal to
LE †	<=	Less than or equal to
GE †	>=	Greater than or equal to
NE †	< >	Not equal to
	¬= †	Not equal to (EBCDIC)
	^= †	Not equal to (ASCII)

84

† Non-ANSI standard

Subsetting with the WHERE Clause

Use only one WHERE clause in a SELECT statement. To specify multiple subsetting criteria, combine expressions with logical operators.

Mnemonic	Symbol	Definition
OR	| †	or, either
AND	& †	and, both
NOT	¬ †	not, negation (EBCDIC)
NOT	^ †	not, negation (ASCII)

85

† Non-ANSI standard

Subsetting with the WHERE Clause

Common WHERE clause operators with examples:

Operator	Example
IN	where JobCategory in ('PT','NA','FA')
CONTAINS or ? †	where word ? 'LAM'
IS NULL or IS MISSING †	where Product_ID is missing
BETWEEN – AND	where Salary between 70000 and 80000
SOUNDS LIKE (=*) †	where LastName =* 'SMITH'
LIKE using % or _	where Employee_Name like 'H%' where JobCategory like '__1'

86

† Non-ANSI standard

Alternative statements for using the IS NULL or IS MISSING operator are as follows:

- `where Product_ID = ' '`

- `where Product_ID = .`

With the = operator, you must know whether **Product_ID** is character or numeric. However, if you use IS MISSING, you do not need advance knowledge of the column type.

2.08 Quiz

Modify program **s102a03** to provide a WHERE
expression that selects only those rows where
the employees' first names begin with N.

Desired Output

```
                    The SAS System

Employee_Name                          Employee_ID

Apr, Nishan                                 120759
James, Narelle                              120155
Kokoszka, Nikeisha                          120765
Plybon, Nicholas                            120276
Post, Nahliah                               120748
Smith, Nasim                                121032
```

88

Subsetting with the WHERE Clause

Select all SA job codes that contain an underscore (_).

```
proc sql;
   select Employee_ID, Job_Code
      from work.Employee_Organization2
      where Job_Code like 'SA_%';
quit;
```

Partial PROC SQL Output

Employee_ID	Job_Code
120115	SAI
120116	SA_II
120669	SAIV
120671	SAIII
120673	SA_II
120678	SAII

90   s102d13a

2.09 Quiz

Why do you see all SA job codes and not only the ones that contain an underscore (_)?

Employee_ID	Job_Code
120115	SAI
120116	SA_II
120669	SAIV
120671	SAIII
120673	SA_II
120678	SAII

```
proc sql;
   select Employee_ID, Job_Code
      from work.Employee_Organization2
      where Job_Code like 'SA_%';
quit;
```

92

ESCAPE Clause

To search for actual percent or underscore characters in your text using the LIKE operator, you must use an ESCAPE clause.

The ESCAPE clause in the LIKE condition enables you to designate a single character string literal, known as an *escape character*, to indicate how PROC SQL should interpret the LIKE wildcards (% and _) when SAS is searching within a character string.

94

ESCAPE Clause

```
proc sql;
   select Employee_ID, Job_Code
      from work.Employee_Organization2
      where Job_Code like 'SA/_%' ESCAPE '/';
quit;
```

Partial PROC SQL Output

Employee_ID	Job_Code
120116	SA_II
120673	SA_II
120681	SA_II
120692	SA_II
120792	SA_II
121012	SA_II

95   s102d13b

2.10 Multiple Choice Poll

Which of the following WHERE clauses correctly selects rows with a **Job_Code** value that begins with an underscore?

a. **where Job_Code like '_%'**

b. **where Job_Code contains '_%'**

c. **where Job_Code like '%_'**
   escape '/_'

d. **where Job_Code like '/_%'**
   escape '/'

97

Business Scenario

Return to the original 10% bonus program.

You want to create a report that includes only those employees who receive bonuses less than $3000.

99

Subsetting with Calculated Values

First attempt:

```
proc sql;
   select Employee_ID, Employee_Gender,
          Salary, Salary * .10 as Bonus
      from orion.Employee_Payroll
      where Bonus < 3000;
quit;
```

100   s102d14

Subsetting with Calculated Values

Because a WHERE clause is evaluated before the SELECT clause, columns used in the WHERE clause must exist in the table or be derived from existing columns.

Because the **Bonus** column is not in the source table, an error was generated.

```
ERROR: The following columns were not found in the contributing
tables: Bonus.
```

101

Subsetting with Calculated Values

One solution is to repeat the calculation in the WHERE clause.

```
proc sql;
    select Employee_ID, Employee_Gender,
            Salary, Salary * .10 as Bonus
        from orion.Employee_Payroll
        where Salary * .10 < 3000;
quit;
```

102   s102d14

Subsetting with Calculated Values

An alternate method is to use the CALCULATED keyword to refer to an already calculated column in the SELECT clause.

```
proc sql;
   select Employee_ID, Employee_Gender,
          Salary, Salary * .10 as Bonus
      from orion.Employee_Payroll
      where calculated Bonus < 3000;
quit;
```

103   s102d14

Subsetting with Calculated Values

Partial PROC SQL Output

```
                    The SAS System

              Employee_
Employee_ID   Gender        Salary      Bonus

     120105   F              27110       2711
     120106   M              26960       2696
     120108   F              27660       2766
     120109   F              26495      2649.5
     120110   M              28615      2861.5
     120111   M              26895      2689.5
     120112   F              26550       2655
```

104

Subsetting with Calculated Values

You can also use the CALCULATED keyword in other parts of a query.

```
proc sql;
   select Employee_ID, Employee_Gender,
          Salary, Salary * .10 as Bonus,
          calculated Bonus/2 as Half
      from orion.Employee_Payroll
      where calculated Bonus < 3000;
quit;
```

105   s102d14

The CALCULATED keyword is also required when referring to any column, character or numeric that is created in the query expression.

Example:

```
proc sql;
   select Employee_ID, Salary,
          (scan(Job_Title,-1,' ')) as Job_Level
      from orion.Staff
      where calculated Job_Level='IV';
quit;
```

Subsetting with Calculated Values

Partial PROC SQL Output

```
                     The SAS System

            Employee_
Employee_ID Gender     Salary     Bonus       Half

    120105  F           27110      2711      1355.5
    120106  M           26960      2696       1348
    120108  F           27660      2766       1383
    120109  F           26495     2649.5    1324.75
    120110  M           28615     2861.5    1430.75
    120111  M           26895     2689.5    1344.75
    120112  F           26550      2655      1327.5
```

106

 **Exercises**

Level 1

4. Eliminating Duplicates

Write a query that generates a report that displays the cities where the Orion Star employees reside. The report should do the following:

- include the title **Cities Where Employees Live**
- display one unique row per **City**
- use the **orion.Employee_Addresses** table

PROC SQL Output

```
                      Cities Where Employees Live

          City
          _____

          Melbourne
          Miami-Dade
          Philadelphia
          San Diego
          Sydney
```

Level 2

5. Subsetting Data

Write a query that generates a report that displays Orion Star employees whose charitable contributions exceed $90.00. The report should have the following characteristics:

- include the title **Donations Exceeding $90.00 in 2007**
- display **Employee_ID**, **Recipients**, and the new column **Total** that represents the total charitable contribution for each employee over the four quarters
- use the **orion.Employee_donations** table
- include only employees whose charitable contribution **Total** for all four quarters exceeds $90.00

Hint: The total charitable contribution is calculated by adding the amount of **Qtr1**, **Qtr2**, **Qtr3**, and **Qtr4**. Use the SUM function to ensure that missing values are ignored.

PROC SQL Output

```
                         Donations Exceeding $90.00 in 2007

 Employee ID  Recipients                                                    Total
 ────────────────────────────────────────────────────────────────────────────────
      120660  Disaster Assist, Inc.                                           100
      120677  EarthSalvors 60%, Vox Victimas 40%                             100
      120753  Conserve Nature, Inc. 50%, AquaMissions International 50%       100
      120766  Mitleid International 80%, Save the Baby Animals 20%            100
      120791  Child Survivors                                                120
      120814  Child Survivors 80%, Disaster Assist, Inc. 20%                 100
      121142  AquaMissions International 10%, Child Survivors 90%             140
      121143  Mitleid International 60%, Save the Baby Animals 40%            140
      121145  Save the Baby Animals                                          140
```

Level 3

6. Subsetting Data Using the ESCAPE Clause

Create a report that displays the **Employee_ID** and **Recipients** for all employees who contributed 90% of their charitable contributions to a single company that was incorporated (Inc.). Use the **orion.Employee_donations** table. Add a title to the report as shown in the output below.

Hint: Use the ESCAPE clause in the WHERE clause to solve this problem.

 Alternative methods can be used to solve this problem, but for this exercise, use the LIKE operator with an ESCAPE clause.

PROC SQL Output

```
                    Employees who contributed 90%
                    To Charitable Companies That Are
                         Also Incorporated (Inc.)

      Employee ID  Recipients
     _____

          120783  Disaster Assist, Inc. 10%, Cancer Cures, Inc. 90%
          121012  Child Survivors 10%, Disaster Assist, Inc. 90%
          121058  Disaster Assist, Inc. 90%, Cancer Cures, Inc. 10%
          121136  Disaster Assist, Inc. 10%, Cancer Cures, Inc. 90%
```

2.4 Chapter Review

Chapter Review

1. What SQL statement is used to display the values from columns in a table?

2. What expression is used to conditionally calculate column values?

3. Name the clause that selects a subset of rows in a query.

4. If your query returns multiple rows with identical content, what keyword can eliminate duplicate rows?

108

2.5 Solutions

Solutions to Exercises

1. **Querying a Table**

   a.

   ```
   *** s102s01 ***;
   proc sql;
      select *
         from orion.Employee_Payroll;
   quit;
   ```

   b.

   ```
   proc sql;
      select Employee_ID, Employee_Gender, Marital_Status, Salary
         from orion.Employee_Payroll;
   quit;
   ```

2. **Calculating a Column**

   ```
   *** s102s02 ***;
   proc sql;
      select Employee_ID, Employee_Gender, Marital_Status,
             Salary, Salary/3 as Tax
         from orion.Employee_Payroll;
   quit;
   ```

3. Conditional Processing

```
*** s102s03 ***;
proc sql;
title "Salary Ranges For Orion Star Management";
   select Employee_ID,
          case (scan(Job_Title,-1," "))
             when "Manager" then "Manager"
             when "Director" then "Director"
             when "Officer" then "Executive"
             when "President" then "Executive"
             else "N/A"
          end as Level,
          Salary,
          case (calculated Level)
             when "Manager" then
                 case
                     when (Salary>72000) then "High"
                     when (Salary>52000) then "Medium"
                     else "Low"
                 end
             when "Director" then
                 case
                     when (Salary>135000) then "High"
                     when (Salary>108000) then "Medium"
                     else "Low"
                 end
             when "Executive" then
                 case
                     when (Salary>300000) then "High"
                     when (Salary>240000) then "Medium"
                     else "Low"
                 end
             else "N/A"
          end as Salary_Range
       from orion.Staff
       where calculated level ne "N/A"
       order by Level, Salary desc
   ;
quit;
```

4. Eliminating Duplicates

```
*** s102s04 ***;
proc sql;
title 'Cities Where Employees Live';
   select distinct City
       from orion.Employee_Addresses;
quit;
title;
```

5. Subsetting Data

```
*** s102s05 ***;
proc sql;
title 'Donations Exceeding $90.00 in 2007';
   select Employee_ID, Recipients,
            sum(Qtr1,Qtr2,Qtr3,Qtr4) as Total
      from orion.Employee_Donations
      where calculated Total > 90;
quit;
title;
```

6. Subsetting Data Using the ESCAPE Clause

```
*** s102s06 ***;
proc sql;
title 'Employees Who Contributed 90% ';
title2 'To Charitable Companies That Are ';
title3 'Also Incorporated (Inc.)';
   select Employee_ID, Recipients
      from orion.Employee_Donations
      where Recipients like "% Inc. 90~%%" ESCAPE "~";
quit;
title;
```

Solutions to Student Activities (Polls/Quizzes)

2.01 Multiple Choice Poll – Correct Answer

Which step generated errors?

a. Step 1
(b.) Step 2
c. Step 3

12

2.02 Quiz – Correct Answer

What error message was generated in Step 2?

ERROR: Statement is not valid or it is used out of proper order.

```
 /* Step 2 */
proc sql;
   from orion.Employee_Payroll
   select Employee_ID, Employee_Gender,
          Salary
   where Employee_Gender = 'M'
   order by EmpID;
quit;
```

15   s102a01

2.03 Multiple Choice Poll – Correct Answer

How are the column names represented in the expanded log?

a. The column names are preceded by the table name (**EMPLOYEE_PAYROLL**).

b. The column names are preceded by the library reference (**ORION**).

c. The column names are preceded by **Work**.

32

2.04 Multiple Choice Poll – Correct Answer

Which of these SAS character functions will be the most useful for identifying the level value for conditional processing?

a. CHAR( )

b. FIND( )

c. SCAN( )

d. SUBSTR( )

44

2.05 Quiz – Correct Answer

What numeric function would you use to create the **Birth_Month** column for the following rows from the **Employee_Payroll** table?

The MONTH Function

```
proc sql;
   select Employee_ID, Birth_Date,
        month(Birth_Date) as Birth_Month,
        Employee_gender
      from orion.Employee_Payroll;
quit;
```

63   s102d10a

2.07 Multiple Answer Poll – Correct Answer

Which SELECT clauses select only the unique combinations of **Employee_Gender** and **Job_Title**?

a. `select distinct Employee_Gender,`
   `distinct Job_Title...`

(b.) `select unique Employee_Gender,`
   `Job_Title...`

(c.) `select distinct Employee_Gender,`
   `Job_Title...`

d. `select distinct Employee_Gender`
   `Job_Title...`

80

2.08 Quiz – Correct Answer

Modify program **s102a03** to provide a WHERE expression that selects only those rows where the employees' first names begin with N.

One possible solution:

```
select Employee_Name, Employee_ID
   from orion.Employee_Addresses
   where Employee_Name contains ', N';
quit;
```

s102a03a

89

2.09 Quiz – Correct Answer

Why do you see all SA job codes and not only the ones that contain an underscore (_)?

You see all the SAS job codes because the WHERE expression uses the LIKE operator. The underscore represents any one character, not an underscore (_) in the third position.

```
proc sql;
   select Employee_ID, Job_Code
      from work.Employee_Organization2
      where Job_Code like 'SA_%';
quit;
```

93

2.10 Multiple Choice Poll – Correct Answer

Which of the following WHERE clauses correctly selects rows with a **Job_Code** value that begins with an underscore?

a. `where Job_Code like '_%'`

b. `where Job_Code contains '_%'`

c. `where Job_Code like '%_'`
   `escape '/_'`

d. `where Job_Code like '/_%'`
   `escape '/'`

98

Solutions to Chapter Review

Chapter Review Answers

1. What SQL statement is used to display the values from columns in a table?

   The SELECT statement

2. What expression is used to conditionally calculate column values?

   The CASE expression

3. Name the clause that selects a subset of rows in a query.

   The WHERE clause

4. If your query returns multiple rows with identical content, what keyword can eliminate duplicate rows?

   The DISTINCT keyword

109

Chapter 3   Displaying Query Results

3.1 Presenting Data

Objectives

- Display a query's results in a specified order.
- Use SAS formats, labels, and titles to enhance the appearance and usability of a query's output.

3

Business Scenario

You need a report that shows the employee ID of each Orion Star employee who makes charitable donations, and lists the amount of the highest quarterly donation. Rows should be sorted first in descending order of amount, and then by employee ID.

Here is a sketch of the desired report:

Employee ID	
120005	25
120006	25
120001	20
120002	20
120003	20

4

Ordering Data

Use the ORDER BY clause to sort query results in a specific order.

- Ascending order (No keyword; this is the default.)
- Descending order (by following the column name with the DESC keyword)

5

The order of your output is only guaranteed if you include an ORDER BY clause in your query.

Ordering Data

In an ORDER BY clause, order the query results by specifying the following:

- any column name from any table in the FROM clause, even if the column is not in the SELECT list
- a column name or a number representing the position of an item in the SELECT list
- an expression
- a combination of any of the above, with individual items separated by commas

6

Ordering Data

Example: From the **orion.Employee_payroll** table, list the employee ID and salary of all employees hired prior to January 1, 1979, in descending salary order.

```
proc sql;
   select Employee_ID, Salary
      from orion.Employee_payroll
      where Employee_Hire_Date < '01JAN1979'd
      order by Salary desc;
quit;
```

7   s103d01

Ordering Data

Partial PROC SQL Output

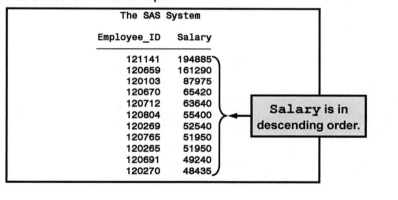

```
              The SAS System

      Employee_ID    Salary
      _____    _____

          121141     194885
          120659     161290
          120103      87975
          120670      65420
          120712      63640
          120804      55400
          120269      52540
          120765      51950
          120265      51950
          120691      49240
          120270      48435
```

Salary is in descending order.

8

3.01 Multiple Choice Poll

Which ORDER BY clause orders a report by descending `State` and descending `City`?

a. `order by state, city`

b. `order by desc state, city`

c. `order by state, city desc`

d. `order by state desc, city desc`

e. `order by desc state, desc city`

10

Producing an Ordered Report

Remember to sort output in descending order of amount and then by employee ID.

```
proc sql;
select Employee_ID,
       max(Qtr1,Qtr2,Qtr3,Qtr4)
    from orion.Employee_donations
    where Paid_By="Cash or Check"
    order by 2 desc, Employee_ID;
quit;
```

Mix and match!

12   s103d02

Producing an Ordered Report

Partial PROC SQL Output

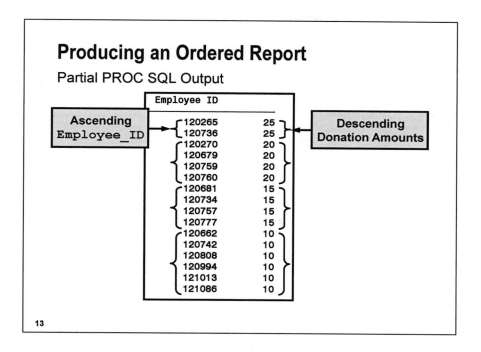

13

Enhancing Query Output

You can use SAS formats and labels to customize PROC SQL output. In the SELECT list, after the column name, but before the commas that separate the columns, you can include the following:

- text in quotation marks (ANSI) or the LABEL= column modifier (SAS enhancement) to alter the column heading
- the FORMAT= column modifier to alter the appearance of the values in that column

14

Enhancing Query Output

You can enhance a report by displaying column labels instead of variable names, and formatting cash amounts with dollar signs and commas.

```
proc sql;
   select Employee_ID
          label='Employee Identifier',
          sum(Qtr1,Qtr2,Qtr3,Qtr4)
          'Annual Donation' format=dollar7.2,
          Recipients
   from orion.Employee_donations
   where Paid_By="Cash or Check"
   order by 2 desc
;
quit;
```

15   s103d03

Enhancing Query Output

Partial PROC SQL Output

```
Employee    Annual
Identifier  Donation  Recipients

   120736   $45.00    Cuidadores Ltd.
   120759   $40.00    Child Survivors
   120681   $40.00    EarthSalvors 60%, Vox Victimas 40%
   120679   $40.00    Cancer Cures, Inc.
   120777   $40.00    Cuidadores Ltd. 80%, Mitleid International 20%
   120760   $35.00    Cancer Cures, Inc. 40%, Cuidadores Ltd. 60%
```

16

Business Scenario

Produce a report of bonus values for all active employees. Bonuses are 5% of salary. The requestor provided this sketch of the desired report.

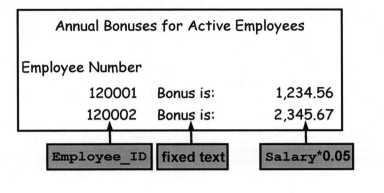

17

Enhancing Query Output

You can also enhance the appearance of the query output by doing the following:

- defining a new column containing the same constant character value for every row
- using SAS titles and footnotes

Use a combination of these techniques to produce the Annual Bonuses for Active Employees report.

18

Enhancing Query Output

The code:

```
proc sql;
title 'Annual Bonuses for Active Employees';
    select Employee_ID label='Employee Number',
            'Bonus is:',
            Salary *.05 format=comma12.2
        from orion.Employee_Payroll
        where Employee_Term_Date is missing
        order by Salary desc
    ;
quit;
title;
```

19   s103d04

✎   TITLE and FOOTNOTE statements must precede the SELECT statement.

PROC SQL has an option, DQUOTE=, which specifies whether PROC SQL treats values within double quotation marks (" ") as variables or strings.

With the default, DQUOTE=SAS, values within double quotation marks are treated as text strings.

With DQUOTE=ANSI, PROC SQL treats a quoted value as a variable. This feature enables you to use reserved words such as AS, JOIN, GROUP, or DBMS names and other names that are not normally permissible in SAS, such as table names, column names, or aliases. The quoted value can contain any character.

Values in single quotation marks are **always** treated as text strings.

Enhancing Query Output

Partial PROC SQL Output

```
Annual Bonuses for Active Employees

Employee
  Number

  120259   Bonus is:     21,690.00
  120262   Bonus is:     13,422.75
  120261   Bonus is:     12,159.50
  120260   Bonus is:     10,394.25
  121141   Bonus is:      9,744.25
  120101   Bonus is:      8,152.00
  120659   Bonus is:      8,064.50
  121142   Bonus is:      7,803.25
  120102   Bonus is:      5,412.75
  121143   Bonus is:      4,754.50
  120103   Bonus is:      4,398.75
  120719   Bonus is:      4,371.00
```

20

 **Exercises**

If you restarted SAS since the last exercise, submit a LIBNAME statement to assign the libref `orion` to the SAS data library for this course.

```
libname orion '_____';
```

Level 1

1. **Enhancing Output with Titles and Formats**

    Open program **s103e01** and modify the query.

    a. Select only the **Employee_ID**, **Salary**, and **Tax** columns.

    b. Display the **Tax** and **Salary** columns using the COMMA10.2 format.

    c. Order the report by **Salary** in descending order.

    d. Add this title to the report: **Single Male Employee Salaries**.

    Partial PROC SQL Output

    Single Male Employee Salaries

Employee_ID	Salary	Tax
121141	194,885.00	64,961.67
120101	163,040.00	54,346.67
120268	76,105.00	25,368.33
120724	63,705.00	21,235.00
120660	61,125.00	20,375.00
120810	58,375.00	19,458.33
120804	55,400.00	18,466.67
120691	49,240.00	16,413.33
120769	47,990.00	15,996.67
120793	47,155.00	15,718.33
120753	47,000.00	15,666.67

Level 2

2. Using Formats to Limit the Width of Columns in the Output

Write a query that retrieves the `Supplier_Name`, `Product_Group`, and `Product_Name` columns from the table `orion.Product_dim`.

   a. Add this title to the report: `Australian Clothing Products`.

   b. Include only rows where `Product_Category` = "Clothes" and `Supplier_Country` = "AU" (Australia).

   c. To enable the report to print in portrait orientation, use formats to limit the width of column `Supplier_Name` to 18, `Product_Group` to 12, and `Product_Name` to 30 characters.

   d. Label the columns `Supplier`, `Group`, and `Product`, respectively.

   e. Order the report by `Product_Name`.

PROC SQL Output

```
                       Australian Clothing Products

          Supplier              Group          Product

          Typhoon Clothing      Street Wear    Tyfoon Flex Shorts
          Typhoon Clothing      Street Wear    Tyfoon Ketch T-Shirt
          Typhoon Clothing      Street Wear    Tyfoon Oliver Sweatshirt
```

Level 3

3. Enhancing Output with Multiple Techniques

Create a report that displays `Customer_ID`, the customer's name written as `Customer_LastName, Customer_FirstName`, and `Gender`, as well as the customer's age as of 31DEC2007. Use the data contained in the `orion.Customer` table. Include only U.S. customers who were more than 50 years old on 31DEC2007. Present the data ordered by descending age, last name, and first name. Give the report an appropriate title. Limit the space used to display the customer's name to a maximum of 20 characters, so that the report can be printed in portrait orientation. The `Customer_ID` values must be displayed with leading zeros as shown in this sample report.

Partial PROC SQL Output

```
            US Customers >50 Years Old as of 31DEC2007

         Customer  Last Name,
               ID  First Name          Gender     Age

         0000089   Lewis, Wynella        F         73
         0000056   Siferd, Roy           M         73
         0000092   Celii, Lendon         M         63
         0000023   Devereaux, Tulio      M         58
         0000018   Asmussen, Tonie       M         53
         0000017   Evans, Jimmie         M         53
```

3.2 Summarizing Data

Objectives

- Use functions to create summary queries.
- Group data and produce summary statistics for each group.

24

Summary Functions

How a summary function works in SQL depends on the number of columns specified.

- If the summary function specifies only one column, the statistic is calculated for the column (using values from one or more rows).
- If the summary function specifies more than one column, the statistic is calculated for the row (using values from the listed columns).

25

The SUM Function (Review)

The SUM function returns the sum of the non-missing arguments.

General form of the SUM function:

> **SUM**(*argument1*<,*argument2*, ...>)

argument   includes numeric constants, expressions, or variable names. Only when all arguments are missing will the SUM function return a missing value.

26

Summary Functions

Example: Total each individual's annual cash donations.
             Order the results by decreasing total donation.

```
proc sql;
   select Employee_ID
          label='Employee Identifier',
          Qtr1,Qtr2,Qtr3,Qtr4,
          sum(Qtr1,Qtr2,Qtr3,Qtr4)
          label='Annual Donation'
          format=comma9.2
      from orion.Employee_donations
      where Paid_By="Cash or Check"
      order by 6 desc
   ;
quit;
```

27   s103d05

Summary Functions

Non-missing values are totaled across columns by row.
In SQL, specifying multiple columns in a summary
function returns results similar to that of a DATA step.

Partial PROC SQL Output

Employee Identifier	Qtr1	Qtr2	Qtr3	Qtr4	Annual Donation
120736	25	.	.	20	45.00
120759	15	20	5	.	40.00
120681	10 +	10 +	5 +	15 =	40.00
120679	.	20	5	15	40.00
120777	5	15	5	15	40.00
120760	.	15	20	.	35.00
120270	20	10	5	.	35.00
120994	5	5	10	10	30.00

28

Summary Functions

If a summary function specifies only one column name,
the statistic is calculated down the column (across rows).
This technique compares to using the MEANS procedure.

Example: Determine the total of all charitable donations
in quarter 1.

```
proc sql;
   select sum(Qtr1)
           'Total Quarter 1 Donations'
       from orion.Employee_Donations
;
quit;
```

29   s103d06

Summary Functions

SUM(Qtr1) calculates the sum of the values in this column for all rows in the table.

Partial Listing of `orion.Employee_Donations`

Employee Identifier	Qtr1	Qtr2	Qtr3	Qtr4
120265	.	.	.	25
120270	20	10	5	.
120662	10	.	5	5
120663	.	.	5	.
120679	.	20	5	15
120681	10	10	5	15
120734	.	.	15	10
120736	25	.	.	20
120742	.	.	10	10
120757	.	.	15	5
120759	15	20	5	.

30

Summary Functions

PROC SQL Output

Total Quarter 1 Donations
1515

31

Summary Functions

Example: Determine the total of all charitable donations
in quarter 1.

```
proc means data=orion.Employee_donations
           sum maxdec=0;
   var Qtr1;
run;
```

PROC MEANS Output

Analysis Variable : Qtr1
Sum
1515

s103d06

32

The COUNT Function

The COUNT function returns the number of rows returned
by a query.

General form of the COUNT function:

COUNT(*|*argument*)

argument   can be the following:

- * (asterisk), which counts all rows
- a column name, which counts the number
of non-missing values in that column

33

Summary Functions

Example: Determine the total number of current
employees.

```
proc sql;
   select count(*) as Count
      from orion.Employee_Payroll
      where Employee_Term_Date is missing
;
quit;
```

PROC SQL Output

Count
308

34   s103d07

Summary Functions

A few commonly used summary functions are listed. Both
ANSI SQL and SAS functions can be used in PROC SQL.

SQL	SAS	Description
AVG	MEAN	returns the mean (average) value.
COUNT	FREQ, N	returns the number of non-missing values.
MAX	MAX	returns the largest value.
MIN	MIN	returns the smallest non-missing value.
SUM	SUM	returns the sum of non-missing values.
	NMISS	counts the number of missing values.
	STD	returns the standard deviation.
	VAR	returns the variance.

35

🖋   SQL aggregate functions do not round, so the order in which values are encountered by a
summary function produces results that might vary from one execution to another, and might
differ from those returned by other SAS procedures such as PROC MEANS.

You can ensure consistent results through the use of numeric truncation functions such as INT,
ROUND, CEIL, and FLOOR.

3.02 Quiz

Open the program file **s103a01**. Submit the program and review the output.

1. How many rows did the first query create?
2. How many rows did the second query create?
3. In the second query's results, was the value in the average column different for every gender listed?

37   s103a01

Remerging Summary Statistics

When a SELECT list contains both a column created by a summary function and a column that is **not** summarized, by default, the summarized data is appended to each row of the original data table (remerged) in order to produce the output.

SAS informs you of this by placing this note in the log.

Partial SAS Log

```
NOTE: The query requires remerging summary statistics back
      with the original data.
```

41

Remerging Summary Statistics

To change the default behavior, use either of the following:

- NOSQLREMERGE SAS system option
- PROC SQL NOREMERGE option

Resubmitting the query with the NOREMERGE option in effect produces no output and results in this SAS log error message:

```
ERROR: The query requires remerging summary statistics back with the
       original data. This is disallowed due to the NOREMERGE proc
       option or NOSQLREMERGE system option.
```

42   s103d07a

 Most DBMS systems do not enable remerging summary statistics; they generate an error instead. SAS 9.2 includes new options that can be used to control remerging. They are the PROC SQL NOREMERGE option and the NOSQLREMERGE SAS system option. When these options are used, PROC SQL produces an error if remerging is attempted.

3.03 Quiz

Open the program file **s103a02**. Submit the query and review the output and the log. Answer the following questions:

1. How many rows of output were created?
2. What major difference was there in the log between this query's results and the second query in the previous activity?

44

Grouping Data

You can use the GROUP BY clause to do the following:

- classify the data into groups based on the values of one or more columns
- calculate statistics for each unique value of the grouping columns

48

Grouping Data

Example: Calculate the average salary by gender.

```
proc sql;
title "Average Salary by Gender";
   select Employee_Gender as Gender,
          avg(Salary) as Average
      from orion.Employee_Payroll
      where Employee_Term_Date is missing
      group by Employee_Gender
;
quit;
title;
```

49   s103d08

Grouping Data

PROC SQL Output

Average Salary by Gender	
Gender	Average
F	37002.88
M	43334.26

50

3.04 Poll

Can you group by more than one column?

O Yes

O No

52

Analyzing Groups of Data

Example: Determine the total number of employees
             in each department.

```
proc sql;
   select Department, count(*) as Count
      from orion.Employee_Organization
      group by Department
;
quit;
```

54   s103d09

Analyzing Groups of Data

PROC SQL Output

Department	Count
Accounts	17
Accounts Management	9
Administration	34
Concession Management	11
Engineering	9
Executives	4
Group Financials	3
Group HR Management	18
IS	25
Logistics Management	14
Marketing	20
Purchasing	18
Sales	201
Sales Management	11
Secretary of the Board	2
Stock & Shipping	26
Strategy	2

55

Analyzing Groups of Data

Example: Calculate each male employee's salary as
          a percentage of all male employees' salaries.
          Display the employee ID, salary, and
          percentage in decreasing order of percentage.

```
proc sql;
title "Male Employee Salaries";
   select Employee_ID, Salary format=comma12.,
          Salary / sum(Salary)
          format=percent6.2
      from orion.Employee_Payroll
      where Employee_Gender="M"
            and Employee_Term_Date is missing
      order by 3 desc
   ;
quit;
title;
```

56   s103d10
                                                            ...

Analyzing Groups of Data

Example: Calculate each male employee's salary as a
          percentage of all male employees' salaries.
          Display the employee ID, salary, and
          percentage in decreasing order of percentage.

```
proc sql;
title "Male Employee Salaries";
   select Employee_ID, Salary format=comma12.,
          Salary / sum(Salary)
          format=percent6.2
      from orion.Employee_Payroll
      where Employee_Gender="M"
            and Employee_Term_Date is missing
      order by 3 desc
   ;
quit;
title;
```

Select only the group
of rows that you want
to analyze.

57   s103d10
                                                            ...

Analyzing Groups of Data

Example: Calculate each male employee's salary as
a percentage of all male employees' salaries.
Display the employee ID, salary, and
percentage in decreasing order of percentage.

```
proc sql;
title "Male Employee Salaries";
   select Employee_ID, Salary format=comma12.,
          Salary / sum(Salary)
          format=percent6.2
   from orion.Employee_Payroll
   where Employee_Gender="M"
          and Employee_Term_Date is missing
   order
;
quit;
title;
```

| Individual salary value for each row | Divided by a remerged summary value (sum of all salaries) |

58   s103d10

Analyzing Groups of Data

Partial PROC SQL Output

```
              Male Employee Salaries

   Employee_ID        Salary

       120259        433,800    5.9%
       120262        268,455    3.7%
       120261        243,190    3.3%
       121141        194,885    2.7%
       120101        163,040    2.2%
       120659        161,290    2.2%
       121142        156,065    2.1%
       120102        108,255    1.5%
       121143         95,090    1.3%
       120103         87,975    1.2%
       121145         84,260    1.2%
       120268         76,105    1.0%
       120724         63,705    .87%
       120714         62,625    .86%
       120660         61,125    .83%
```

59

This is a good example of SQL simplifying code. The following traditional SAS code produces similar results:

```
proc means data=orion.Employee_Payroll
                (where=(Employee_Gender="M" and Employee_Term_Date
                is missing)) sum noprint;
   output out=summary sum=TotalSalary;
   var salary;
run;
data report;
   merge orion.Employee_Payroll (where=(Employee_Gender="M"
                                 and Employee_Term_Date is
                                 missing)) summary
                                 (keep=TotalSalary);
   retain Total 0;
   if _n_=1 then Total=TotalSalary;
   Percent=Salary / Total;
   keep Employee_ID Salary Percent;
   format salary comma12.2 Percent percent6.2;
run;
proc sort data=report;
   by descending Percent;
run;
title "Male Employee Salaries - Traditional SAS Programming";
proc print data=report noobs split='*';
   label Percent='*';
run;
title;
```

Selecting Groups with the HAVING Clause

- The WHERE clause is processed **before** a GROUP BY clause and determines which individual rows are available for grouping.
- The HAVING clause is processed **after** the GROUP BY clause and determines which groups will be displayed.

60

Selecting Groups with the HAVING Clause

Example: Display the names of the departments and the number of employees for departments with 25 or more employees. List the department with the highest count first.

```
proc sql;
   select Department, count(*) as Count
      from orion.Employee_Organization
      group by Department
      having Count ge 25
      order by Count desc
;
quit;
```

s103d11

61

Selecting Groups with the HAVING Clause

PROC SQL Output

Department	Count
Sales	201
Administration	34
Stock & Shipping	26
IS	25

62

3.05 Quiz

Which syntax will select employee IDs having bonuses greater than $1000?

1. ```
   select Employee_ID, Salary*0.1 as Bonus
          from orion.Employee_Payroll
          where calculated Bonus > 1000;
   ```
2. ```
   select Employee_ID, Salary*0.1 as Bonus
          from orion.Employee_Payroll
          having Bonus > 1000;
   ```
3. Both of the above
4. Neither of the above

64

Business Scenario

Create a report that lists, for each department, the total number of managers, total number of employees, and the Manager-to-Employee (M/E) ratio. Calculate the M/E ratio as follows:

M/E Ratio= # Managers / # non-Manager Employees

Below is a rough sketch of the desired report.

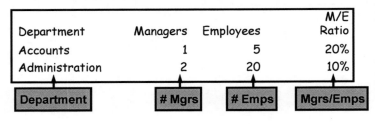

66

Counting Rows Meeting a Specified Criteria

This request is complicated by the need, in the same query, to count rows that **do** have **Manager** in the title, as well as rows that **do not**. You cannot use a WHERE clause to exclude either group.

Instead, use the FIND function in a Boolean expression to simplify the query.

67

The FIND Function

The FIND function returns the starting position of the first occurrence of a substring within a string (character value).

General form of the FIND function:

> **FIND**(*string, substring<,modifier(s)><,startpos>*)

string   constant, variable, or expression to be searched

substring constant, variable, or expression sought within the string

modifiers i=ignore case, t=trim trailing blanks

startpos   an integer specifying the start position and direction of the search

68

The FIND Function

Example: Find the starting position of the substring **Manager** in the character variable **Job_Title**.

> `find(Job_Title,"manager","i")`

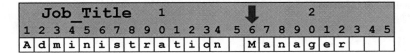

The value returned by the FIND function is 16.

69

Using Boolean Expressions

Boolean expressions evaluate to TRUE (1) or FALSE (0).
They are used in this SELECT list to distinguish rows that
have **Manager** in the **Job_Title** column.

```
proc sql;
    select Department,Job_Title,
           (find(Job_Title,"manager","i") >0)
           "Manager"
       from orion.Employee_Organization
;
quit;
```

The Boolean expression will produce the value 1 when
Job_Title contains the word **Manager** and 0 when
it does not.

70   s103d12

Using Boolean Expressions

Partial PROC SQL Output (Rows 4–14)

Department	Job_Title	Manager
Administration	Administration Manager	1
Administration	Secretary I	0
Administration	Office Assistant II	0
Administration	Office Assistant III	0
Administration	Warehouse Assistant II	0
Administration	Warehouse Assistant I	0
Administration	Warehouse Assistant III	0
Administration	Security Guard II	0
Administration	Security Guard I	0
Administration	Security Guard II	0
Administration	Security Manager	1

To count the managers, you can add the values in the
column produced by the Boolean expression. In this
segment, the Administration department has two
managers.

71

Using Boolean Expressions

Example: For each department, calculate the percentage
of people with the word *Manager* in the job title.

```
proc sql;
title "Manager to Employee Ratios";
   select Department,
          sum((find(Job_Title,"manager","i") >0))
             as Managers,
          sum((find(Job_Title,"manager","i") =0))
             as Employees,
          calculated Managers/calculated Employees
          "M/E Ratio" format=percent8.1
      from orion.Employee_Organization
      group by Department
;
quit;
```

72   s103d13

Using Boolean Expressions

PROC SQL Output

```
              Manager to Employee Ratios

                                                M/E
    Department            Managers  Employees   Ratio

    Accounts                  3        14       21.4%
    Accounts Management       1         8       12.5%
    Administration            5        29       17.2%
    Concession Management     1        10       10.0%
    Engineering               1         8       12.5%
    Executives                0         4        0.0%
    Group Financials          0         3        0.0%
    Group HR Management       3        15       20.0%
    IS                        2        23        8.7%
    Logistics Management      6         8       75.0%
    Marketing                 6        14       42.9%
    Purchasing                3        15       20.0%
    Sales                     0       201        0.0%
    Sales Management          5         6       83.3%
    Secretary of the Board    0         2        0.0%
    Stock & Shipping          5        21       23.8%
    Strategy                  0         2        0.0%
```

73

 **Exercises**

If you restarted SAS since the last exercise, submit a LIBNAME statement to assign the libref **orion** to the SAS data library for this course.

    libname orion '.';

Level 1

4. Summarizing Data

Create a report that displays the number of employees residing in each city.

a. Use the **City** column and the COUNT(*) function.

b. Use the **orion.Employee_Addresses** table.

c. Group the data and order the output by **City**.

d. Add this title to the report: **Cities Where Employees Live**.

PROC SQL Output

Cities Where Employees Live	
City	Count
Melbourne	41
Miami-Dade	109
Philadelphia	95
San Diego	112
Sydney	67

5. Using SAS Functions

Create a report that includes each employee's age at time of employment.

a. The report should contain the columns **Employee_ID**, **Birth_Date**, **Employee_Hire_Date**, and **Age**.

b. Obtain the data for the report from the **orion.Employee_Payroll** table.

c. Calculate **Age** as INT((**Employee_Hire_Date** – **Birth_Date**)/365.25).

d. Add this title to the report: **Age at Employment**.

e. Display **Birth_Date** and **Employee_Hire_Date** values using the MMDDYY10. format.

f. Label each column as shown in the following sample report:

Partial PROC SQL Output

```
                       Age at Employment

            Employee ID  Birth Date   Hire Date      Age
            ───────────────────────────────────────────
                 120101  08/18/1976  07/01/2003       26
                 120102  08/11/1969  06/01/1989       19
                 120103  01/22/1949  01/01/1974       24
                 120104  05/11/1954  01/01/1981       26
                 120105  12/21/1974  05/01/1999       24
                 120106  12/23/1944  01/01/1974       29
```

Hint: For the purpose of this report, an employee's age when hired can be computed by taking the integer portion of (**Employee_Hire_Date** − **Birth_Date**)/365.25.

Level 2

6. Summarizing Data

   a. Using data contained in the **orion.Customer** table, create a report that shows the following statistics for each country:

   1) total number of customers

   2) total number of male customers

   3) total number of female customers

   4) percent of all customers that are male (**Percent Male**)

   b. Add this title to the report: **Customer Demographics: Gender by Country**.

   c. Arrange the report by value of **Percent Male** so that the country with the lowest value is listed first, with the remaining countries following in ascending order.

```
              Customer Demographics: Gender by Country

       Customer                                      Percent
       Country    Customers      Men      Women        Male
       ──────────────────────────────────────────────────────
       ZA                4         1          3         25%
       CA               15         7          8         47%
       US               28        15         13         54%
       AU                8         5          3         63%
       DE               10         7          3         70%
       IL                5         5          0        100%
       TR                7         7          0        100%
```

Hint: The Boolean expression (**Customer_Gender="M"**) evaluates as 1 when true and 0 when false.

7. Summarizing Data in Groups

Use the **orion.Customer** table to determine the number of Orion Star customers of each gender in each country. Display columns titled **Country**, **Male Customers**, and **Female Customers**. Display only those countries that have more female customers than male customers. Order the report by descending female customers. Add this title to the report: **Countries with more Female than Male Customers**.

PROC SQL Output

```
                   Countries with more Female than Male Customers

                           Male       Female
              Country    Customers   Customers
              ─────────────────────────────────
              CA             7           8
              ZA             1           3
```

Level 3

8. Advanced Summarizing Data in Groups

Use the **orion.Employee_Addresses** table to create a report that displays the countries and cities where Orion Star employees reside, and the number of employees in each city. Include only one row per country/city combination. Display the values in country/city order, and give the report an appropriate title.

PROC SQL Output

```
                   Countries and Cities Where Employees Live

            Country  City                          Employees
            ─────────────────────────────────────────────────
            AU       Melbourne                        41
            AU       Sydney                           67
            US       Miami-Dade                      109
            US       Philadelphia                     95
            US       San Diego                       112
```

Hint: Some data might not have consistent capitalization.

3.3 Chapter Review

Chapter Review

1. Which of these ORDER BY clauses will display the results ordered by decreasing **Salary** and then by increasing **Name**?

   a. `order by descending Salary, Name`

   b. `order by Salary desc, Name`

   c. `order by desc Salary, ascending Name`

76

Chapter Review

2. How would you modify this SELECT statement to display the **Salary** column using the EUROX10. format?

```
proc sql;
   select First_Name, Last_Name,
          Job_Title,
          Salary
      from orion.Sales
;
quit;
```

78

Chapter Review

3. The SAS RANGE() function returns the difference between the largest and the smallest of the non-missing arguments. What clause can you add to this query to produce a listing of the salary range for each value of **Job_Title**?

```
proc sql;
   select Job_Title, range(Salary)
      from orion.Sales

;
quit;
```

80

3.4 Solutions

Solutions to Exercises

1. **Enhancing Output with Titles and Formats**

```
*** s103s01 ***;
proc sql;
title "Single Male Employee Salaries";
   select Employee_ID,
          Salary format=comma10.2,
          Salary/3 format=comma9.2 as Tax
      from orion.Employee_Payroll
      where Marital_Status="S"
        and Employee_Gender ="M"
        and Employee_Term_Date is missing
      order by Salary desc
   ;
quit;
title;
```

2. **Using Formats to Limit the Width of Columns in the Output**

```
*** s103s02 ***;
proc sql;
title "Australian Clothing Products";
   select Supplier_Name 'Supplier' format=$18.,
          Product_Group 'Group' format=$12.,
          Product_Name 'Product' format=$30.
      from orion.Product_dim
      where Supplier_Country="AU"
        and Product_Category="Clothes"
      order by Product_Name
   ;
quit;
title;
```

3. Enhancing Output with Multiple Techniques

```
*** s103s03 ***;
proc sql;
title "US Customers >50 Years Old as of 31DEC2007";
    select Customer_ID format=z7. 'Customer ID',
           catx(', ',Customer_LastName,Customer_FirstName)
           format=$20. 'Last Name, First Name' as Name,
           Gender 'Gender',
           int(('31dec2007'd-Birth_Date)/365.25) as Age
        from orion.Customer
        where Country="US"
          and calculated Age > 50
        order by Age desc, Name
    ;
quit;
title;
```

4. Summarizing Data

```
*** s103s04 ***;

proc sql;
title "Cities Where Employees Live";
    select City, Count(*) as Count
        from orion.Employee_addresses
        group by city
        order by city
    ;
quit;
title;
```

5. Using SAS Functions

```
*** s103s05 ***;

proc sql;
title "Age at Employment";
    select Employee_ID 'Employee ID',
           Birth_Date format=mmddyy10. 'Birth Date',
           Employee_Hire_Date format=mmddyy10. 'Hire Date',
           int((Employee_Hire_Date - Birth_Date)/365.25) 'Age' as Age
        from orion.Employee_payroll
    ;
quit;
title;
```

6. Summarizing Data

```
*** s103s06 ***;

proc sql;
title "Customer Demographics: Gender by Country";
    select Country, Count(*) as Customers,
            sum(Gender="M") as Men,
            sum(Gender = "F") as Women,
            calculated Men/calculated Customers 'Percent Male'
                format=percent6.1
        from orion.Customer
        group by Country
        order by 5,Country
    ;
quit;
title;
```

7. Summarizing Data in Groups

```
*** s103s07 ***;

proc sql;
title "Countries with more Female than Male Customers";
    select Country 'Country',
            sum(Gender="M") as M "Male Customers",
            sum(Gender="F") as F "Female Customers"
        from orion.Customer
        group by Country
        having F > M
        order by F desc
    ;
quit;
title;
```

8. Advanced Summarizing Data in Groups

```
*** s103s08 ***;

proc sql;
title "Countries and Cities Where Employees Live";
    select upcase(Country) 'Country',
            propcase(City) 'City',
            count(*) 'Employees'
        from orion.Employee_addresses
        group by 1,2
        order by 1,2
    ;
quit;
title;
```

Items of interest:

- **Country** and **City** columns – The case of the data values is inconsistent. Sorting by column position uses the data in the intermediate results set, which was already corrected for case using SAS functions.

- Sorting by column name, even if you use column aliases (as **Country**, as **City**), produces duplicates in the output, although the data displayed appears to be identical. This happens because, by default, the ORDER BY and GROUP BY clauses operate on the **Country** and **City** data values found in the original table, before case correction. To ensure that you get the desired results, specify column position numbers in the GROUP BY and ORDER BY clauses instead of column names. This causes SQL to group by and sort by the values in the intermediate result set (corrected data) instead of the values in the original table.

Code demonstrating **incorrect** results:

```
*** s103s08 ***;
proc sql;
title "Countries and Cities Where Employees Live";
title2 "Incorrect Solution: Improper grouping due to Case issues";
title3 "Even with DISTINCT specified, duplicates remain";
   select upcase(Country),
          propcase(City),
          count(*) 'Employees'
      from orion.Employee_addresses
      group by country, city
      order by country, city
   ;
quit;
title;
```

Solutions to Student Activities (Polls/Quizzes)

3.01 Multiple Choice Poll – Correct Answer

Which ORDER BY clause orders a report by descending `State` and descending `City`?

a. `order by state, city`
b. `order by desc state, city`
c. `order by state, city desc`
d. `order by state desc, city desc`
e. `order by desc state, desc city`

11

3.02 Quiz – Correct Answer

1. How many rows did the first query create?

```
proc sql;
   select 'The Average Salary is:',
          avg(Salary)
      from orion.Employee_Payroll
      where Employee_Term_Date is missing
;
quit;
```

Only one row, which displays the average salary for the entire table, was created.

```
                The SAS System
       ---------------------------------
       The Average Salary is:  40476.92
```

38   s103a01

3.02 Quiz – Correct Answer

2. How many rows did the second query create?

```
proc sql;
   select Employee_Gender,
          avg(Salary) as Average
      from orion.Employee_Payroll
      where Employee_Term_Date is missing
;
quit;
```

The output contains 308 rows. This is the number of rows returned by the COUNT(*) function in program s103d07.

39   s103a01

3.02 Quiz – Correct Answer

3. In the second query's results, was the value in the average column different for every gender listed? **No.**

Every row contained the same Average value, which is the overall average salary for the entire table.

	Employee_
Gender	Average
M	40476.92
M	40476.92
M	40476.92
F	40476.92
F	40476.92

40   s103a01

3.03 Quiz – Correct Answer

1. How many rows of output were created?

```
proc sql;
   select Employee_Gender,
          avg(Salary) as Average
      from orion.Employee_Payroll
      where Employee_Term_Date is missing
      group by Employee_Gender
;
quit;
```

Two rows

| | Employee_ | |
Row	Gender	Average
1	F	37002.88
2	M	43334.26

45   s103a02

3.03 Quiz – Correct Answer

2. What major difference was there in the log between this query's results and the second query in the previous activity?

SAS log notes from the previous activity:

```
NOTE: The query requires remerging summary statistics back
with the original data.
NOTE: PROCEDURE SQL used (Total process time):
      real time           0.01 seconds
      cpu time            0.01 seconds
```

SAS log notes from this activity:

```
NOTE: PROCEDURE SQL used (Total process time):
      real time           0.01 seconds
      cpu time            0.01 seconds
```

There was no note about remerging statistics.

46   s103a02

3.04 Poll – Correct Answer

Can you group by more than one column?

(○) Yes
○ No

53

3.05 Quiz – Correct Answer

Which syntax will select employee IDs having bonuses greater than $1000?

1. ```
   select Employee_ID, Salary*0.1 as Bonus
            from orion.Employee_Payroll
            where calculated Bonus > 1000;
   ```

2. ```
   select Employee_ID, Salary*0.1 as Bonus
            from orion.Employee_Payroll
            having Bonus > 1000;
   ```

Both of the these queries produce the desired results.

In the second query, the HAVING clause can be used without the GROUP BY clause to filter the calculated columns row-by-row without specifying the CALCULATED keyword.

65

Solutions to Chapter Review

Chapter Review Answers

1. Which of these ORDER BY clauses will display the results ordered by decreasing **Salary** and then by increasing **Name**?

    a. `order by descending Salary, Name`
    b. `order by Salary desc, Name`
    c. `order by desc Salary, ascending Name`

77

Chapter Review Answers

2. How would you modify this SELECT statement to display the **Salary** column using the EUROX10. format? **format=eurox10.**

```
proc sql;
   select First_Name, Last_Name,
          Job_Title,
          Salary format=eurox10.
      from orion.Sales
;
quit;
```

79

Chapter Review Answers

3. The SAS RANGE() function returns the difference between the largest and the smallest of the non-missing arguments. What clause can you add to this query to produce a listing of the salary range for each value of **Job_Title**? **GROUP BY clause**

```
proc sql;
   select Job_Title, range(Salary)
      from orion.Sales
      group by Job_Title
;
quit;
```

81

Chapter 4 Subqueries

4.1 Noncorrelated Subqueries

Objectives

- Define PROC SQL subqueries.
- Differentiate between correlated and noncorrelated subqueries.
- Subset data based on values returned a subquery.

3

Queries versus Subqueries

A query corresponds to a single SELECT statement within a PROC SQL step.

```
proc sql;
    select *
        from orion.Staff;

    select avg(Salary) as MeanSalary
        from orion.Staff;

    select Job_Title, avg(Salary) as MeanSalary
        from orion.Staff
        group by Job_Title
        having avg(Salary) > 38041.51;
quit;
```

4

Queries versus Subqueries

A *subquery* is a query (SELECT statement) that resides within an outer query (the main SELECT statement). The subquery must be resolved before the main query can be resolved.

```
proc sql;

   select Job_Title, avg(Salary) as MeanSalary       Main Query
      from orion.Staff
      group by Job_Title
      having avg(Salary) >
          (select ...    ...   ...
              from ...   ...   ... );      Subquery

quit;
```

5

Subqueries

Subqueries

- return values to be used in the outer query's WHERE or HAVING clause
- can return single or multiple values
- must return only a single column.

6

Subqueries are also known as nested queries, inner queries, and sub-selects.

Subqueries

There are two types of subqueries:

- In a *noncorrelated subquery*, values are passed from the inner query to the outer query.

```
proc sql;

   select Job_Title, avg(Salary) as MeanSalary
      from orion.Staff
      group by Job_Title
      having avg(Salary) >
         (select avg(Salary) as MeanSalary
             from orion.Staff);    Stand-alone query

quit;
```

7   *continued...*

Subqueries

- In a *correlated subquery*, the outer query must provide information to the subquery before it can be successfully resolved.

```
proc sql;
   select Employee_ID, avg(Salary) as MeanSalary
      from orion.Employee_Addresses
      where 'AU'=
        (select Country
            from Work.Supervisors
            where Employee_Addresses.Employee_ID=
                  Supervisors.Employee_ID);
quit;
```

8

Correlated subqueries are discussed in this chapter's Self-Study section.

Business Scenario

Create a report that displays **Job_Title** for job groups with an average salary greater than the average salary of the company as a whole.

9

Using a Noncorrelated Subquery

s104d01

1. Retrieve the program **s104d01**.

2. Submit the first PROC SQL step to get the average salary from the query results.

```
/* Step 1: Get average salary number from query.*/
proc sql;
   select avg(Salary) as MeanSalary
      from orion.Staff;
quit;
```

3. Review the results in the Output window.

```
               MeanSalary
               _____

                38041.51
```

4. In the Output window, hold down the CTRL key and press the C key to copy the value of average salary.

5. Manually change **xxxxx.xx** in the second step by pasting the average salary value into the HAVING clause.

```
  /* Step 2: Manually change xxxxx.xx to average
     salary from Step1 above. */
proc sql;
   select Job_Title,avg(Salary) as MeanSalary
      from orion.Staff
      group by Job_Title
      having avg(Salary) > xxxxx.xx;
quit;
```

6. Submit the second PROC SQL step with the hardcoded average salary figure.

```
  /* Step 2: Manually change xxxxx.xx to average
     salary from Step1 above. */
proc sql;
   select Job_Title,avg(Salary) as MeanSalary
      from orion.Staff
      group by Job_Title
      having avg(Salary) > 38041.51;
quit;
```

7. Review the results in the Output window.

    Partial PROC SQL Output

Employee Job Title	MeanSalary
Account Manager	46090
Administration Manager	47415
Applications Developer I	42760
Applications Developer II	47315
Applications Developer IV	55751.67
Auditing Manager	53400
Auditor I	42190
Auditor II	46545
Auditor III	51950
BI Administrator IV	58530

8. Submit the third PROC SQL step. Notice that the hardcoded average salary figure was replaced by the query in the first step. The query is placed inside parentheses and is now a noncorrelated subquery.

```
/* Step 3: Use a noncorrelated subquery to return the average
   salary for the HAVING clause. */
proc sql;
   select Job_Title, avg(Salary) as MeanSalary
      from orion.Staff
      group by Job_Title
      having avg(Salary) >
         (select avg(Salary) as MeanSalary
             from orion.Staff);
quit;
```

9. Review the results in the Output window. Notice that the results are identical to the results above in step 7. Now the subquery is populating the value of **avg**.

    Partial PROC SQL Output

Employee Job Title	MeanSalary
Account Manager	46090
Administration Manager	47415
Applications Developer I	42760
Applications Developer II	47315
Applications Developer IV	55751.67
Auditing Manager	53400
Auditor I	42190
Auditor II	46545
Auditor III	51950
BI Administrator IV	58530

Noncorrelated Subqueries

```
proc sql;
    select Job_Title,
            avg(Salary) as MeanSalary
        from orion.Staff
        group by Job_Title
        having avg(Salary) >
            (select avg(Salary)
                from orion.Staff)
    ;
quit;
```

Evaluate the subquery first.

s104d01

11

Noncorrelated Subqueries

```
proc sql;
    select Job_Title,
            avg(Salary) as MeanSalary
        from orion.Staff
        group by Job_Title
        having avg(Salary) > (38041.51)
    ;
quit;
```

Then pass the results to the outer query.

s104d01

12

Noncorrelated Subqueries

Partial PROC SQL Output

Employee Job Title	MeanSalary
Account Manager	46090
Administration Manager	47415
Applications Developer I	42760
Applications Developer II	47315
Applications Developer IV	55751.67
Auditing Manager	53400
Auditor I	42190
Auditor II	46545
Auditor III	51950
BI Administrator IV	58530
BI Architect II	47155
BI Specialist II	44425

13

4.01 Poll

Can a subquery contain a subquery?

○ Yes

○ No

15

Business Scenario

Each month, the CEO sends a birthday card to each employee having a birthday in that month.

Create a report listing the names and addresses of employees with February birthdays.

17

Noncorrelated Subqueries

The `orion.Employee_Addresses` table contains names and addresses. Birth dates are found in the `orion.Employee_Payroll` table.

```
proc sql;
   select Employee_ID,
          Employee_Name, City,
          Country
      from orion.Employee_Addresses
      where Employee_ID in
         (select Employee_ID
             from orion.Employee_Payroll
             where month(Birth_Date)=2)
      order by 1;
quit;
```

s104d02

18

Noncorrelated Subqueries:
How Do They Work?

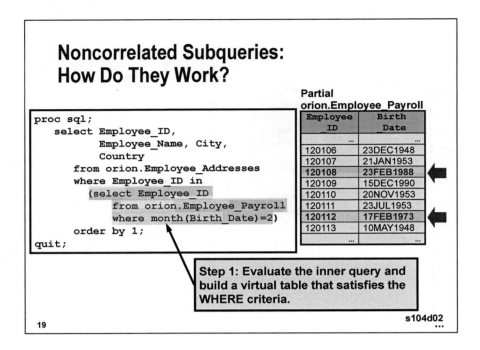

**Partial
orion.Employee_Payroll**

```
proc sql;
   select Employee_ID,
          Employee_Name, City,
          Country
      from orion.Employee_Addresses
      where Employee_ID in
         (select Employee_ID
             from orion.Employee_Payroll
             where month(Birth_Date)=2)
      order by 1;
quit;
```

Employee ID	Birth Date
...	...
120106	23DEC1948
120107	21JAN1953
120108	23FEB1988
120109	15DEC1990
120110	20NOV1953
120111	23JUL1953
120112	17FEB1973
120113	10MAY1948
...	...

Step 1: Evaluate the inner query and build a virtual table that satisfies the WHERE criteria.

19   s104d02
...

Noncorrelated Subqueries:
How Do They Work?

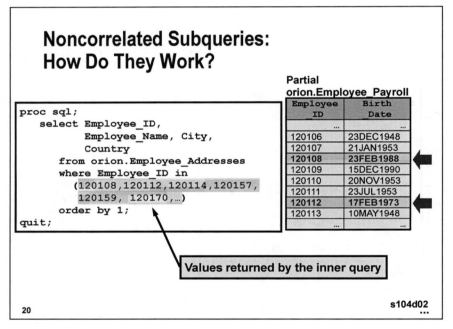

**Partial
orion.Employee_Payroll**

```
proc sql;
   select Employee_ID,
          Employee_Name, City,
          Country
      from orion.Employee_Addresses
      where Employee_ID in
         (120108,120112,120114,120157,
          120159, 120170,…)
      order by 1;
quit;
```

Employee ID	Birth Date
...	...
120106	23DEC1948
120107	21JAN1953
120108	23FEB1988
120109	15DEC1990
120110	20NOV1953
120111	23JUL1953
120112	17FEB1973
120113	10MAY1948
...	...

Values returned by the inner query

20   s104d02
...

Noncorrelated Subqueries: How Do They Work?

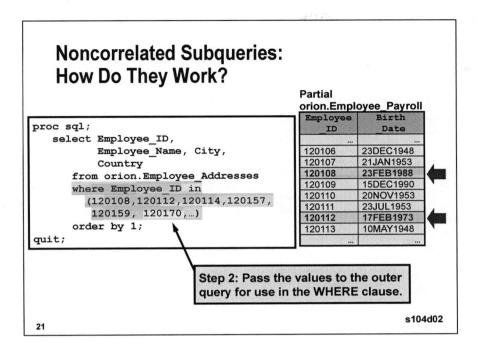

Partial orion.Employee_Payroll

Employee ID	Birth Date
...	...
120106	23DEC1948
120107	21JAN1953
120108	23FEB1988
120109	15DEC1990
120110	20NOV1953
120111	23JUL1953
120112	17FEB1973
120113	10MAY1948
...	...

```
proc sql;
   select Employee_ID,
          Employee_Name, City,
          Country
      from orion.Employee_Addresses
      where Employee_ID in
         (120108,120112,120114,120157,
          120159, 120170,…)
      order by 1;
quit;
```

Step 2: Pass the values to the outer query for use in the WHERE clause.

21   s104d02

Noncorrelated Subqueries: Output

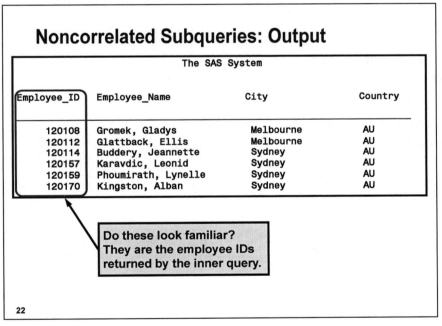

```
                        The SAS System

Employee_ID   Employee_Name          City           Country

    120108    Gromek, Gladys         Melbourne      AU
    120112    Glattback, Ellis       Melbourne      AU
    120114    Buddery, Jeannette     Sydney         AU
    120157    Karavdic, Leonid       Sydney         AU
    120159    Phoumirath, Lynelle    Sydney         AU
    120170    Kingston, Alban        Sydney         AU
```

Do these look familiar? They are the employee IDs returned by the inner query.

22

Setup for the Poll

- Open the program **s104a01**.
- Change the IN operator to an equal sign (=) in the code as shown on the previous slide.
- Run the changed program and review the SAS log for messages.
- What happens when you change the comparison operator to an equal sign?

```
proc sql;
   select Employee_Name, City, Country
      from orion.Employee_Addresses
      where Employee_ID in
        (select Employee_ID
            from orion.Employee_Payroll
            where month(Birth_Date)=2)
      order by 1;
quit;
```

24

4.02 Multiple Choice Poll

What happens when you change the comparison operator to an equal sign?

a. Nothing special; the program runs fine.
b. You get multiple rows returned in your output.
c. You get an error message.
d. a and b.

25

Subqueries That Return Multiple Values

When a subquery returns multiple values and the EQUAL operator is used, an ERROR message is generated. The EQUAL operator does not accept any expression that resolves to more than a single value.

Example:

```
where Employee_ID=120108, 120112, 120114...
```

```
ERROR: Subquery evaluated to more than one row.
```

✎ If the subquery returns multiple values, you must use the IN operator or a comparison operator with the ANY or ALL keywords.

27

The ANY Keyword (Self-Study)

If you specify the ANY keyword before a subquery, the comparison is true if it is true for any of the values that the subquery returns.

Keyword ANY	Signifies...
= ANY(20,30,40)	=20 or =30 or =40
> ANY(20,30,40)	> 20
< ANY(20,30,40)	< 40

✎ The values 20,30,40 represent values returned from a subquery.

28

✎ You can use the = ANY comparison instead of the IN operator.

The ANY Keyword (Self-Study)

Example: Do any Level IV sales representatives have a
          salary that is lower than any of the lower-level
          sales representatives?

```
proc sql;
select Employee_ID, Salary
   from orion.Staff
   where Job_Title='Sales Rep. IV'
         and salary < any
      (select Salary
         from orion.Staff
         where Job_Title in
               ('Sales Rep. I','Sales Rep. II',
                'Sales Rep. III'));
quit;
```

Think < select
max(salary).

s104d03

29

An alternative WHERE clause is shown below:

```
where Job_Title='Sales Rep. IV' and salary <
   (select max(salary) from ...);
```

The ANY Keyword (Self-Study)

Partial PROC SQL Output

Level IV Sales Reps Who Earn Less Than Any Lower Level Sales Rep	
Employee ID	Employee Annual Salary
120125	$32,040
120128	$30,890
120135	$32,490
120159	$30,765
120166	$30,660
121019	$31,320
121020	$31,750

30

The ALL Keyword (Self-Study)

The ALL keyword is true only if the comparison is true for all returned values.

Keyword ALL	Signifies
> ALL(20,30,40)	> 40
< ALL(20,30,40)	< 20

✎ The values 20,30,40 represent values returned from a subquery.

31

The ALL Keyword (Self-Study)

Example: What are the job titles and salaries of the employees who earn more than all Level IV employees?

```
proc sql;
   select Job_Title, Salary
      from orion.Staff
      where Salary > all
      (select Salary
         from orion.Staff
         where Job_Title contains 'IV');

quit;
```

Think > select max(salary).

s104d04

32

An alternative WHERE clause is shown below:

```
where salary >
   (select max(Salary) from ...);
```

Selecting Data (Self-Study)

Partial PROC SQL Output

```
        Job Titles and Salaries of Employees
                 That Earn More Than
                All level IV Employees

                                     Employee
                                      Annual
        Employee Job Title            Salary

        Director                     $163,040
        Sales Manager                $108,255
        Sales Manager                 $87,975
        Chief Executive Officer      $433,800
        Chief Marketing Officer      $207,885
        Chief Sales Officer          $243,190
        Chief Financial Officer      $268,455
        Senior Strategist             $76,105
```

33

 **Exercises**

Submit a LIBNAME statement to assign the libref **orion** to the SAS data library for this course.

```
libname orion '_____';
```

Level 1

1. **Using Subqueries**

   The **orion.Order_Fact** table contains information about orders that were placed by Orion Star Sales staff. Create a report that lists the Sales staff whose average quantity of items sold exceeds the company average quantity of items sold.

   a. Write a query that displays the average **Quantity** for all rows in the table.

   - Use **AVG(Quantity)** to calculate the average.
   - Use the **orion.Order_Fact** table.

   PROC SQL Output

1.747164

   b. Write a query that displays **Employee_ID** and **AVG(Quantity)** for those employees whose average exceeds the company average. The query should do the following:

   - Display the values for **Employee_ID** and **AVG(Quantity)**. Name the second column **MeanQuantity**.
   - Use the **orion.Order_Fact** table.
   - Group the data by **Employee_ID**.
   - Include only groups where the employee's average quantity of items sold exceeds the company average. Use the query from step **1.a.** as a subquery in the HAVING clause.
   - Add a title to the report as shown.

   Partial PROC SQL Output

Employees whose Average Quantity Items Sold Exceeds the Company's Average Items Sold	
Employee_ID	MeanQuantity
120127	2.20
120128	2.00
120134	1.83

Level 2

2. Using a Noncorrelated Subquery

Each month a memo is posted that lists the employees who have employment anniversaries for that month. Create the report for February and list **Employee_ID** and the first and last names for all employees hired during the month of February of any year.

You can find **Employee_Name** in the **orion.Employee_Addresses** table and **Employee_Hire_Date** in the **orion.Employee_Payroll** table. Both tables contain the column **Employee_ID**. Order the report by an employee's last name.

a. Create a query that returns a list of employee IDs for employees with a February anniversary. The query should do the following:

- Display **Employee_ID** numbers.
- Use the **orion.Employee_Payroll** table.
- Return only employees whose **Employee_Hire_Date** isin February.
- Add a title to the report as shown.

```
                Employee IDs for February Anniversaries

                              Employee_ID
                              _____

                                120107
                                120116
                                120136
                                120162
                                120164
                                120167
                                120177
                                120194
                                120267
                                120658
                                120667
                                120671
                                120677
                                120715
                                120719
                                120750
                                120778
                                120806
                                121005
                                121007
                                121022
                                121030
                                121053
                                121070
                                121090
                                121106
                                121130
```

b. Using the query in step **2.a.** as a noncorrelated subquery, write a query that displays the employee IDs and names of employees who have February anniversaries. The final query should do the following:

- Display **Employee_ID** and split **Employee_Name** into two new columns: **FirstName** and **LastName**. Both new columns should have a length of $15 and appropriate labels. (See the report below.) The original **Employee_Name** is stored as **Lastname, Firstname**.

- Use the **orion.Employee_Addresses** table.

- Select only employee IDs for employees who had February anniversary months.

- Order the final results by **LastName**.

- Create an appropriate title.

```
             Employees with February Anniversaries

        Employee_ID  First Name         Last Name
        ─────────────────────────────────────────────
             121030  Jeryl              Areu
             121007  John               Banaszak
             120667  Edwin              Droste
             120778  Angela             Gardner
             120194  Reece              Harwood
             121130  Gary               Herndon
             121106  James              Hilburger
             121070  Agnieszka          Holthouse
             120658  Kenneth            Kennedy
             120177  Franca             Kierce
             121090  Betty              Klibbe
             120671  William            Latty
             120136  Atul               Leyden
             121053  Tywanna            Mcdade
             121005  Yuh-Lang           Mclamb
             120715  Angelia            Neal
             120806  Lorna              Ousley
             120116  Austen             Ralston
             120719  Roya               Ridley
             120267  Belanda            Rink
             120162  Randal             Scordia
             120107  Sherie             Sheedy
             120677  Suad               Sochacki
             120164  Ranj               Stamalis
             121022  Robert             Stevens
             120167  Kimiko             Tilley
             120750  Connie             Woods
```

Level 3

3. Creating Subqueries Using the ALL Keyword

In most companies, you can assume that the higher-level job titles have employees that are older than employees with a lower-level job title. Using the **orion.Staff** table, determine whether there are any lower-level purchasing agents (Purchasing Agent I and Purchasing Agent II) that are older than all the higher-level purchasing agents (Purchasing Agent III). The final report should display **Employee_ID**, **Job_Title**, **Birth_Date**, and a calculated **Age** column for the employee as of 24Nov2007.

Hint: Use the SAS date constant ('24Nov2007'd) in the calculation for **Age**. If you use the TODAY function to calculate the age, the values might differ from the results below:

```
                       Level I or II Purchasing Agents
                     Who are older than ALL Purchasing Agent IIIs


                                                      Employee
                                                        Birth
                 Employee ID  Employee Job Title         Date      Age
                 ---------------------------------------------------------
                      120742  Purchasing Agent I     04FEB1948      59
```

4. Using Nested Subqueries

Orion Star Sales managers are interested in rewarding the top sales person at the company. The **orion.Order_Fact** table contains information about all sales, including the employee ID of the staff member responsible for making the sale. The **orion.Employee_Addresses** table contains the ID and name of every employee in the company.

Generate a report that shows **Employee_ID** and the respective staff member's calculated total sales figures from the **orion.Order_Fact** table. Calculate the total sales figures by summing the product of **Total_retail_price*Quantity**. The **Employee_ID** number 99999999 is a generic employee ID number that indicates an Internet sale for which no staff member can take credit. Exclude the **Employee_ID** number 99999999 when you determine the employee with the highest total sales.

a. Generate a report that shows **Employee_ID** and calculated **Total_Sales** from the **orion.Order_Fact** table.

```
                       Employee with the Highest Total Sales

                         Employee_ID    Total_Sales
                         -------------------------------
                              121045     $8,446.70
```

b. Generate another report that displays **Employee_ID** and **Employee_Name** of the employee with the highest sales. The **orion.Employee_Addresses** table contains the employee names.

```
                    Name of the Employee with the Highest Total Sales

                    Employee_ID  Employee_Name
                    ---------------------------------------
                         121045  Hampton, Cascile
```

c. Write a query that combines the two queries above in order to generate a report that adds the **Total_Sales** column with **Employee_ID** and **Employee_Name** and the calculated **Total_Sales** column.

Hint: To solve this problem, you can use an in-line view.

```
                         Employee with the Highest Sales

            Employee
        Identification
            Number   Employee Name                          Total Sales
        ───────────────────────────────────────────────────────────────
            121045   Hampton, Cascile                        $8,446.70
```

4.2 Correlated Subqueries (Self-Study)

Objectives

- Define correlated subqueries.
- Describe how data is subset using correlated subqueries.

37

Correlated Subqueries

Correlated subqueries

- cannot be evaluated independently
- require values to be passed to the inner query from the outer query
- are evaluated for each row in the outer query.

38

Business Scenario

Create a report listing the employee identifier and the first name followed by the last name for all managers in Australia.

Considerations:

- You have a temporary table, **Supervisors**, containing **Employee_ID** and **Country** for all managers.

- The table **orion.Employee_Addresses** contains **Employee_Name** for all employees, but the names are stored as Last, First.

- You used SCAN() to separate first and last names before. Now you need a new technique to concatenate the pieces into First, Last order.

39

The CATX Function

The CATX function concatenates the values in *argument-1* through *argument-n* by stripping leading and trailing spaces, and inserting the value of *argument-1* between each segment.

General form of the CATX function:

CATX(*delimiter,argument-1,argument-2<, ...argument-n>*)

delimiter a character string that is used as a delimiter between concatenated arguments.

argument a character variable's name, a character constant, or an expression yielding a character value.

40

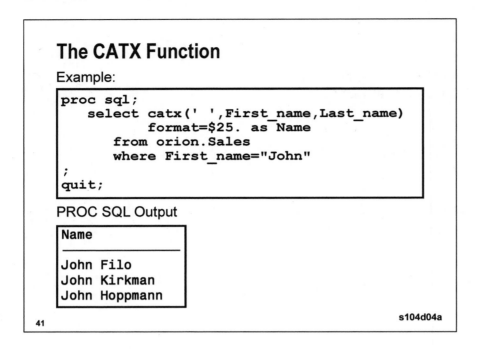

The CATX Function

Example:

```
proc sql;
    select catx(' ',First_name,Last_name)
            format=$25. as Name
        from orion.Sales
        where First_name="John"
;
quit;
```

PROC SQL Output

Name
John Filo
John Kirkman
John Hoppmann

41   s104d04a

Correlated Subqueries

In a correlated subquery, the outer query provides information so that the subquery resolves successfully.

```
proc sql;
  select Employee_ID,
         catx(' ',scan(Employee_Name,2),
         scan(Employee_Name,1) as Manager_Name
         length=25
      from orion.Employee_Addresses
      where 'AU'=
        (select Country
            from Work.Supervisors
            where Employee_Addresses.Employee_ID=
                  Supervisors.Employee_ID);
quit;
```

You must qualify each column with a table name.

42   s104d05

What does it mean to qualify a column?

When a column appears in more than one table, the column name is preceded with the table name or alias to avoid ambiguity. In this example, you use the table names **Employee_Addresses** and **Supervisors** in front of the **Employee_ID** column name.

Correlated Subqueries

```
proc sql;
   select Employee_ID,
          catx(' ',scan(Employee_Name,2),
          scan(Employee_Name,1) as Manager_Name
          length=25
   from orion.Employee_Addresses
   where 'AU'=
       (select Country
           from Work.Supervisors
           where Employee_Addresses.Employee_ID=
               Supervisors.Employee_ID) ;
quit;
```

Partial Listing of
orion.Employee_Addresses

Employee ID	Employee_Name
120145	Aisbitt, Sandy
120798	Ardskin, Elizabeth
120656	Amos, Salley
120104	Billington, Kareen
121035	Blackley, James
121141	Bleu, Henri Le
120679	Cutucache, Chrisy
120103	Dawes, Wilson
120672	Guscott, Verne

Work.Supervisors

Employee ID	Country
120798	US
120800	US
120104	AU
120735	US
121141	US
...	...
120262	US
120679	US
120103	AU
120668	US
121143	US
120260	US
120672	AU

...

Step 1: The outer query takes the first row in `orion.Employee_Addresses` and finds `Employee_ID` and `Employee_Name`.

43

Correlated Subqueries

```
proc sql;
   select Employee_ID,
          catx(' ',scan(Employee_Name,2),
          scan(Employee_Name,1) as Manager_Name
          length=25
   from orion.Employee_Addresses
   where 'AU'=
       (select Country
           from Work.Supervisors
           where Employee_Addresses.Employee_ID=
               Supervisors.Employee_ID) ;
quit;
```

Partial Listing of
orion.Employee_Addresses

Employee ID	Employee_Name
120145	Aisbitt, Sandy
120798	Ardskin, Elizabeth
120656	Amos, Salley
120104	Billington, Kareen
121035	Blackley, James
121141	Bleu, Henri Le
120679	Cutucache, Chrisy
120103	Dawes, Wilson
120672	Guscott, Verne

Work.Supervisors

Employee ID	Country
120798	US
120800	US
120104	AU
120735	US
121141	US
...	...
120262	US
120679	US
120103	AU
120668	US
121143	US
120260	US
120672	AU

...

Step 2: In the subquery, try to match `Employee_Addresses.Employee_ID` of 120145 with the value of `Supervisors.Employee_ID` to find a qualifying row in `Work.Supervisors`.

NO MATCH

44

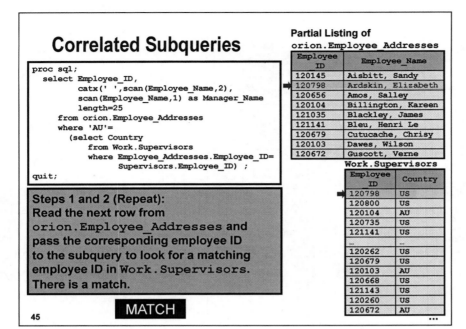

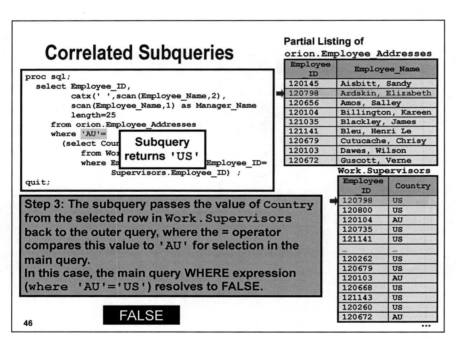

4.03 Quiz

Given the following query, subquery, and data in
Work.Supervisors, what is the maximum number
of rows that will be selected by the outer query?

```
proc sql;
   select Employee_ID,
          catx(' ',scan(Employee_Name,2),
          scan(Employee_Name,1) as Manager_Name
          length=25
      from orion.Employee_Addresses
      where 'AU'=
          (select Country
              from Work.Supervisors
              where Employee_Addresses.Employee_ID=
                  Supervisors.Employee_ID) ;
quit;
```

Work.Supervisors

Employee ID	Country
120798	US
120800	US
120104	AU
120735	US
121141	US
...	...
120262	US
120679	US
120103	AU
120668	US
121143	US
120260	US
120672	AU

48

The Outer Query Controls the Result Set

The outer query determines which rows cause the inner
query to resolve successfully.

```
proc sql;
   select Employee_ID,
          catx(' ',scan(Employee_Name,2),
          scan(Employee_Name,1) as Manager_Name
          length=25
      from orion.Employee_Addresses
      where 'AU'=
          (select Country
              from Work.Supervisors
              where Employee_Addresses.Employee_ID=
                  Supervisors.Employee_ID) ;
quit;
```

Work.Supervisors

Employee ID	Country
120798	US
120800	US
120104	AU
120735	US
121141	US
...	...
120262	US
120679	US
120103	AU
120668	US
121143	US
120260	US
120672	AU

50

Correlated Subqueries

```
proc sql;
  select Employee_ID,
         catx(' ',scan(Employee_Name,2),
         scan(Employee_Name,1) as Manager_Name
         length=25
    from orion.Employee_Addresses
    where 'AU'=
        (select Country
            from Work.Supervisors
            where Employee_Addresses.Employee_ID=
                  Supervisors.Employee_ID) ;
quit;
```

Continue repeating steps 1, 2, and 3 until all `orion.Employee_Addresses` rows are read.

`Employee_ID` **120656** has no match.

NO MATCH

51

Partial Listing of
`orion.Employee_Addresses`

Employee ID	Employee_Name
120145	Aisbitt, Sandy
120798	Ardskin, Elizabeth
120656	Amos, Salley
120104	Billington, Kareen
121035	Blackley, James
121141	Bleu, Henri Le
120679	Cutucache, Chrisy
120103	Dawes, Wilson
120672	Guscott, Verne

Work.Supervisors

Employee ID	Country
120798	US
120800	US
120104	AU
120735	US
121141	US
...	...
120262	US
120679	US
120103	AU
120668	US
121143	US
120260	US
120672	AU

Correlated Subqueries

```
proc sql;
  select Employee_ID,
         catx(' ',scan(Employee_Name,2),
         scan(Employee_Name,1) as Manager_Name
         length=25
    from orion.Employee_Addresses
    where 'AU'=
        (select Country
            from Work.Supervisors
            where Employee_Addresses.Employee_ID=
                  Supervisors.Employee_ID) ;
quit;
```

Continue repeating steps 1, 2, and 3 until all rows are read from `orion.Employee_Addresses`. For `Employee_ID` **120104**, which is passed from the main query to the subquery, there is a match.

MATCH

52

Partial Listing of
`orion.Employee_Addresses`

Employee ID	Employee_Name
120145	Aisbitt, Sandy
120798	Ardskin, Elizabeth
120656	Amos, Salley
120104	Billington, Kareen
121035	Blackley, James
121141	Bleu, Henri Le
120679	Cutucache, Chrisy
120103	Dawes, Wilson
120672	Guscott, Verne

Work.Supervisors

Employee ID	Country
120798	US
120800	US
120104	AU
120735	US
121141	US
...	...
120262	US
120679	US
120103	AU
120668	US
121143	US
120260	US
120672	AU

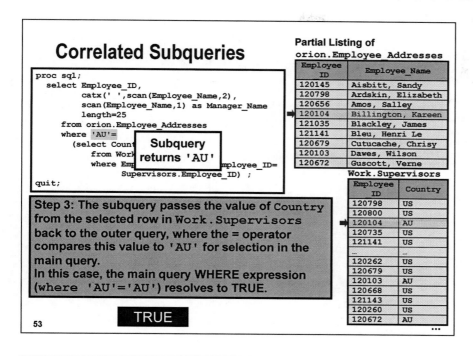

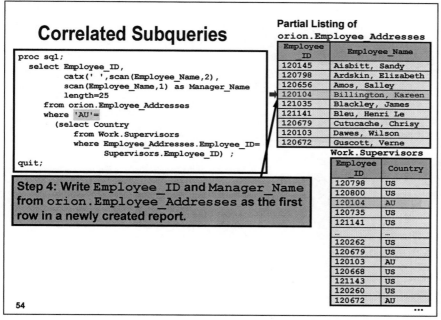

SAS continues this process until all rows are read from the table referred to in the outer query, **orion.Employee_Addresses**. At that point, the final (third) row of the report is written, as seen in the following slide.

Correlated Subqueries

Build third (and final) row of report:

```
Employee_ID   Manager_Name

     120104   Kareen Billington
     120103   Wilson Dawes
     120672   Verne Guscott
```

68

Business Scenario

Create a report showing **Employee_ID** and **Job_Title** columns of all sales personnel who did not make any sales.

The table **orion.Sales** contains **Employee_ID** and **Job_Title** columns for all sales personnel.

The table **orion.Order_Fact** holds information about all sales, and the **Employee_ID** column contains the employee identifier of the staff member who made the sale.

70

The EXISTS and NOT EXISTS Condition

The EXISTS condition tests for the existence of a set of values returned by the subquery.

- The EXISTS condition is true if the subquery returns at least one row.
- The NOT EXISTS condition is true if the subquery returns no data.

71

Correlated Subqueries

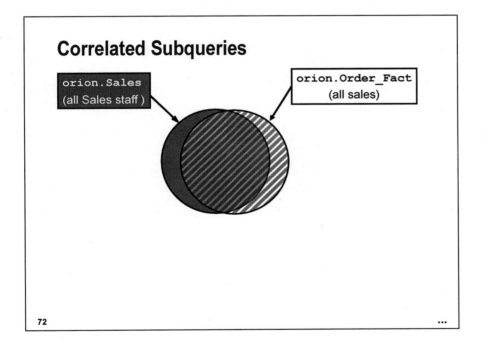

72   ...

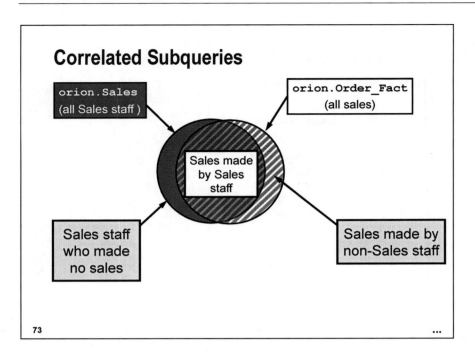

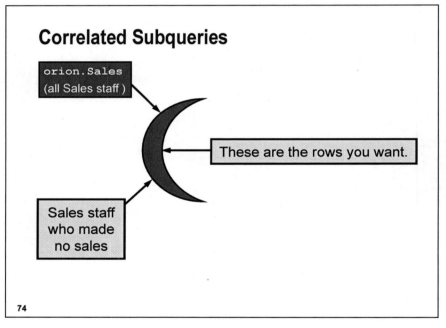

Correlated Subqueries

The table **orion.Sales** contains the employee IDs, job titles, and other demographic information about the Orion Star Sales staff.

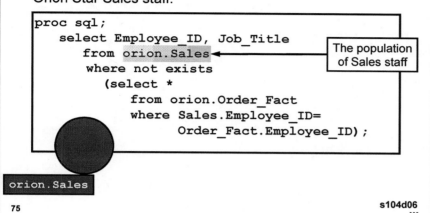

```
proc sql;
   select Employee_ID, Job_Title
      from orion.Sales          ←——  The population
      where not exists                of Sales staff
         (select *
             from orion.Order_Fact
             where Sales.Employee_ID=
                   Order_Fact.Employee_ID);
```

orion.Sales

75   s104d06
                                                        ...

Correlated Subqueries

The **orion.Order_Fact** table contains a row for each product sold to a customer.

```
proc sql;
   select Employee_ID, Job_Title
      from orion.Sales
      where not exists
         (select *                       Staff who
             from orion.Order_Fact  ←——   placed
             where Sales.Employee_ID=     orders
                   Order_Fact.Employee_ID);
```

orion.Order_Fact

76   s104d06
                                                        ...

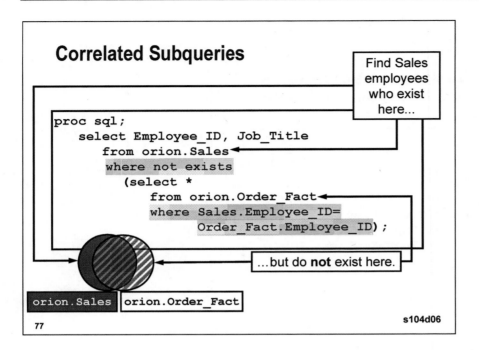

Correlated Subqueries

Find Sales employees who exist here...

```
proc sql;
   select Employee_ID, Job_Title
      from orion.Sales
      where not exists
        (select *
            from orion.Order_Fact
            where Sales.Employee_ID=
                 Order_Fact.Employee_ID);
```

...but do **not** exist here.

orion.Sales orion.Order_Fact

77

s104d06

Testing Concepts: Referencing Columns

Are the highlighted column references equivalent?
Will they result in the same output?

```
proc sql;
   select Employee_ID, Job_Title
      from orion.Sales
      where not exists
        (select *
            from orion.Order_Fact
            where Sales.Employee_ID =
                 Order_Fact.Employee_ID);
quit;
```

```
proc sql;
   select Employee_ID, Job_Title
      from orion.Sales
      where not exists
        (select *
            from orion.Order_Fact
            where Employee_ID=Employee_ID);
quit;
```

78

Setup for the Poll

1. Submit the program **s104a02** and review the results.
2. Change the original code to the code shown below.
3. Submit the changed program and review the results.

Your instructor will review the log results with you.

```
proc sql;
    select Employee_ID, Job_Title
        from orion.Sales
        where not exists
         (select *
               from orion.Order_Fact
               where Employee_ID=Employee_ID);
quit;
```

80

4.04 Poll

Is it necessary to qualify the column names in the inner WHERE clause as follows?

```
where sales.Employee_ID=Order_Fact.Employee_ID
```

○ Yes
○ No

81

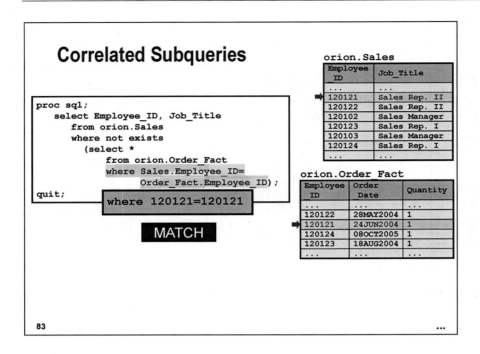

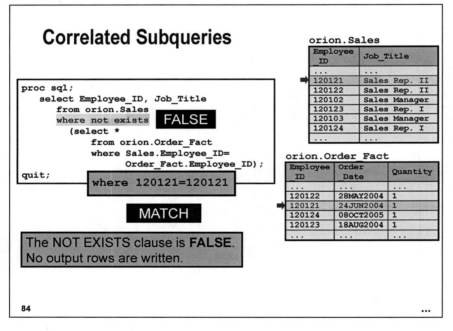

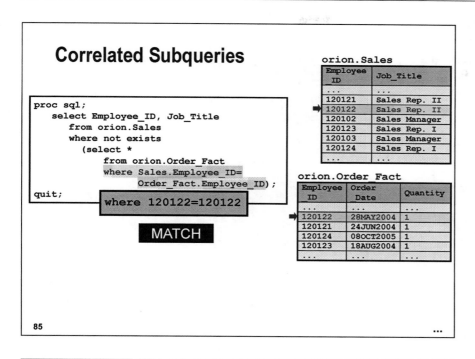

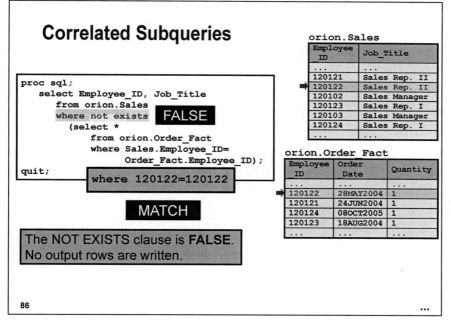

Correlated Subqueries

```
proc sql;
   select Employee_ID, Job_Title
      from orion.Sales
      where not exists
         (select *
            from orion.Order_Fact
            where Sales.Employee_ID=
               Order_Fact.Employee_ID);
quit;
```

NO MATCH

orion.Sales

Employee ID	Job_Title
...	...
120121	Sales Rep. II
120122	Sales Rep. II
➡ 120102	Sales Manager
120123	Sales Rep. I
120103	Sales Manager
120124	Sales Rep. I
...	...

orion.Order_Fact

Employee ID	Order Date	Quantity
...	...	...
120122	28MAY2004	1
120121	24JUN2004	1
120124	08OCT2005	1
120123	18AUG2004	1
...	...	...

87

...

Correlated Subqueries

```
proc sql;
   select Employee_ID, Job_Title
      from orion.Sales
      where not exists        TRUE
         (select *
            from orion.Order_Fact
            where Sales.Employee_ID=
               Order_Fact.Employee_ID);
quit;
```

NO MATCH

The NOT EXISTS clause
evaluates as **TRUE**.
The first output row is written.

orion.Sales

Employee ID	Job_Title
...	...
120121	Sales Rep. II
120122	Sales Rep. II
➡ 120102	Sales Manager
120123	Sales Rep. I
120103	Sales Manager
120124	Sales Rep. I
...	...

orion.Order_Fact

Employee ID	Order Date	Quantity
...	...	...
120122	28MAY2004	1
120121	24JUN2004	1
120124	08OCT2005	1
120123	18AUG2004	1
...	...	...

Partial PROC SQL Output

Employee_ID	Job_Title
120102	Sales Manager

88

...

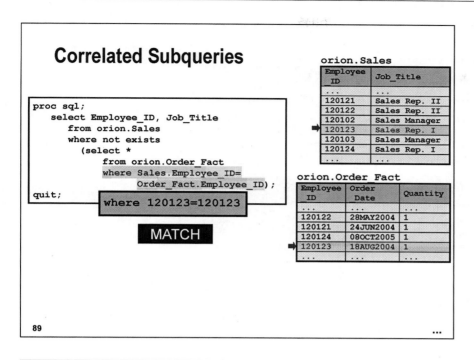

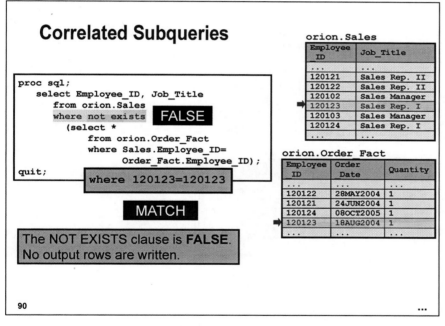

Correlated Subqueries

```
proc sql;
   select Employee_ID, Job_Title
      from orion.Sales
      where not exists
        (select *
            from orion.Order_Fact
            where Sales.Employee_ID=
                  Order_Fact.Employee_ID);
quit;
```

NO MATCH

orion.Sales

Employee ID	Job_Title
...	...
120121	Sales Rep. II
120122	Sales Rep. II
120102	Sales Manager
120123	Sales Rep. I
120103	Sales Manager
120124	Sales Rep. I
...	...

orion.Order_Fact

Employee ID	Order Date	Quantity
...	...	...
120122	28MAY2004	1
120121	24JUN2004	1
120124	08OCT2005	1
120123	18AUG2004	1
...	...	...

Partial PROC SQL Output

Employee_ID	Job_Title
120102	Sales Manager

91   ...

Correlated Subqueries

```
proc sql;
   select Employee_ID, Job_Title
      from orion.Sales
      where not exists    TRUE
        (select *
            from orion.Order_Fact
            where Sales.Employee_ID=
                  Order_Fact.Employee_ID);
quit;
```

NO MATCH

The NOT EXISTS clause
evaluates as **TRUE**.
The next output row is written.

orion.Sales

Employee ID	Job_Title
...	...
120121	Sales Rep. II
120122	Sales Rep. II
120102	Sales Manager
120123	Sales Rep. I
120103	Sales Manager
120124	Sales Rep. I
...	...

orion.Order_Fact

Employee ID	Order Date	Quantity
...	...	...
120122	28MAY2004	1
120121	24JUN2004	1
120124	08OCT2005	1
120123	18AUG2004	1
...	...	...

Partial PROC SQL Output

Employee_ID	Job_Title
120102	Sales Manager
120103	Sales Manager

92   ...

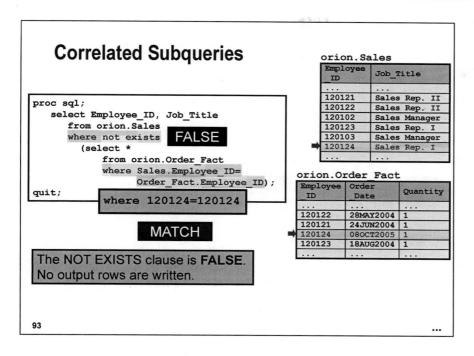

Correlated Subqueries

```
proc sql;
   select Employee_ID, Job_Title
      from orion.Sales
      where not exists   FALSE
         (select *
             from orion.Order_Fact
             where Sales.Employee_ID=
                 Order_Fact.Employee_ID);
quit;

         where 120124=120124

              MATCH
```

The NOT EXISTS clause is **FALSE**.
No output rows are written.

orion.Sales

Employee ID	Job_Title
...	...
120121	Sales Rep. II
120122	Sales Rep. II
120102	Sales Manager
120123	Sales Rep. I
120103	Sales Manager
120124	Sales Rep. I
...	...

orion.Order_Fact

Employee ID	Order Date	Quantity
...	...	...
120122	28MAY2004	1
120121	24JUN2004	1
120124	08OCT2005	1
120123	18AUG2004	1
...	...	...

93

...

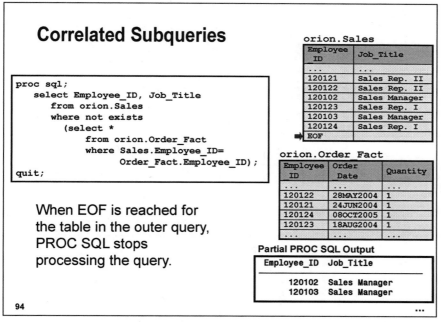

Correlated Subqueries

```
proc sql;
   select Employee_ID, Job_Title
      from orion.Sales
      where not exists
         (select *
             from orion.Order_Fact
             where Sales.Employee_ID=
                 Order_Fact.Employee_ID);
quit;
```

When EOF is reached for
the table in the outer query,
PROC SQL stops
processing the query.

orion.Sales

Employee ID	Job_Title
...	...
120121	Sales Rep. II
120122	Sales Rep. II
120102	Sales Manager
120123	Sales Rep. I
120103	Sales Manager
120124	Sales Rep. I
EOF	

orion.Order_Fact

Employee ID	Order Date	Quantity
...	...	...
120122	28MAY2004	1
120121	24JUN2004	1
120124	08OCT2005	1
120123	18AUG2004	1
...	...	...

Partial PROC SQL Output

Employee_ID	Job_Title
120102	Sales Manager
120103	Sales Manager

94

...

 **Exercises**

Submit a LIBNAME statement to assign the libref **orion** to the SAS data library for this course.

```
libname orion '_____';
```

Level 1

5. **Creating a Simple Correlated Subquery**

   Create a report showing **Employee_ID** and the birth month (calculated as
   month(Birth_date)) for all Australian employees, using a correlated subquery.

   The table **orion.Employee_Payroll** contains **Employee_ID** and **Birth_Date**.

   In the subquery, select only **Country** from **orion.Employee_Addresses**. Use a WHERE
   clause to return only rows where the **EmployeeID** in **orion.Employee_Addresses** matches
   the **EmployeeID** in **orion.Employee_Payroll**.

   Order the report by birth month.

   Partial PROC SQL Output

```
                    Australian Employees' Birth Months

                                    Birth
                   Employee_ID      Month
                  _____

                        120145        1
                        120198        1
                        120147        1
                        120127        1
                        120191        1
```

Level 2

6. Using a Correlated Subquery

Generate a report that displays **Employee_ID**, **Employee_Gender**, and **Marital_Status** for all employees who donate more than 0.02 of their salary. The table **orion.Employee_donations** contains **Employee_ID**, quarterly donations (**Qtr1-Qtr4**), and charities (**Recipients**). The **orion.Employee_Payroll** table contains **Employee_ID** and **Salary** information.

Partial PROC SQL Output

```
                    Employees With Donations > 0.02 Of Their Salary

                                 Employee_        Marital_
                    Employee_ID  Gender           Status
                    ─────────────────────────────────────────
                        120267   F                M
                        120680   F                S
                        120686   F                M
                        120689   F                S
                        120753   M                S
```

4.3 Chapter Review

Chapter Review

True or False:

1. SQL subqueries can return values to be used in an outer query's FROM clause.

2. A subquery can return several rows of data, but must only return values from a single column.

3. Correlated subqueries use very few resources and are inexpensive to execute.

96

4.4 Solutions

Solutions to Exercises

1. **Using Subqueries**

   a.

```
*** s104s01 ***;

title;
proc sql;
   select avg(Quantity) as MeanQuantity
      from orion.Order_Fact;
quit;
```

   b.

```
title "Employees whose Average Quantity Items Sold";
title2 "Exceeds the Company's Average Items Sold";
proc sql;
   select Employee_ID,
          avg(Quantity) as MeanQuantity format=4.2
      from orion.Order_Fact
      group by Employee_ID
      having MeanQuantity >
         (select avg(Quantity)
             from orion.Order_Fact);
quit;
title;
```

2. **Using Noncorrelated Subqueries**

   a.

```
*** s104s02***;

 /*a */
proc sql;
title "Employee IDs for February Anniversaries";
   select Employee_ID
      from orion.Employee_Payroll
      where month(Employee_Hire_Date)=2;
quit;
title;
```

b.

```
    /* b */
proc sql;
title "Employees with February Anniversaries";
    select  Employee_ID,
            scan(Employee_name,2,', ') length=15
                as FirstName 'First Name',
            scan(Employee_name,1,', ') length=15
                as LastName 'Last Name'
        from orion.Employee_Addresses
        where Employee_ID in
            (select Employee_ID
                from orion.Employee_Payroll
                where month(Employee_Hire_Date)=2)
        order by LastName;
quit;
title;
```

3. **(Optional) Creating Subqueries Using the ALL Keyword**

```
*** s104s03***;

proc sql;
title "Level I or II Purchasing Agents";
title2 "Who are older than ALL Purchasing Agent IIIs";
    select Employee_ID, Job_Title, Birth_Date,
            int(('24Nov2007'd-Birth_Date)/365.25) as Age
        from orion.Staff
        where Job_Title  in ('Purchasing Agent I',
                             'Purchasing Agent II')
          and Birth_Date < all
                (select Birth_Date
                    from orion.Staff
                    where Job_Title='Purchasing Agent III')
;
quit;
title;
```

Alternate Solution

```
proc sql;
title "Level I or II Purchasing Agents";
title2 "Who are older than ALL Purchasing Agent IIIs";
    select Employee_ID, Job_Title, Birth_Date,
            int(('24Nov2007'd-Birth_Date)/365.25) as Age
        from orion.Staff
        where Job_Title  in ('Purchasing Agent I',
                             'Purchasing Agent II')
          and Birth_Date <
                (select min(Birth_Date)
                    from orion.Staff
                    where Job_Title='Purchasing Agent III')
;
quit;
title;
```

4. Using Nested Subqueries

a.

```
*** s104s04 ***;

/* a */
proc sql;
title "Employee With The Highest Total Sales";
   select Employee_ID,
          sum(Total_Retail_Price*quantity) as Total_Sales
          format=dollar12.2
       from orion.Order_Fact
       where Employee_ID ne 99999999
       group by Employee_ID
       having Total_Sales =
         (select max(Total_Sales)
             from (select sum(Total_retail_price*quantity)
                         as Total_Sales
                      from orion.Order_Fact
                      where Employee_ID ne 99999999
                      group by Employee_ID))
    ;
quit;
title;
```

b.

```
proc sql;
title "Name Of The Employee With The Highest Sales";
   select Employee_ID, Employee_Name
       from orion.Employee_Addresses
       where Employee_ID=
         (select Employee_ID
             from orion.Order_Fact
             where Employee_ID ne 99999999
             group by Employee_ID
             having  sum(Total_Retail_Price*quantity) =
               (select max(Total_Sales)
                   from (select sum(Total_retail_price*quantity)
                               as Total_Sales
                            from orion.Order_Fact
                            where Employee_ID ne 99999999
                            group by Employee_ID)))
    ;
quit;
title;
```

c.

```sas
proc sql;
title "Employee with the Highest Sales";
   select E.Employee_ID label='Employee Identification Number',
          Employee_Name label='Employee Name',
          Total_Sales format=dollar12.2 label='Total Sales'
      from orion.Employee_Addresses as E,
         (select Employee_ID,
                 sum(Total_Retail_Price*quantity) as
                 Total_Sales format=dollar12.2
            from orion.Order_Fact
            where Employee_ID ne 99999999
            group by Employee_ID
            having Total_Sales =
               (select max(Total_Sales)
                   from (select sum(Total_retail_price*quantity)
                                as Total_Sales
                           from orion.Order_Fact
                           where Employee_ID ne 99999999
                           group by Employee_ID
                        )
               )
         ) as O
      where E.Employee_ID=O.Employee_ID
   ;
quit;
title;
```

5. Creating a Simple Correlated Subquery

```
*** s104s05 ***;
proc sql;
title "Australian Employees' Birth Months";
   select Employee_ID,
          month(Birth_Date) as BirthMonth format=3.
      from orion.Employee_Payroll as EP
      where 'AU' =
         (select Country
             from orion.Employee_Addresses as EA
             where EA.Employee_ID=EP.Employee_ID
         )
      order by 2
   ;
quit;
title;
```

Alternate Solution with Non-Correlated Query

```
proc sql;
title "Australian Employees' Birth Months";
   select Employee_ID, month(Birth_Date) as BirthMonth
      from orion.Employee_Payroll
      where Employee_ID in
         (select Employee_ID
             from orion.Employee_Addresses
             where country='AU'
         )
      order by BirthMonth
   ;
quit;
title;
```

6. Using a Correlated Subquery

```
*** s104s06 ***:
proc sql;
title  "Employees With Donations >  0.02 Of Their Salary";
   select Employee_ID, Employee_Gender,
          Marital_Status
      from orion.Employee_Payroll
      where Employee_ID in
         (select Employee_ID
             from orion.Employee_Donations
             where Employee_Payroll.Employee_ID=
                   Employee_Donations.Employee_ID
                   and sum(qtr1,qtr2,qtr3,qtr4)/salary > .002
         )
      order by Employee_ID
   ;
quit;
title;
```

(Continued on the next page.)

Alternate Solution Using the EXISTS Condition

```
proc sql;
title  "Employees With Donations >  0.02 Of Their Salary";
   select Employee_ID, Employee_Gender,
          Marital_Status
      from orion.Employee_Payroll
      where exists
        (select *
            from orion.Employee_Donations
            where Employee_Payroll.Employee_ID=
                  Employee_Donations.Employee_ID
                  and sum(qtr1,qtr2,qtr3,qtr4)/salary > .002
        )
      order by Employee_ID
   ;
quit;
title;
```

Solutions to Student Activities (Polls/Quizzes)

4.01 Poll – Correct Answer

Can a subquery contain a subquery?

◉ Yes
○ No

16

4.02 Multiple Choice Poll – Correct Answer

What happens when you change the comparison operator to an equal sign?

a. Nothing special; the program runs fine.
b. You get multiple rows returned in your output.
ⓒ You get an error message.
d. a and b.

26

4.03 Quiz – Correct Answer

Given the following query, subquery, and data in **Work.Supervisors**, what is the maximum number of rows that will be selected by the outer query?

Only the three managers where Country='AU' would be selected.

```
proc sql;
   select Employee_ID,
          catx(' ',scan(Employee_Name,2),
          scan(Employee_Name,1) as Manager_Name
          length=25
      from orion.Employee_Addresses
      where 'AU'=
          (select Country
               from Work.Supervisors
               where Employee_Addresses.Employee_ID=
                    Supervisors.Employee_ID) ;
quit;
```

Work.Supervisors

Employee ID	Country
120798	US
120800	US
120104	AU
120735	US
121141	US
...	...
120262	US
120679	US
120103	AU
120668	US
121143	US
120260	US
120672	AU

49

4.04 Poll – Correct Answer

Is it necessary to qualify the column names in the inner WHERE clause as follows?

```
where sales.Employee_ID=Order_Fact.Employee_ID
```

◉ Yes
○ No

82

Solutions to Chapter Review

Chapter Review Answers

True or False:

1. SQL subqueries can return values to be used in an outer query's FROM clause.

   False – Subqueries are used only in WHERE and HAVING clauses.

2. A subquery can return several rows of data, but must only return values from a single column.

   True

3. Correlated subqueries use very few resources and are inexpensive to execute.

   False – Correlated subqueries are resource intensive and can be very expensive to execute.

97

Chapter 5 SQL Joins

5.1 Introduction to SQL Joins

Objectives

- Horizontally combine data from multiple tables.
- Distinguish between inner and outer SQL joins.
- Compare SQL joins to DATA step merges.

3

Combining Data from Multiple Tables

SQL uses set operators to combine tables vertically.

This produces results that can be compared to a DATA step concatenation.

4

Combining Data from Multiple Tables

SQL uses joins to combine tables horizontally.

| Table A | Table B |

This produces results that can be compared to a DATA step merge.

5

5.01 Multiple Choice Poll

Which of these DATA step statements is used to combine tables horizontally?

a. SET
b. APPEND
c. MERGE
d. INPUT
e. INFILE

7

Types of Joins

PROC SQL supports two types of joins:

- inner joins
- outer joins

9

Types of Joins

Inner joins

- return only matching rows
- enable a maximum of 256 tables to be joined at the same time.

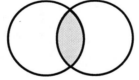

10

If the join involves views, the number of tables underlying the views, not the views themselves, counts toward the limit of 256. SAS 9.1 Service Pack 3 and earlier versions are limited to a maximum of 32 tables.

Types of Joins

Outer joins

- return all matching rows, plus nonmatching rows from one or both tables
- can be performed on only two tables or views at a time.

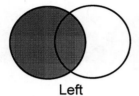 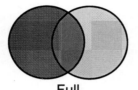 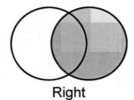

Left   Full   Right

11

Cartesian Product

To understand how SQL processes a join, it is important to understand the concept of the Cartesian product.

A query that lists multiple tables in the FROM clause without a WHERE clause produces all possible combinations of rows from all tables. This result is called the *Cartesian product*.

```
select *
   from one, two;
```

12   s105d01

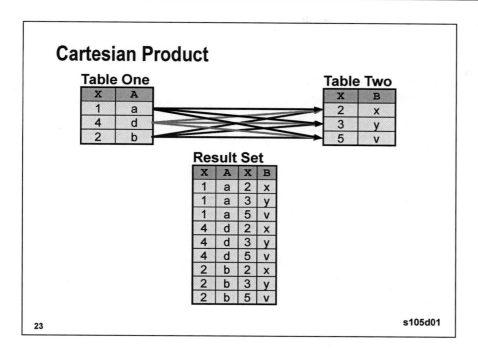

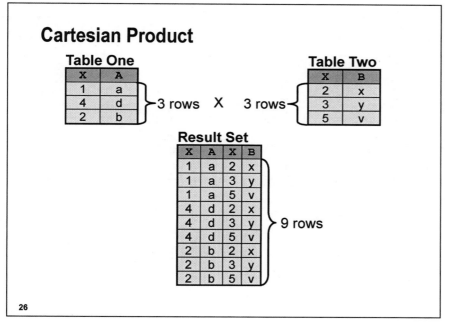

Cartesian Product

The number of rows in a Cartesian product is the product of the number of rows in the contributing tables.

3 x 3 = 9
1,000 x 1,000 = 1,000,000
100,000 x 100,000 = 10,000,000,000

A Cartesian product is rarely the **desired** result of a query.

27

Alternatively, CROSS JOIN syntax can be used to produce the Cartesian product of two tables:

```
proc sql;
   select *
      from one cross join two
;
quit;
```

 When a Cartesian product is generated, the SQL processor prints a note in the SAS log:

```
NOTE: The execution of this query involves performing one or more
Cartesian product joins that cannot be optimized.
```

5.02 Quiz

How many rows are returned from this query?

```
select *
   from three, four;
```

Table Three

X	A
1	a1
1	a2
2	b1
2	b2
4	d

Table Four

X	B
2	x1
2	x2
3	y
5	v

29

s105a01

Inner Joins

Inner join syntax resembles Cartesian product syntax, but a WHERE clause restricts which rows are returned.

General form of an inner join:

SELECT *column-1<, ...column-n>*
   FROM *table-1|view-1<, ... table-n|view-n>*
   WHERE *join-condition(s)*
      <AND other subsetting conditions>
      <other clauses>;

Significant syntax changes from earlier queries:

- The FROM clause references multiple tables.
- The WHERE clause includes join conditions in addition to other subsetting specifications.

32

The distinguishing characteristics of inner join syntax are
- a list of two or more table names in the FROM clause
- one or more join conditions in the WHERE clause.

Inner Joins

Conceptually, when processing an inner join, PROC SQL does the following:

1. builds the Cartesian product of all the tables listed
2. applies the WHERE clause to limit the rows returned

33

In reality, the SQL Procedure Optimizer breaks the Cartesian product into smaller pieces. SAS data sets are stored in pages that contain a certain number of observations. To reduce input/output, the SQL Procedure Optimizer uses these pages in its processing.

During a two-way join, the following tasks are completed:

1. The first page from table A is read into memory with as many of the first pages from table B that can fit into available memory.

2. Valid rows are selected.

3. The first page of table A is kept in memory. All subsequent pages from table B that can fit into memory are read and step 2 is repeated.

4. All pages from table B are processed in combination with page 1 from table A. Steps 1 through 4 are repeated for page 2 from table A. The entire process stops when all rows in both tables are processed.

The SQL Procedure Optimizer can process an *equijoin* (a join on an equal condition, for example, **where x.idnum=y.idnum**) more efficiently than a join involving an inequality.

During a two-way equijoin, the following tasks are completed:

1. Both tables are sorted by the matching column (if necessary) and are grouped by the matching column's value into chunks.

2. The Cartesian product is only performed on matching portions of data.

3. After a section of data is processed, it is not processed again.

   The SQL Procedure Optimizer has other algorithms from which to select to optimize a join. For example, the optimizer might use a hashing algorithm when joining a small table with a large table.

In a multiway join (more than two tables), in order to minimize the Cartesian product, the SQL Procedure Optimizer does the following:

- splits the join into a number of two-way joins, and eliminates rows and columns from the intermediate tables as soon as they are no longer required

- decides the order in which the tables are processed

- processes the joins in the order that minimizes the intermediate Cartesian product

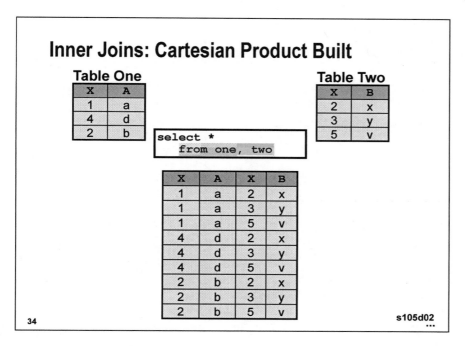

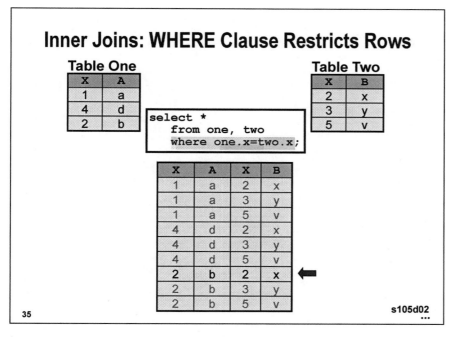

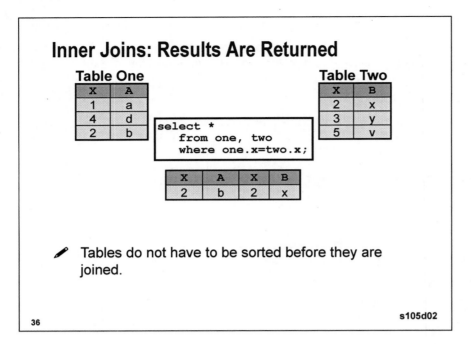

Inner Joins: Results Are Returned

Table One

X	A
1	a
4	d
2	b

```
select *
    from one, two
    where one.x=two.x;
```

Table Two

X	B
2	x
3	y
5	v

X	A	X	B
2	b	2	x

✎ Tables do not have to be sorted before they are joined.

36   s105d02

✎ When same-named columns exist in more than one table used in a query, you must qualify those names to avoid ambiguity. A qualified column name consists of the table name and column name separated by a period. In the example above, both tables contain a column named **X**, so you must qualify the name of column **X**. The qualified name for the **X** column from table **one** is **one.x**. The qualified name for the **X** column from table **two** is **two.x**.

✎ Because column **X** exists in both tables, there are two **X** columns in the query result.

Inner Joins

One method of displaying the X column only once is to use a table qualifier in the SELECT list.

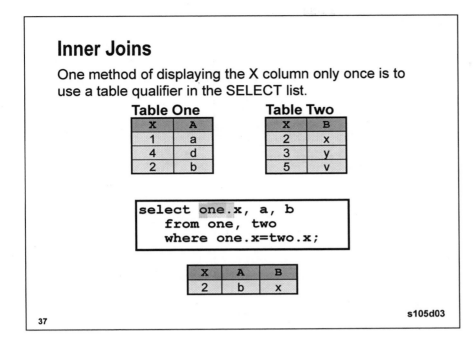

Table One

X	A
1	a
4	d
2	b

Table Two

X	B
2	x
3	y
5	v

```
select one.x, a, b
    from one, two
    where one.x=two.x;
```

X	A	B
2	b	x

s105d03

37

Equijoins are specialized inner joins where the join criteria specify equality for the identifying variables. The above query is an example of an equijoin. Natural joins are even more specialized equijoins in which SQL compares the values of all same-name columns in both tables and produces output containing **only one column** for results from same-name columns in the source tables. The rows in the tables are joined, based on matching values in same-name columns.

For example, the following natural join code would produce results identical to the query above:

```
proc sql;
    select *
        from one natural join two
;
quit;
```

Inner Joins

Display all combinations of rows with matching keys, including duplicates.

Table Three

X	A
1	a1
1	a2
2	b1
2	b2
4	d

Table Four

X	B
2	x1
2	x2
3	y
5	v

```
proc sql;
   select *
       from three, four
       where three.x=four.x;
quit;
```

38   s105d04
                                       ...

Inner Joins

Display all combinations of rows with matching keys, including duplicates.

Table Three

X	A
1	a1
1	a2
2	b1
2	b2
4	d

Table Four

X	B
2	x1
2	x2
3	y
5	v

Results Set

X	A	X	B
2	b1	2	x1
2	b1	2	x2
2	b2	2	x1
2	b2	2	x2

```
proc sql;
   select *
       from three, four
       where three.x=four.x;
quit;
```

39   s105d04

Setup for the Poll

Run program **s105a02** and review the results to determine how many rows (observations) the DATA step MERGE statement produces in the output table.

Three

X	A
1	a1
1	a2
2	b1
2	b2
4	d

Four

X	B
2	x1
2	x2
3	y
5	v

```
data new;
   merge three (in=InThree)
         four (in=InFour);
   by x;
   if InThree and InFour;
run;

proc print data=new;
run;
```

41   s105a02

5.03 Multiple Choice Poll

How many rows (observations) result from the DATA step MERGE statement in program **s105a02**?

a. 4

b. 2

c. 6

d. 20

e. None of the above

42

Business Scenario

Display the name, city, and birth month of all Australian employees. Here is a sketch of the desired report:

Australian Employees' Birth Months		
Name	City	Birth Month
Last, First	City Name	1

44

Business Scenario

Considerations:

- **orion.Employee_Addresses** contains employee name, country, and city data.
- **orion.Payroll** contains employee birth dates.
- Both **orion.Employee_Addresses** and **orion.Payroll** contain **Employee_ID**.
- Names are stored in the **Employee_Name** column as Last, First.

45

Inner Joins

```
proc sql;
title "Australian Employees' Birth Months";
select Employee_Name as Name format=$25.,
       City format=$25.,
       month(Birth_Date) 'Birth Month' format=3.
   from orion.Employee_Payroll,
        orion.Employee_Addresses
   where Employee_Payroll.Employee_ID=
         Employee_Addresses.Employee_ID
         and Country='AU'
   order by 3,City, Employee_Name;
quit;
```

46   s105d05

Inner Joins

Partial PROC SQL Output

```
           Australian Employees Birthday Months

                                          Birth
Name                      City            Month

Aisbitt, Sandy            Melbourne         1
Graham-Rowe, Jannene      Melbourne         1
Hieds, Merle              Melbourne         1
Sheedy, Sherie            Melbourne         1
Simms, Doungkamol         Melbourne         1
Tannous, Cos              Melbourne         1
Body, Meera               Sydney            1
Clarkson, Sharryn         Sydney            1
Dawes, Wilson             Sydney            1
Rusli, Skev               Sydney            1
Glattback, Ellis          Melbourne         2
Gromek, Gladys            Melbourne         2
```

47

Inner Join Alternate Syntax

An inner join can also be accomplished using an alternate syntax, which limits the join to a maximum of two tables.

General form of an inner join:

```
SELECT column-1 <, ...column-n>
     FROM table-1
     INNER JOIN
          table-2
     ON join-condition(s)
     <other clauses>;
```

✐   This syntax is common in SQL code produced by code generators such as SAS Enterprise Guide. The ON clause specifies the JOIN criteria; a WHERE clause **can** be added to subset the results.

48

Inner Join Alternate Syntax

```
proc sql;
title "Australian Employees' Birth Months";
select Employee_Name as Name format=$25.,
       City format=$25.,
       month(Birth_Date) 'Birth Month' format=3.
  from orion.Employee_Payroll
       inner join
       orion.Employee_Addresses
       on Employee_Payroll.Employee_ID=
          Employee_Addresses.Employee_ID
  where Country='AU'
  order by 3,City, Employee_Name;
quit;
```

49   s105d06

5.04 Multiple Choice Poll

How many tables can be combined using a single inner join?

a. 2
b. 32
c. 256
d. 512
e. Limited only by my computer's resources
f. No limit

51

Outer Joins

Inner joins returned only matching rows. When you join tables, you might want to include nonmatching rows as well as matching rows.

54

Outer Joins

You can retrieve both nonmatching and matching rows using an outer join.

Outer joins include left, full, and right outer joins. Outer joins can process only two tables at a time.

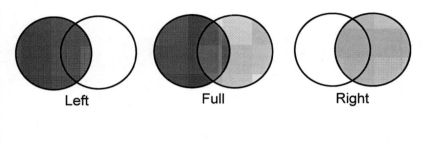

| Left | Full | Right |

55

✎ An outer join is an augmentation of an inner join. It returns all the rows generated by an inner join, plus others.

Compare Inner Joins And Outer Joins

The following table is a comparison of inner and outer join syntax and limitations:

Key Point	Inner Join	Outer Join
Table Limit	256	2
Join Behavior	Returns matching rows only	Returns matching and nonmatching rows
Join Options	Matching rows only	LEFT, FULL, RIGHT
Syntax changes	▪ Multiple tables in the FROM clause ▪ WHERE clause that specifies join criteria	ON clause that specifies join criteria

56

✎ A single SELECT statement can include more than one outer join, but the joins are processed one at a time.

Outer Joins

Outer join syntax is similar to the inner join alternate syntax.

General form of an outer join:

```
SELECT column-1 <, ...column-n>
    FROM table-1
    LEFT|RIGHT|FULL JOIN
        table-2
    ON join-condition(s)
        <other clauses>;
```

The ON clause specifies the join criteria in outer joins.

57

The distinguishing characteristics of outer join syntax are as follows:

- a FROM clause containing a single table name, one of the three OUTER JOIN operators, and then another single table name, in that order
- an ON clause specifying the join condition(s)

Outer joins are usually referred to as LEFT, RIGHT, or FULL joins.

In outer joins, the WHERE and ON clauses operate independently.

- The ON clause specifies the rows to be joined.
- The WHERE clause produces a subset of the results.

Determining Left and Right

Consider the position of the tables in the FROM clause.

- Left joins include all rows from the first (left) table, even if there are no matching rows in the second (right) table.
- Right joins include all rows from the second (right) table, even if there are no matching rows in the first (left) table.
- Full joins include all rows from both tables, even if there are no matching rows in either table.

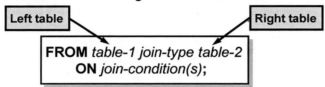

| Left table | | Right table |

```
FROM table-1 join-type table-2
      ON join-condition(s);
```

58

Left Join

Table One	
X	A
1	a
4	d
2	b

Table Two	
X	B
2	x
3	y
5	v

```
select *
   from one left join two
      on one.x = two.x;
```

X	A	X	B
1	a	.	
2	b	2	x
4	d	.	

59

s105d07

Right Join

Table Two	
X	B
2	x
3	y
5	v

Table One	
X	A
1	a
4	d
2	b

```
select *
   from two right join one
      on one.x = two.x;
```

X	B	X	A
.		1	a
2	x	2	b
.		4	d

60

s105d08

Full Join

Table One	
X	A
1	a
4	d
2	b

Table Two	
X	B
2	x
3	y
5	v

```
select *
   from one full join two
      on one.x = two.x;
```

X	A	X	B
1	a	.	
2	b	2	x
.		3	y
4	d	.	
.		5	v

61

s105d09

Business Scenario

List the employee ID and gender for all married employees. Include the names of any charities to which the employee donates via the company program.

62

Business Scenario

Considerations:

- The **orion.Employee_Payroll** table contains gender and marital status information.
- The **orion.Employee_Donations** table contains records only for those employees who donate to a charity via the company program.
- Less than half of all employees are married.

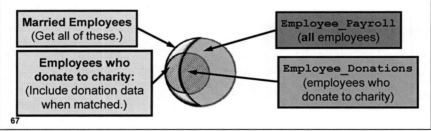

Married Employees
(Get all of these.)

Employees who donate to charity:
(Include donation data when matched.)

Employee_Payroll
(all employees)

Employee_Donations
(employees who donate to charity)

67

5.05 Multiple Choice Poll

For the report, you need the data for all married employees from `orion.Employee_Payroll`. You also want to include the charity names from the `orion.Employee_Donations` table if `Employee_ID` matches. What type of join should you use to combine the information from these two tables?

a. Inner Join
b. Left Join
c. Full Join
d. None of the above

69

Outer Joins

```
proc sql;
   select Employee_payroll.Employee_ID,
          Employee_Gender, Recipients
      from orion.Employee_payroll
           left join
           orion.Employee_donations
      on Employee_payroll.Employee_ID=
         Employee_donations.Employee_ID
      where Marital_Status="M"
;
quit;
```

71   s105d10

Outer Joins

Partial PROC SQL Output (Rows 203-215)

```
               Employee_
Employee_ID    Gender    Recipients
_____

    121128     F         Cancer Cures, Inc.
    121131     M         Vox Victimas 40%, Conserve Nature, Inc. 60%
    121132     M         EarthSalvors 50%, Vox Victimas 50%
    121133     M         Disaster Assist, Inc.
    121138     M         Cuidadores Ltd.
    121139     F
    121142     M         AquaMissions International 10%, Child Survivors 90%
    121143     M         Mitleid International 60%, Save the Baby Animals 40%
    121144     F
    121145     M         Save the Baby Animals
    121146     F
    121147     F         Cuidadores Ltd. 50%, Mitleid International 50%
    121148     M
```

✎ Remember that output order is not guaranteed unless
   you use an ORDER BY clause.

72

Using a Table Alias

An *alias* is a table nickname. You can assign an alias to a table by following the table name in the FROM clause with the AS keyword and a nickname for the table. Then use the alias in other clauses of the QUERY statement.

General form of the FROM clause:

```
SELECT alias-1.column-1<, ...alias-2.column-n>
    FROM table-1 AS alias-1
            join-type
            table-2 AS alias-2
    ON join-condition(s)
        <other clauses>;
```

73

Using a Table Alias

```
proc sql;
   select p.Employee_ID, Employee_Gender,
          Recipients
      from orion.Employee_payroll as p
          left join
          orion.Employee_donations as d
      on p.Employee_ID=d.Employee_ID
      where Marital_Status="M"
;
quit;
```

74   s105d11

🖉   A table alias is primarily used to reduce the amount of typing required to write a query.
It is usually optional. There are, however, other situations that require a table alias:

- creating a self join (a table is joined to itself); for example:

```
from orion.Staff as s1, orion.Staff as s2
```

- referencing same-named columns from multiple in-line views or from same-named tables in
different libraries.

🖉   The AS keyword is optional in a table alias. The alias can directly follow the table name in the
FROM clause.

DATA Step Merge (Review)

A DATA step with MERGE and BY statements automatically overlays same-name columns.

Table One

X	A
1	a
4	d
2	b

Table Two

X	B
2	x
3	y
5	v

Table One must be sorted or indexed on column X before a merge can be performed.

```
data merged;
   merge one two;
   by x;
run;
proc print data=merged;
run;
```

Output

X	A	B
1	a	
2	b	x
3		y
4	d	
5		v

s105d12

75

SQL Join versus DATA Step Merge

SQL joins do not automatically overlay same-named columns.

Table One

X	A
1	a
4	d
2	b

Table Two

X	B
2	x
3	y
5	v

```
proc sql;
   select one.x, a, b
      from one full join two
      on one.x=two.x
;
quit;
```

Output

X	A	B
1	a	
2	b	x
○		y
4	d	
○		v

s105d12

76

The COALESCE Function

The COALESCE function returns the value of the first non-missing argument.

General form of the COALESCE function:

> **COALESCE**(*argument-1,argument-2<, ...argument-n*)

argument   can be a constant, expression, or variable name. When all arguments are missing, COALESCE returns a missing value.

✎ All arguments must be of the same type (character or numeric).

77

SQL Join versus DATA Step Merge

You can use the COALESCE function to overlay columns.

Table One

X	A
1	a
4	d
2	b

Table Two

X	B
2	x
3	y
5	v

```
proc sql;
   select coalesce(one.x,two.x)
          as x,a,b
      from one full join two
      on one.x=two.x;
quit;
```

Output

```
X  A  B
1  a
2  b  x
3     y
4  d
5     v
```

s105d12

78

SQL Join versus DATA Step Merge

Key Points	SQL Join	DATA Step Merge
Explicit sorting of data before join/merge	Not required	Required
Same-named columns in join/merge expressions	Not required	Required
Equality in join or merge expressions	Not required	Required

79

Tables can be joined on inequalities; for example:

```
proc sql;
title "List of things I could buy";
   select Item_name, Price
       from budget, wish_list
       where budget.cash_available > wish_list.Price
;
quit;
```

 **Exercises**

If you restarted SAS since the last exercise, submit a LIBNAME statement to assign the libref **orion** to the SAS data library for this course.

```
libname orion '_____';
```

Level 1

1. **Inner Joins**

    Produce a report containing **Employee_Name** and calculated years of service (YOS) as of December 31, 2007, by joining **orion.Employee_Addresses** and **orion.Employee_Payroll** on **Employee_ID**. Label the columns and provide two title lines, as shown in the sample output. Limit the report to employees where YOS > 30. Order the output alphabetically by **Employee_Name**.

    - The **orion.Employee_Addresses** table contains the **Employee_Name** column.
    - The **orion.Employee_Payroll** table contains the **Employee_Hire_Date** column.
    - Both **orion.Employee_Addresses** and **orion.Employee_Payroll** contain columns named **Employee_ID**.
    - Use TITLE1 and TITLE2 statements to produce title lines as indicated in the sample report:

    Partial PROC SQL Output

    ```
                    Employees With More Than 30 Years of Service
                              As of December 31, 2007


                                                    Years of
                    Name                            Service

                    Abbott, Ray                        32
                    Banchi, Steven                     33
                    Blackley, James                    33
                    Bleu, Henri Le                     33
                    Branly, Wanda                      33
                    Buddery, Jeannette                 33
                    Campbell, Carston                  33
                    Capps, Ramond                      33
    ```

 Age/years of service calculations can be difficult to render precisely. In this course, you use the following:

```
YOS=int(('31DEC2007'd= Employee_Hire_Date)/365.25)
```

Others might leverage the INTCK function, like this:

```
YOS=intck('year',Employee_Hire_Date,'31DEC2007'd)
```

For a more in-depth discussion, see "Accurately Calculating Age with Only One Line of Code" at support.sas.com/kb/24/808.html.

2. Outer Joins

Join `orion.Sales` and `orion.Employee_Addresses` on `Employee_ID` to create a report showing the names and cities of all Orion Star employees, and if an employee is in Sales, the job title. Present the report in alphabetical order by city, job title, and name.

- The `orion.Sales` table contains a record for every employee in the Sales Department and includes columns `Employee_ID` and `Job_Title`.

- The `orion.Employee_Addresses` table contains a record for every employee and includes `Employee_ID`, `Employee_Name`, and `City`.

Partial PROC SQL Output

Name	City	Job_Title
Blanton, Brig	Melbourne	
Catenacci, Reyne	Melbourne	
Dillin, Kerrin	Melbourne	
Fiocca, Jina	Melbourne	
Fouche, Madelaine	Melbourne	
Glattback, Ellis	Melbourne	
Graham-Rowe, Jannene	Melbourne	
Gromek, Gladys	Melbourne	
Harwood, Reece	Melbourne	
Hieds, Merle	Melbourne	
Horsey, Riu	Melbourne	
Mccleary, Bill	Melbourne	
Moffat, Trent	Melbourne	
Pettolino, Peter	Melbourne	
Povey, Liz	Melbourne	
Santomaggio, Pearl	Melbourne	
Sheedy, Sherie	Melbourne	
Streit, Russell	Melbourne	
Zhou, Tom	Melbourne	Sales Manager
Barcoe, Selina	Melbourne	Sales Rep. I
Chantharasy, Judy	Melbourne	Sales Rep. I
Duckett, Shani	Melbourne	Sales Rep. I
Osborn, Hernani	Melbourne	Sales Rep. I
Pa, Koavea	Melbourne	Sales Rep. I
Scordia, Randal	Melbourne	Sales Rep. I
Simms, Doungkamol	Melbourne	Sales Rep. I
Aisbitt, Sandy	Melbourne	Sales Rep. II
George, Vino	Melbourne	Sales Rep. II
Magrath, Brett	Melbourne	Sales Rep. II

Level 2

3. **Joining Multiple Tables**

Create a report showing Orion Star Internet customers residing in the U.S. or Australia who purchased foreign manufactured products, that is, a product that was not manufactured in their country of residence. The report should be titled `US and Australian Internet Customers Purchasing Foreign Manufactured Products` and should display the customers' names and the number of foreign purchases made. Present the information so that those with the largest number of purchases appear at the top of the report, and customers who have the same number of purchases are displayed in alphabetical order.

`Employee_ID` 99999999 is a dummy ID that can be used to identify Internet orders. The data that you need can be found in the listed columns of the following tables:

- `orion.Product_Dim` contains
  - `Product_ID`
  - `Supplier_Country`
- `orion.Order_Fact` contains
  - `Product_ID`
  - `Customer_ID`
- `orion.Customer` contains
  - `Customer_ID`
  - `Country`

Partial PROC SQL Output

```
                  US and Australian Internet Customers
                  Purchasing Foreign Manufactured Products


        Name                              Purchases
        _____

        Candy Kinsey                            10
        Phenix Hill                              7
        Cynthia Mccluney                         5
        Korolina Dokter                          5
        Najma Hicks                              4
        Robert Bowerman                          4
```

Level 3

4. Joining Multiple Tables

Create a report of Orion Star employees with more than 30 years of service as of December 31, 2007. Display the employee's name, years of service, and the employee's manager's name. Order the report alphabetically by manager name, by descending years of service, and then alphabetically by employee name. Label the columns and title the report as shown in the sample output.

The data that you need can be found in the listed columns of the following tables:

- orion.**Employee_Addresses** contains

  - **Employee_ID**

  - **Employee_Name**

- orion.**Employee_Payroll** contains

  - **Employee_ID**

  - **Employee_Hire_Date**

- orion.**Employee_Organization** contains

  - **Employee_ID**

  - **Manager_ID** (**Employee_ID** of the person's manager)

Partial PROC SQL Output

```
                   Employees with more than 30 years of service
                             as of December 31, 2007

                                            Years of
            Employee Name                    Service  Manager Name
            _____

            Marion, Chiorene                     33   Ardskin, Elizabeth
            Zied, Ahmed                          33   Ardskin, Elizabeth
            Buddery, Jeannette                   33   Billington, Kareen
            Hornsey, John                        33   Billington, Kareen
            Horsey, Riu                          33   Billington, Kareen
```

5.2 Complex SQL Joins

Objectives

- Create and use in-line views.
- Use in-line views and subqueries to simplify coding a complex query.

83

In-Line Views

In-line views are often useful when you build complex SQL queries.

An *in-line view* is

- a temporary "virtual table" that exists only during query execution
- created by placing a query expression in a FROM clause where a table name would normally be used.

84

In-Line Views

An in-line view is a query expression (SELECT statement) that resides in a FROM clause. It acts as a virtual table, used in place of a physical table in a query.

```
proc sql;
   select *
      from
        (in-line view query expression)
quit;
```

85

 An in-line view consists of any valid SQL query, except that it must **not** contain an ORDER BY clause. In-line views can be independently tested while building a complex query, which can simplify troubleshooting.

Business Scenario

List all active Sales employees having annual salaries significantly (more than 5%) lower than the average salary for everyone with the same job title.

86

Considerations

First, you must calculate the average salaries for active employees in the Sales department, grouped by job title.

Next, you must match each employee to a GROUP-BY job title.

Finally, you must compare the employee's salary to the group's average to determine if it is more than 5% below the group average.

87

In-Line Views

Build a query to produce the aggregate averages.

```
proc sql;
title   'Sales Department Average Salary';
title2 'By Job Title';
   select Job_Title,
          avg(Salary) as Job_Avg
          format=comma7.
      from orion.Employee_payroll as p,
           orion.Employee_organization as o
      where p.Employee_ID=o.Employee_ID
            and not Employee_Term_Date
            and o.Department="Sales"
   group by Job_Title;
quit;
```

88   s105d13

In-Line Views

PROC SQL Output

Sales Department Average Salary by Job Title	
Job_Title	Job_Avg
Sales Rep. I	26,576
Sales Rep. II	27,348
Sales Rep. III	29,214
Sales Rep. IV	31,589

89

In-Line Views

If you create a table from the results of the query, you can join this table and the **orion.Employee_payroll** table and subset the appropriate rows to get the answer. This adds unnecessary I/O.

Would it be useful to use only the query itself in place of a table?

In SQL, you can with an in-line view!

90

In-Line Views

Using a query in the FROM clause in place of a table
causes the query output to be used as an in-line view.

```
proc sql;
title  'Employees with salaries less than';
title2 '95% of the average for their job';
   select Employee_Name, emp.Job_Title,
          Salary format=comma7., Job_Avg format=comma7.
      from (select Job_Title,
                   avg(Salary) as Job_Avg format=comma7.
               from orion.Employee_payroll as p,
                    orion.Employee_organization as o
               where p.Employee_ID=o.Employee_ID
                 and not Employee_Term_Date
                 and o.Department="Sales"
               group by Job_Title) as job,
           orion.Salesstaff as emp
      where emp.Job_Title=job.Job_Title
        and Salary < Job_Avg*.95
      order by Job_Title, Employee_Name;
```

91   s105d14

In-Line Views

PROC SQL Output

```
              Employees with salaries less than
              95% of the average for their job

                                    Employee
                                     Annual
   Employee_Name    Employee Job Title   Salary   Job_Avg

   Ould, Tulsidas   Sales Rep. I        22,710   26,576
   Polky, Asishana  Sales Rep. I        25,110   26,576
   Tilley, Kimiko   Sales Rep. I        25,185   26,576
   Voron, Tachaun   Sales Rep. I        25,125   26,576
```

92

Business Scenario

In 2003, Top Sports launched a premium line of sleeping bags called Expedition Zero, which was sold through Orion Star.

The CEO of Top Sports wants to send a letter of thanks to the manager of each employee who sold Expedition Zero sleeping bags in 2003, with a $50 reward certificate (in U.S. dollars) to be presented by the manager to the employee.

The Task:
Prepare a list of the managers' names and the cities in which they are located.

94

Because this query involves four tables, it might not be easy to code all at once. To simplify the task, split the query into small parts. Test each part individually, and test the overall query each time that a new segment is added.

The tables required for this query are listed below:

- `orion.Order_Fact`
- `orion.Product_Dim`
- `orion.Employee_Organization`
- `orion.Employee_Addresses`

The columns required for this query are listed below:

- `Product_ID`
- `Employee_ID`
- `Manager_ID`
- `Product_Name`
- `Order_Date`

Planning the Complex Query

| Step 1 | Identify the employees who sold Expedition Zero merchandise in 2003. |

| Step 2 | Find the employee identifier for the managers of these employees |

| Step 3 | Obtain the managers' names and city information. |

95

Complex Query: Step 1 Considerations

| Step 1 | Get employee IDs for employees who sold Expedition Zero merchandise in 2003. |

Select the employee's identifier (**Employee_ID**) from the results of joining the **Order_Fact** and **Product_Dim** tables on **Product_ID**, where **Product_Name** contains Expedition Zero. Exclude Internet orders (**Employee_ID NE 99999999**).

96

Coding the Complex Query

 Step 1 Write a query to obtain the employee ID of all employees who sold Expedition Zero merchandise in 2003.

```
select distinct Employee_ID
   from orion.Order_Fact as o,
        orion.Product_Dim as p
   where o.Product_ID=p.Product_ID
         and year(Order_Date)=2003
         and Product_Name contains
         'Expedition Zero'
         and Employee_ID ne 99999999;
```

97   s105d15

Coding the Complex Query

Step 1 PROC SQL Output

Employee ID
120145
120732

98

Complex Query: Step 2 Considerations

 Find the employee identifier for the managers of these employees.

Select the manager's identifier (**Manager_ID**) from the results of joining the **Employee_Organization** table with the first query's results on **Employee_ID**.

99

5.06 Multiple Choice Poll

To join the **Employee_Organization** table with the Step 1 query results, you use the query from Step 1 as which of the following?

  a. an in-line view
  b. a subquery

101

Coding the Complex Query

Step 2   Write a query to obtain the manager ID of the employee's manager.

```
select Manager_ID
   from orion.Employee_Organization as o,
      (<Step 1 query results>) as ID
   where o.Employee_ID=ID.Employee_ID;
```

Employee_ID
120145
120732

103

✎   You can assign an alias to an in-line view as if it were a table.

Coding the Complex Query

Step 2   Write a query to obtain the manager ID of the employee's manager.

```
select Manager_ID
   from orion.Employee_Organization as o,
      (select distinct Employee_ID
          from orion.Order_Fact as o,
                orion.Product_Dim as p
          where o.Product_ID=p.Product_ID
               and year(Order_Date)=2003
               and Product_Name
               contains 'Expedition Zero'
               and Employee_ID ne 99999999)as ID
   where o.Employee_ID=ID.Employee_ID;
```

104   s105d16

Coding the Complex Query

Step 2   PROC SQL Output

Manager_ID
120103
120736

105

Complex Query: Step 3 Considerations

Step 3   Find the managers' names and cities.

Select the employee's name (**Employee_Name**) and
City from the **Employee_Addresses** table, where
Employee_ID matches **Manager_ID**
in the results of the previous query.

106

7

5.07 Poll

Is it possible to use the entire query in Step 2 as
a subquery?

○ Yes

○ No

108

Coding the Complex Query

| Step 3 | Write a query to obtain the managers' names and city information. |

```
proc sql;
select Employee_Name format=$25. as Name, City
    from orion.Employee_Addresses
    where Employee_ID in
        (<Step 2 query results>);
```

Manager_ID
120145
120732

110

Coding the Complex Query

```
proc sql;
select Employee_Name format=$25. as Name
      , City
   from orion.Employee_Addresses
   where Employee_ID in
       (select Manager_ID
            from orion.Employee_Organization as o,
            (select distinct Employee_ID
                 from orion.Order_Fact as o,
                      orion.Product_Dim as p
            where o.Product_ID=p.Product_ID
            and year(Order_Date)=2003
            and Product_Name contains
                'Expedition Zero'
            and Employee_ID ne 99999999) as ID
          where o.Employee_ID=ID.Employee_ID);
```

s105d17

111

Coding the Complex Query

 PROC SQL Output

Name	City
Dawes, Wilson	Sydney
Kiemle, Parie	Miami-Dade

112

Coding the Complex Query

You can also solve this problem using a multiway join.

```
proc sql;
   select distinct Employee_Name format=$25. as Name
                 , City
      from orion.Order_Fact as of,
           orion.Product_Dim as pd,
           orion.Employee_Organization as eo,
           orion.Employee_Addresses as ea
      where of.Product_ID=pd.Product_ID
            and of.Employee_ID=eo.Employee_ID
            and ea.Employee_ID=eo.Manager_ID
            and Product_Name contains 'Expedition Zero'
            and year(Order_Date)=2003
            and eo.Employee_ID ne 99999999
   ;
quit;
```

113   s105d18

This code provides a more efficient solution to the query, but many people find this syntax more difficult to build and troubleshoot.

Comparison with Traditional SAS Programs

Perform the same task using traditional SAS programming.

```
*** s105d19 ***;

   /**************************************************
   Step 1:   Identify the employees who sold Expedition Zero
             merchandise in 2003.
   **************************************************/
proc sort data=orion.Order_Fact
          (keep=Product_ID Employee_ID Order_Date
          where=(YEAR(Order_Date)=2003 and Employee_ID ne 99999999))
          out=Orders_2007 (Drop=Order_Date);
   by Product_ID;
run;
proc sort data=orion.Product_Dim (keep=Product_ID Product_Name)
          out=Products;
   by Product_ID;
run;
data Employees (Keep=Employee_ID);
   merge Orders_2007 (In=KeepMe)
         Products (where=(Product_Name contains 'Expedition Zero'));
   by Product_ID;
   if KeepMe and Product_Name ne '';
run;
proc sort data=Employees nodup;
   by Employee_ID;
run;

   /**************************************************
   Step 2:   Find the employee identifier for the managers of
             these employees
   **************************************************/
data Manager_ID (rename=(Manager_ID=Employee_ID));
   merge Employees (in=KeepMe)
         orion.Employee_Organization (keep=Employee_ID Manager_ID);
   by Employee_ID;
   if KeepMe;
   drop Employee_ID;
run;
proc sort data=Manager_ID nodup;
   by Employee_ID;
run;
```

(Continued on the next page.)

```
/***********************************************************
   Step 3:  Obtain the managers' names and city information
   ***********************************************************/
proc sort data=orion.Employee_Addresses (Keep=Employee_ID Employee_Name City)
        out=Employees;
   by Employee_ID;
run;

data Managers;
   length Manager $28.;
   merge Manager_ID (in=KeepMe)
         Employees;
   by Employee_ID;
   if KeepMe;
   Manager=catx(' ',scan(Employee_Name,2,','),
           scan(Employee_Name,1,','));
   drop Employee_ID Employee_Name;
run;
proc print data=Managers noobs;
run;
```

PROC PRINT Output

Manager	City
Wilson Dawes	Sydney
Parie Kiemle	Miami-Dade

 **Exercises**

If you restarted SAS since the last exercise, submit a LIBNAME statement to assign the libref `orion` to the SAS data library for this course.

```
libname orion '_____';
```

Level 1

5. **Using In-Line Views**

    a. Produce a report of Orion Star sales force employees' aggregate sales in 2007. Select **Country**, **First_Name**, **Last_Name**, **Value_Sold**, **Orders**, and **Avg_Order** columns by joining `orion.Order_Fact` and `orion.Sales` tables on `Employee_ID`. Group the report by `Country`, `First_Name`, `Last_Name`. Include only employees having an aggregate `Value_Sold` of $200.00 or more. Order the results by `Country`, `Value_Sold` (descending), and `Orders` (descending).

        1) Calculate `Value_Sold` by summing `Total_Retail_Price`.

        2) Calculate `Orders` by using the COUNT(*) function to count the number of rows returned for each employee.

        3) Calculate `Avg_Order` by dividing `Value_Sold` by `Orders`.

        4) Title the report as indicated in the sample output.

        Partial PROC SQL Output

```
                    2007 Sales Force Sales Statistics
                   For Employees With 200.00 or More In Sales

        Country   First_Name   Last_Name      Value_Sold   Orders   Avg_Order
        ─────────────────────────────────────────────────────────────────────
        AU        Lucian       Daymond            880.10        5      176.02
        AU        Ranj         Stamalis           697.60        3      232.53
        AU        Sharryn      Clarkson           400.40        3      133.47
        AU        Marinus      Surawski           398.80        2      199.40
        AU        Sian         Shannan            306.20        1      306.20
        AU        Monica       Kletschkus         239.30        2      119.65
        US        Tywanna      Mcdade           1,387.90        2      693.95
```

b. Using the query created in step **a** as an in-line view, select <u>**Country**</u>, the maximum <u>**Value_Sold**</u>, <u>**Orders**</u>, and <u>**Avg_Order**</u> as well as the minimum <u>**Avg_Order**</u> for each country. Name the report `2007 Sales Summary by Country`.

Hint: An in-line view must not use the ORDER BY clause.

PROC SQL Output

		2007 Sales Summary by Country			
	Country	Max Value Sold	Max Orders	Max Average	Min Average
	AU	880.10	5.00	306.20	119.65
	US	1,387.90	6.00	693.95	66.50

Level 2

6. **Building Complex Queries with In-Line Views**

Your ultimate goal in this exercise is to create a report showing each employee's salary expressed as a percentage of the total salary for his department. The report should be sorted by department and, within each department, in descending order of salary percentage.

- The `orion.Employee_Payroll` table contains `Salary`.
- The `orion.Employee_Addresses` table contains `Employee_Name`.
- The `orion.Employee_Organization` table contains `Department`.

Sketch of desired report:

Employee Salaries as a percent of Department Total		
Department	Employee_Name	Salary Percent
Accounts	Mea, Azavi0us	58,200.00 8.6%
Accounts	Miller, Pamela	53,475.00 7.9%
Accounts	Asta, Wendy	52,295.00 7.7%

a. Create a report aggregating the sum of all salaries for each department. The report should include **Department** and the sum of all associated salary values as **Dept_Salary_Total**. Join `orion.Employee_Payroll` and `orion.Employee_Organization` by **Employee_ID** to obtain the information you need.

- The `orion.Employee_Payroll` table contains salary values.
- The `orion.Employee_Organization` table contains department information.

Partial PROC SQL Output

Department	Dept_Salary_Total
Accounts	680440
Accounts Management	397175
Administration	1009850
Concession Management	372225
Engineering	276285

b. Create a report that includes the employee ID, name, and department. Join
`orion.Employee_Addresses` and `orion.Employee_Organization` by
`Employee_ID` to obtain the information you need.

- The `orion.Employee_Addresses` table contains `Employee_Name` and
`Employee_ID`.

- The `orion.Employee_Organization` table contains `Employee_ID` and
`Department`.

Partial PROC SQL Output

```
Employee_
      ID  Employee_Name            Department

   121044  Abbott, Ray             Sales
   120145  Aisbitt, Sandy          Sales
   120761  Akinfolarin, Tameaka    Accounts
   120656  Amos, Salley            Logistics Management
   121107  Anger, Rose             Sales
   121038  Anstey, David           Sales
```

c. Use the two queries you created in steps **a** and **b** as in-line views. Join the views with
`orion.Employee_Payroll` by either `Employee_ID` or `Department` to create the final
report.

- The query from step **a** contains `Department` and `Dept_Salary_Total`.

- The query from step **b** contains `Employee_ID`, `Employee_Name`, and `Department`.

- The `orion.Employee_Payroll` table contains `Employee_ID` and individual `Salary`
values.

Partial PROC SQL Output

```
               Employee Salaries as a percent of Department Total

   Department            Employee_Name            Salary   Percent

   Accounts              Mea, Azavious          58,200.00    8.6%
   Accounts              Miller, Pamela         53,475.00    7.9%
   Accounts              Asta, Wendy            52,295.00    7.7%
   Accounts              Post, Nahliah          48,380.00    7.1%
   Accounts              Ferrari, Ralph         47,000.00    6.9%
   Accounts              Kimmerle, Kevie        46,090.00    6.8%
   Accounts              Farthing, Zashia       43,590.00    6.4%
   Accounts              Knopfmacher, Paul      38,545.00    5.7%
   Accounts              Thoits, Elizabeth      36,440.00    5.4%
   Accounts              Apr, Nishan            36,230.00    5.3%
   Accounts              Atkins, John           34,760.00    5.1%
   Accounts              Voltz, Sal             34,040.00    5.0%
   Accounts              Woods, Connie          32,675.00    4.8%
   Accounts              Akinfolarin, Tameaka   30,960.00    4.5%
   Accounts              Leone, Marvin          30,625.00    4.5%
   Accounts              Van Damme, Jean-Claude 30,590.00    4.5%
   Accounts              Niemann, Kevin         26,545.00    3.9%
   Accounts Management   Kempster, Janelle      53,400.00     13%
   Accounts Management   Kokoszka, Nikeisha     51,950.00     13%
   Accounts Management   Lightbourne, Abelino   47,990.00     12%
```

Level 3

7. Building a Complex Query Using a Multi-Way Join

Create a report using a multi-way inner join, which produces the total of the 2007 sales figures for each Orion Star employee. The report should be titled **2007 Total Sales Figures** and must include both the managers' and employees' names (displayed as first name followed by last name), and the total retail value of all sales made by each employee in 2007. Present the information as follows:

- Use one row per employee.
- Organize the report so that the following standards are observed:
  - Employees under one manager are adjacent to each other (grouped together) on the report.
  - Within each manager's group, employees are listed in decreasing order of total sales.
  - The Australian groups are listed first, followed by the U.S. groups.
  - Manager names are in alphabetical order by last name and then first name.

Remember that you can group and order by columns that are not included in the SELECT statement list.

The data that you need can be found in the following tables (variables of interest in parentheses):

- **orion.Order_Fact** (**Employee_ID**, **Total_Retail_Price**)
- **orion.Employee_Organization** (**Employee_ID**, **Manager_ID**)
- **orion.Employee_Addresses** (**Employee_ID**, **Employee_Name**)

Partial PROC SQL Output

```
                         2007 Total Sales Figures

        Manager                    Employee                 Total_Sales

        Wilson Dawes               Jina Fiocca                   223.80
        Wilson Dawes               Phu Sloey                      17.60
        Wilson Dawes               Amanda Liebman                  6.40
        Tom Zhou                   Lucian Daymond                880.10
        Tom Zhou                   Ranj Stamalis                 697.60
        Tom Zhou                   Sharryn Clarkson              400.40
        Tom Zhou                   Marinus Surawski              398.80
        Tom Zhou                   Sian Shannan                  306.20
        Tom Zhou                   Monica Kletschkus             239.30
        Tom Zhou                   Fancine Kaiser                147.10
        Tom Zhou                   Shani Duckett                 101.50
        Tom Zhou                   Atul Leyden                    92.50
        Tom Zhou                   Kevin Lyon                     73.99
        Tom Zhou                   Andrew Conolly                 60.80
        Tom Zhou                   Sean Dives                     19.10
        Tom Zhou                   Lynelle Phoumirath             19.10
        Renee Capachietti          Brienne Darrohn               533.40
        Renee Capachietti          Michael Westlund              366.00
```

5.3 Chapter Review

Chapter Review

1. How many rows are returned by the following query?

```
proc sql;
   select *
      from
      table1,table2;
quit;
```

Table1

X	A
1	a
3	d
2	b

Table2

X	B
2	x
1	y
3	v

114

Chapter Review

2. Which of the following statements describes an advantage of using a PROC SQL view?

   a. Views often save space, because a view is usually quite small compared with the data that it accesses.

   b. Views can provide users a simpler alternative to frequently retrieving and submitting query code to produce identical results.

   c. Views hide complex query details from users.

   d. All of the above

116

Chapter Review

3. Outer and Inner Joins:

   a. An **outer join** can operate on a maximum of ___ tables simultaneously.

   b. An **inner join** can operate on a maximum of ___ tables simultaneously.

118

Chapter Review

4. True or False:
   An in-line view can be used on a WHERE or HAVING clause and can return many rows of data, but must return only one column.

120

5.4 Solutions

Solutions to Exercises

1. **Inner Joins**

```
*** s105s01 ***;

proc sql;
title "Employees With More Than 30 Years of Service";
title2 "As of December 31, 2007";
    select Employee_Name 'Employee Name',
           int(('31DEC2007'd-Employee_Hire_Date)/365.25)
           as YOS 'Years of Service'
        from orion.Employee_Addresses as a,
             orion.Employee_Payroll as p
        where a.Employee_ID=p.Employee_ID
             and calculated YOS gt 30
        order by Employee_Name
    ;
quit;
title;
```

2. **Outer Joins**

```
*** s105s02 ***;

proc sql;
    select Employee_Name 'Name' format=$35.,
           City, Job_Title
        from orion.Employee_Addresses as a
             left join
             orion.Sales as s
        on a.Employee_ID=s.Employee_ID
        order by City, Job_Title, Employee_Name
    ;
quit;
```

3. **Joining Multiple Tables**

```
*** s105s03 ***;

proc sql;
title  "US and Australian Internet Customers";
title2 "Purchasing Foreign Manufactured Products";
    select Customer_Name 'Name', Count(*) 'Purchases'
           as Count
        from orion.Product_Dim as p,
             orion.Order_Fact as o,
             orion.Customer as c
```

(Continued on the next page.)

```
            where p.Product_ID=o.Product_ID
              and o.Customer_ID=c.Customer_ID
              and Employee_ID=99999999
              and p.Supplier_Country ne Country
              and Country in ('US','AU')
           group by Customer_Name
           order by Count desc, Customer_Name
   ;
quit;
title;
```

4. Joining Multiple Tables

```
*** s105s04 ***;

proc sql;
title "Employees With More Than 30 Years of Service";
title2 "As of December 31, 2007";
   select emp.Employee_Name 'Employee Name' format=$35.,
          int(('31DEC2007'd-Employee_Hire_Date)/365.25)
             as YOS 'Years of Service',
          mgr.Employee_Name 'Manager Name' as Manager_Name
      /* Employee_Addresses:
         First copy is required to
         look up Employee information Employee's
         Employee_ID */
      /* Employee_Organization:
         Links Employee_ID to Manager_ID */
      /* Employee_Addresses:
         Second copy is required to
         look up Manager information using Manager's
         Employee_ID */
       from orion.Employee_Addresses as emp,
            orion.Employee_Organization as org,
            orion.Employee_Payroll as pay,
            orion.Employee_Addresses as mgr
       where emp.Employee_ID=pay.Employee_ID
             and emp.Employee_ID=org.Employee_ID
             and org.Manager_ID=mgr.Employee_ID
             and calculated YOS gt 30
       order by Manager_Name, YOS desc, Employee_Name
   ;
quit;
title;
```

5. Using In-Line Views

a.

```
   /* Summarizing by employee */
proc sql;
title "2007 Sales Force Sales Statistics";
title2 "For employees with 200.00 or more in sales";
   select Country, First_Name, Last_Name,
          sum(Total_Retail_Price) as Value_Sold format=comma9.2,
          count(*) as Orders,
          calculated Value_Sold / calculated Orders as Avg_Order
             format=comma7.2
      from orion.Order_Fact as of,
           orion.Sales as s
      where of.Employee_ID=s.Employee_ID
            and year(Order_Date)=2007
      group by Country, First_Name, Last_Name
      having Value_Sold ge 200
      order by Country, Value_Sold desc, Orders desc
   ;
quit;
```

b.

```
   /*  Further summarize by country using
       the previous query as an in-line view */
proc sql;
title "2007 Sales Summary by Country";
   select Country,
          max(Value_Sold) 'Max Value Sold' format=comma9.2,
          max(Orders) 'Max Orders' format=comma7.2,
          max(Avg_Order) 'Max Average' format=comma7.2,
          min(Avg_Order) 'Min Average' format=comma7.2
          /* Begin in-line view */
      from (select Country, First_Name, Last_Name,
                   sum(Total_Retail_Price) as Value_Sold,
                   count(*) as Orders,
                   calculated Value_Sold / calculated Orders
                      as Avg_Order
               from orion.Order_Fact as of,
                    orion.Sales as s
               where of.Employee_ID=s.Employee_ID
                 and year(Order_Date)=2007
               group by Country, First_Name, Last_Name
               having Value_Sold ge 200) /* End in-line view */
   group by Country
   order by Country;
quit;
title;
```

6. Building Complex Queries with In-Line Views

a.

```
*** s105s06 ***;

proc sql;
    select Department, sum(Salary) as Dept_Salary_Total
        from orion.Employee_Payroll as pay,
            orion.Employee_Organization as org
        where org.Employee_ID=pay.Employee_ID
        group by Department;
quit;
```

b.

```
proc sql;
    select adr.Employee_ID, Employee_Name, org.Department
        from orion.Employee_Addresses as adr,
            orion.Employee_Organization as org
        where adr.Employee_ID=org.Employee_ID;
quit;
```

c.

```
proc sql;
title "Employee Salaries as a Percent of Department Total";
    select emp.Department format=$22.,
            emp.Employee_Name format=$28.,
            Salary format=comma9.2,
            Salary/Dept_Salary_Total as Percent
            format=percent6.2
        from orion.Employee_Payroll as pay,
        /* In-line View: Employee ID, name and department */
            (select adr.Employee_ID, Employee_Name,
                    org.Department
                from orion.Employee_Addresses as adr,
                    orion.Employee_Organization as org
                where adr.Employee_ID=org.Employee_ID)
            as emp,
        /* In-line View: Aggregate sum of salary by department */
            (select Department, sum(Salary) as Dept_Salary_Total
                from orion.Employee_Payroll as pay,
                    orion.Employee_Organization as org
                where org.Employee_ID=pay.Employee_ID
                group by Department)
            as sum
        where sum.Department=emp.Department
            and pay.Employee_ID=emp.Employee_ID
        order by Department, Percent desc;
quit;
```

7. Building a Complex Query Using a Multi-Way Join

```
*** s105s07 ***;

proc sql;
title "2007 Total Sales Figures";
   select catx(' ',scan(mgr.Employee_Name,2,','),
               scan(mgr.Employee_Name,1,',')) format=$27.
          as Manager,
          catx(' ',scan(emp.Employee_Name,2,','),
               scan(emp.Employee_Name,1,',')) format=$27.
          as Employee,
          Sum(Total_Retail_Price) format=comma9.2
          as Total_Sales
      from orion.Order_Fact as order,
           orion.Employee_Organization as org,
           orion.Employee_Addresses as emp,
           orion.Employee_Addresses as mgr
     where order.Employee_ID=org.Employee_ID
       and order.Employee_ID=emp.Employee_ID
       and mgr.Employee_ID=org.Manager_ID
       and year(Order_Date)=2007
       and order.Employee_ID ne 99999999
     group by mgr.Country, mgr.Employee_Name, emp.Employee_Name
     order by mgr.Country, mgr.Employee_Name, Total_Sales desc
   ;
quit;
title;
```

Solutions to Student Activities (Polls/Quizzes)

5.01 Multiple Choice Poll – Correct Answer

Which of these DATA step statements is used to combine tables horizontally?

a. SET
b. APPEND
c. MERGE
d. INPUT
e. INFILE

8

5.02 Quiz – Correct Answer

How many rows are returned from this query?

The query produces 20 rows.

```
select *
   from three, four;
```

Table Three

X	A
1	a1
1	a2
2	b1
2	b2
4	d

Table Four

X	B
2	x1
2	x2
3	y
5	v

Partial Results Set

X	A	X	B
1	a1	2	x1
1	a1	2	x2
1	a1	3	y
1	a1	5	v
1	a2	2	x1
1	a2	2	x2
1	a2	3	y
1	a2	5	v
2	b1	2	x1
2	b1	2	x2

5*4=20

30

s105a01

5.03 Multiple Choice Poll – Correct Answer

How many rows (observations) result from the DATA step MERGE statement in program **s105a02**?

a. 4
(b.) 2
c. 6
d. 20
e. None of the above

Three

X	A
1	a1
1	a2
2	b1
2	b2
4	d

Four

X	B
2	x1
2	x2
3	y
5	v

New

X	A	B
2	b1	x1
2	b2	x2

43

5.04 Multiple Choice Poll – Correct Answer

How many tables can be combined using a single inner join?

a. 2
b. 32
(c.) 256
d. 512
e. Limited only by my computer's resources
f. No limit

52

5.05 Multiple Choice Poll – Correct Answer

For the report, you need the data for all married employees from `orion.Employee_Payroll`. You also want to include the charity names from the `orion.Employee_Donations` table if `Employee_ID` matches. What type of join should you use to combine the information from these two tables?

a. Inner Join
b. Left Join
c. Full Join
d. None of the above

70

5.06 Multiple Choice Poll – Correct Answer

To join the `Employee_Organization` table with the Step 1 query results, you use the query from Step 1 as which of the following?

a. an in-line view
b. a subquery

A query used in place of a physical table in a SELECT statement FROM clause is called an in-line view.

102

5.07 Poll – Correct Answer

Is it possible to use the entire query in Step 2 as a subquery?

 Yes

○ No

A subquery can return values for multiple rows, but must return values for only one column. When submitted on its own, the query in Step 2 returns two rows and only one column, so it can be used as a non-correlated subquery.

109

Solutions to Chapter Review

Chapter Review Answers

1. How many rows are returned by the following query?

```
proc sql;
    select *
        from
        table1,table2;
quit;
```

Table1

X	A
1	a
3	d
2	b

Table2

X	B
2	x
1	y
3	v

This query produces a Cartesian product.
Nine rows will be returned.

115

Chapter Review Answers

2. Which of the following statements describes an advantage of using a PROC SQL view?
   a. Views often save space, because a view is usually quite small compared with the data that it accesses.
   b. Views can provide users a simpler alternative to frequently retrieving and submitting query code to produce identical results.
   c. Views hide complex query details from users.
   d. All of the above

117

Chapter Review Answers

3. Outer and Inner Joins:

   a. An **outer join** can operate on a maximum of _2_ tables simultaneously.

   b. An **inner join** can operate on a maximum of _256_ tables simultaneously.

119

Chapter Review Answers

4. True or False:
   An in-line view can be used on a WHERE or HAVING clause and can return many rows of data, but must return only one column.
   False
   An in-line view is a query used in the FROM clause in place of a table. An in-line view can return any number of rows or columns.

121

Chapter 6 Set Operators

6.1   Introduction to Set Operators

Objectives

- Describe SQL set operators and modifiers.

3

Types of Set Operators

Set operators vertically combine rows from two result sets. There are four set operators:

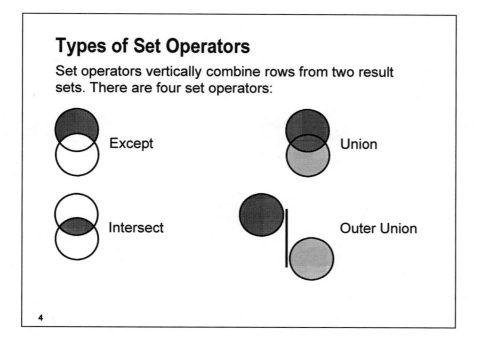

Except

Union

Intersect

Outer Union

4

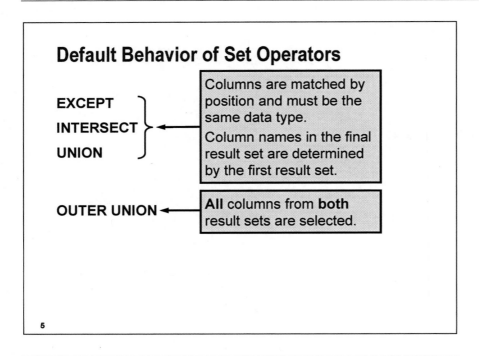

Set Operator Syntax

General form of an SQL query using a set operator:

```
SELECT ...
EXCEPT | INTERSECT | UNION | OUTER UNION <CORR> <ALL>
SELECT ...
```

The set operator operates on the result sets produced
by the two SELECT statements, not on the actual tables
themselves.

6

Many times, when you write a query that operates on all of the rows and columns from the source
tables, you speak about the query as if it were operating on the actual table instead of a result set.
For example, you might describe the function of this code segment as "Select all of the rows from
TABLEA, which are not in **TABLEB**":

```
SELECT * from TABLEA
   EXCEPT
SELECT * from TABLEB;
```

The words aptly describe the desired results, and there is no **practical** difference in this case.

Types of Set Operators

EXCEPT

Unique rows from the first table that are not found in the second table are selected.

```
select *
    from one
except
select *
    from two;
```

7 ...

Types of Set Operators

INTERSECT

Common unique rows from both tables are selected.

```
select *
    from one
intersect
select *
    from two;
```

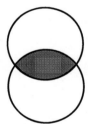

8 ...

Types of Set Operators

UNION

Unique rows from both tables are selected with columns overlaid.

```
select *
   from one
union
select *
   from two;
```

9   ...

Types of Set Operators

OUTER UNION

- All rows from both tables, unique as well as non-unique, are selected.
- Columns are not overlaid.

```
select *
   from one
outer union
select *
   from two;
```

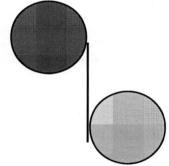

10

Modifiers

You can use two modifiers to modify the behavior
of set operators:

- ALL
- CORRESPONDING

11

Use the ALL keyword when the following conditions occur:

- You do not care if there are duplicates.
- Duplicates are not possible. For example, there is a unique or primary key constraint on the column.

Modifiers

ALL

- does not remove duplicate rows, and thus avoids an extra pass through the data. Use the ALL modifier for better performance when it is possible.
- is not allowed in connection with an OUTER UNION operator. It is implicit.

12

Modifiers

CORRESPONDING

- overlays columns by name, instead of by position
- removes any columns not found in both tables when used in EXCEPT, INTERSECT, and UNION operations
- causes common columns to be overlaid when used in OUTER UNION operations
- can be abbreviated as CORR.

13

6.01 Poll

By default the EXCEPT, INTERSECT, and UNION set operators remove duplicate rows from the query output.

- ○ True
- ○ False

15

6.2 The EXCEPT Operator

Objectives

- Describe the SQL process when you use the EXCEPT set operator and keywords.
- Use the EXCEPT set operator.

19

EXCEPT

Unique rows from the first result set that are not found in the second result set are selected.

20

Business Scenario

Create a report that displays the employee identification number and job title of the non-Sales staff employees.

Considerations:

- The `orion.Employee_organization` table contains information about all current Orion Star employees.
- The `orion.Sales` table contains information about current Sales employees only.

21

The EXCEPT Operator

You need a query that returns information from rows that exist in `orion.Employee_organization`, but not in `orion.Sales`. The EXCEPT operator could be useful.

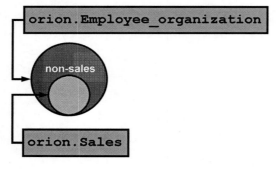

22

Flow Diagram: EXCEPT Operator

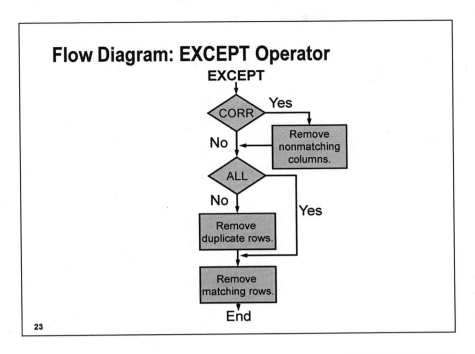

23

The EXCEPT Operator

Display the unique rows in Table ONE that are not found in Table TWO.

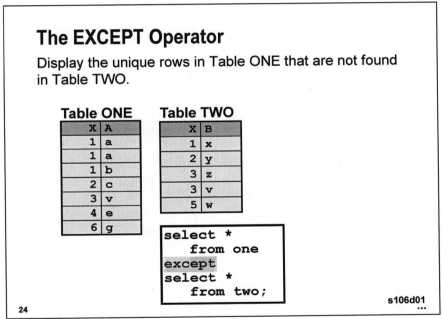

24

s106d01
...

The EXCEPT Operator

The SQL processor removes duplicate rows within the tables.

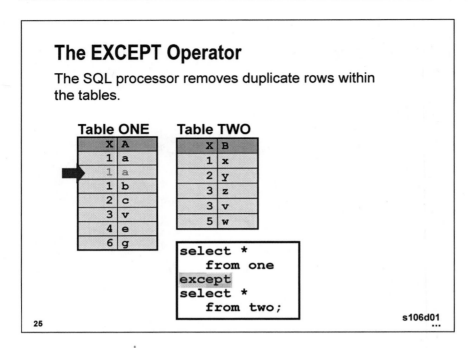

s106d01

25

The EXCEPT Operator

The SQL processor creates an intermediate result set by returning the rows that are found only in Table ONE.

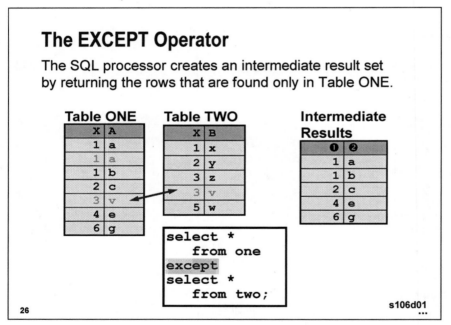

s106d01

26

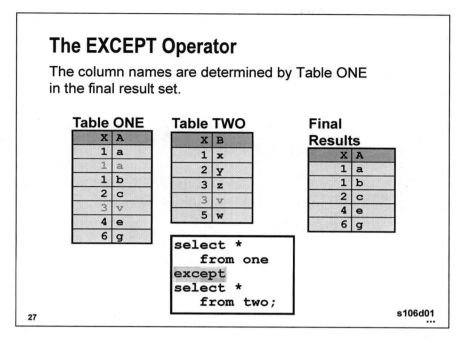

Duplicate rows are omitted.

How can you include duplicate rows?

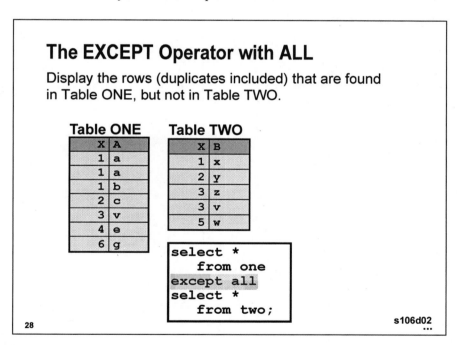

The EXCEPT Operator with ALL

The SQL processor creates an intermediate result set by returning the rows that are found only in Table ONE.

Table ONE

X	A
1	a
1	a
1	b
2	c
3	v
4	e
6	g

Table TWO

X	B
1	x
2	y
3	z
3	v
5	w

Intermediate Results

❶	❷
1	a
1	a
1	b
2	c
4	e
6	g

```
select *
   from one
except all
select *
   from two;
```

29

s106d02
...

The EXCEPT Operator with ALL

The column names are determined by Table ONE in the final result set.

Table ONE

X	A
1	a
1	a
1	b
2	c
3	v
4	e
6	g

Table TWO

X	B
1	x
2	y
3	z
3	v
5	w

Final Results

X	A
1	a
1	a
1	b
2	c
4	e
6	g

```
select *
   from one
except all
select *
   from two;
```

30

s106d02
...

The EXCEPT Operator with CORR

Display the unique rows that exist in Table ONE and
not in Table TWO, based on same-named columns.

Table ONE

X	A
1	a
1	a
1	b
2	c
3	v
4	e
6	g

Table TWO

X	B
1	x
2	y
3	z
3	v
5	w

```
select *
    from one
except corr
select *
    from two;
```

s106d03

31

The EXCEPT Operator with CORR

The SQL processor eliminates any columns not found
in both tables.

Table ONE

X	A
1	a
1	a
1	b
2	c
3	v
4	e
6	g

Table TWO

X	B
1	x
2	y
3	z
3	v
5	w

```
select *
    from one
except corr
select *
    from two;
```

s106d03

32

The EXCEPT Operator with CORR

The SQL processor eliminates duplicate rows.

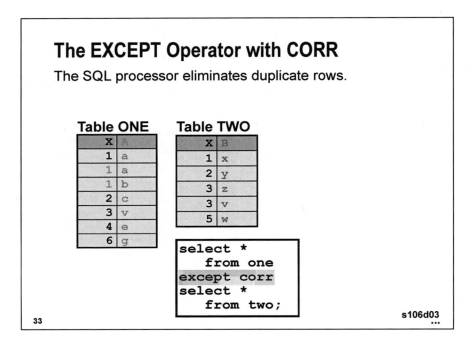

```
select *
   from one
except corr
select *
   from two;
```

33

s106d03

The EXCEPT Operator with CORR

The SQL processor creates an intermediate result set
by returning rows that are found only in Table ONE.

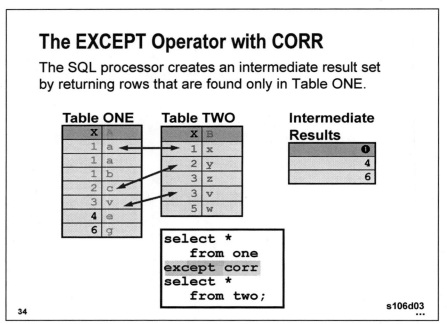

```
select *
   from one
except corr
select *
   from two;
```

34

s106d03

The EXCEPT Operator with CORR

The SQL processor creates an intermediate result set by returning rows that are found only in Table ONE.

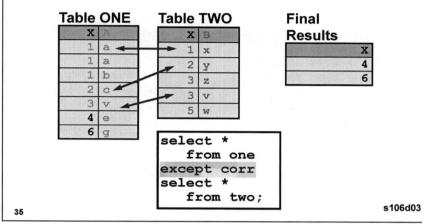

Table ONE

X	A
1	a
1	a
1	b
2	c
3	v
4	e
6	g

Table TWO

X	B
1	x
2	y
3	z
3	v
5	w

Final Results

X
4
6

```
select *
    from one
except corr
select *
    from two;
```

35   s106d03

6.02 Quiz

What are the results when you combine ALL with CORR?

Table ALPHA

X	A
1	x
1	y
3	z
4	v
5	w

Table BETA

X	B
1	x
2	y
3	z
3	v
5	v

```
select *
    from alpha
except all corr
select *
    from beta;
```

Run the program **s106a01** and review the results.

37   s106a01

Step 1: Using ALL with CORR

Step 1 CORR specifies that only same-named columns be used. ALL specifies that all values of **X** be used, including duplicates.

Table ALPHA

X	A
1	x
1	y
3	z
4	v
5	w

Table BETA

X	B
1	x
2	y
3	z
3	v
5	v

```
select *
   from alpha
except all corr
select *
   from beta;
```

39   ...

Step 2: Using ALL with CORR

Step 2 EXCEPT specifies that only **X** values found in ALPHA and not in BETA are used.

Table ALPHA

X	A
1	x
1	y
3	z
4	v
5	w

Table BETA

X	B
1	x
2	y
3	z
3	v
5	v

```
select *
   from alpha
except all corr
select *
   from beta;
```

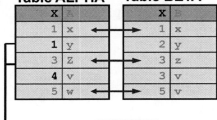

X
1
4

Final result set

40

Business Scenario (Review)

Create a report that displays the employee identification number and job title of the employees who are not Sales staff.

`orion.Employee_organization`

```
proc sql;
   select Employee_ID, Job_Title
      from orion.Employee_organization
   except all
   select Employee_ID, Job_Title
      from orion.Sales;
quit;
```

non-sales

`orion.Sales`

41   s106d04

The EXCEPT Operator

Partial PROC SQL Output (10 out of 259)

```
                Non-Sales Staff Employees

        Employee_ID  Job_Title
        _____

             120101  Director
             120104  Administration Manager
             120105  Secretary I
             120106  Office Assistant II
             120107  Office Assistant III
             120108  Warehouse Assistant II
             120109  Warehouse Assistant I
             120110  Warehouse Assistant III
             120111  Security Guard II
             120112  Security Guard I
```

42

6.03 Quiz

Answer the questions about the following program:

```
select Employee_ID, Job_Title
    from orion.Employee_organization
except all
select Employee_ID, Job_Title
    from orion.Sales;
```

1. Why is the CORR keyword not used in this example?

2. Would adding the CORR keyword to this example change the outcome?

44   s106a02

Using the CORR Keyword

s106d04a

1. Retrieve the program **s106d04a**.

2. Highlight and submit the first PROC SQL step.

```
proc sql;
   select count(*) 'No. Non-Sales Employees'
      from (select *
               from orion.Employee_organization
               except all
            select *
               from orion.Sales);
quit;
```

3. Examine the error message in the SAS log. The EXCEPT operator performs the set operation based on the positions of the columns from **orion.Employee_organization**, not by column names. When columns from the tables have different attributes, you get the error message indicated below:

```
proc sql;
   select count(*) 'No. Non-Sales Employees'
      from (select *
               from orion.Employee_organization
               except all
            select *
                from orion.Sales);
quit;
WARNING: A table has been extended with null columns to perform
         the EXCEPT ALL set operation.
ERROR: Column 4 from the first contributor of EXCEPT ALL is not
       the same type as its counterpart from the second.
301   quit;
NOTE: The SAS System stopped processing this step because of
      errors.
NOTE: PROCEDURE SQL used (Total process time):
      real time            0.01 seconds
      cpu time             0.00 seconds
```

4. Highlight and submit the two PROC CONTENTS steps to examine the descriptor portion of **orion.Employee_organization** and **orion.Sales** by column position.

```
proc contents data=orion.Employee_organization
            position;
   title 'ORION.Employee_organization';
run;
title;

proc contents data=orion.Sales position;
   title 'ORION.Sales';
run;
title;
```

5. Examine the position of the columns in the **orion.Employee_organization** table by selecting **Contents: ORION.Employee_organization** ⇨ **ORION.EMPLOYEE_ORGANIZATION** ⇨ **Position** in the Results window. Notice the attributes of column four in the **orion.Employee_organization** table.

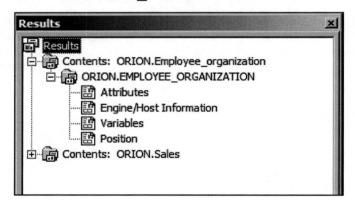

Partial PROC CONENTS Output

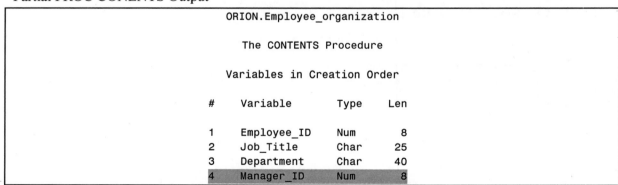

```
              ORION.Employee_organization

              The CONTENTS Procedure

           Variables in Creation Order

     #    Variable       Type    Len

     1    Employee_ID    Num       8
     2    Job_Title      Char     25
     3    Department     Char     40
     4    Manager_ID     Num       8
```

6. Examine the position of the columns in the **orion.Sales** table by selecting
Contents: ORION.Sales ⇨ **ORION.SALES** ⇨ **Position** in the Results window. Compare
the attributes in **orion.Employee_organization** from column four to the same column
attributes in the **orion.Sales** table.

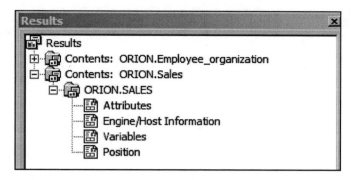

Partial PROC CONTENTS OUTPUT

```
                              ORION.Sales

                           The CONTENTS Procedure

                         Variables in Creation Order

              #      Variable      Type      Len      Format

              1      Employee_ID   Num         8      12.
              2      First_Name    Char       12
              3      Last_Name     Char       18
              4      Gender        Char        1
              5      Salary        Num         8
              6      Job_Title     Char       25
              7      Country       Char        2
              8      Birth_Date    Num         8
              9      Hire_Date     Num         8
```

The columns are matched by position and must have the same type. In this result set, you receive an
error message because the fourth column in **orion.Employee_organization** is numeric and
the same column based on position in **orion.Sales** is character. When columns are overlaid by
position, but do not have same data type, the set operation fails.

7. Submit the next PROC SQL step. This step uses the CORR keyword. The CORR keyword overlays
columns with the same column names.

```
proc sql;
   select count(*) 'No. Non-Sales Employees'
      from (select *
               from orion.Employee_organization
            except all corr
            select *
               from orion.Sales);
quit;
```

8. Examine the notes in the log for any error messages. The CORR keyword is used and there should not be any error messages, as long as all columns with the same name have the same attributes.

Partial SAS Log

```
proc sql;
   select count(*) 'No. Non-Sales Employees'
      from (select *
                from orion.Employee_organization
            except all corr
            select *
                from orion.Sales);
quit;
NOTE: PROCEDURE SQL used (Total process time):
      real time           0.03 seconds
      cpu time            0.01 seconds
```

9. Examine the results in the Output window.

PROC SQL Output

```
              No.
          Non-Sales
          Employees
          _____

              259
```

The EXCEPT Operator

This query can easily become an in-line view used to determine how many managers, who are not Sales staff, are employed at Orion Star.

```
proc sql;
   select count(*) 'No. Non-Sales Managers'
      from (select distinct Manager_ID
               from orion.Employee_organization
            except all
            select Employee_ID
               from orion.Sales)
   ;
quit;
```

✎ A manager might have multiple direct reports, so use the DISTINCT keyword in the first part of the query. You can confidently use the ALL keyword because the first query returns distinct values, and the Sales table contains no duplicate records.

s106d05

48

The EXCEPT Operator

PROC SQL Output

No. Non-Sales Managers
48

49

6.04 Poll

By default, the EXCEPT set operator selects **all** the rows from the first result set that are not in the second result set.

○ True

○ False

51

6.3 The INTERSECT Operator

Objectives

- Describe the SQL process when using the INTERSECT set operator and keywords.
- Use the INTERSECT set operator.

55

INTERSECT

Common unique rows from both result sets are selected.

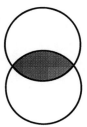

56

Business Scenario

Orion Star frequently hires experienced Sales staff at higher levels on the assumption that they will be more productive than inexperienced personnel.

Create a report that displays the employee identification number of current Level III and Level IV Sales staff hired in 2004, who made at least one sale by the end of 2005.

Considerations:

- The `orion.Order_fact` table contains information on all sales.
- The `orion.Sales` table contains information about current Sales employees, including job titles and hire dates.

57

The INTERSECT Operator

You need a query that returns information from rows that exist in both `orion.Sales` and `orion.Order_fact`.

The INTERSECT operator could be useful.

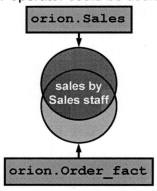

58

Flow Diagram: INTERSECT Operator

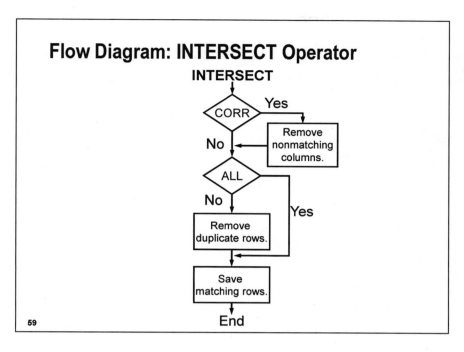

59

The INTERSECT Operator

Display the unique rows common to Table ONE and Table TWO.

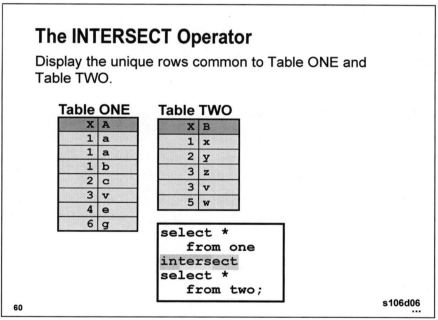

60

s106d06
...

The INTERSECT Operator

The SQL processor removes duplicate rows within the tables.

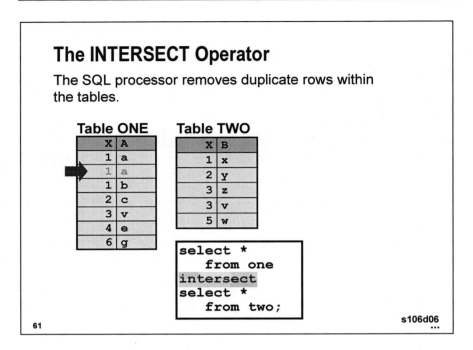

```
select *
   from one
intersect
select *
   from two;
```

61   s106d06
                                              ...

The INTERSECT Operator

The SQL processor creates an intermediate result set by returning the rows that are found in both tables.

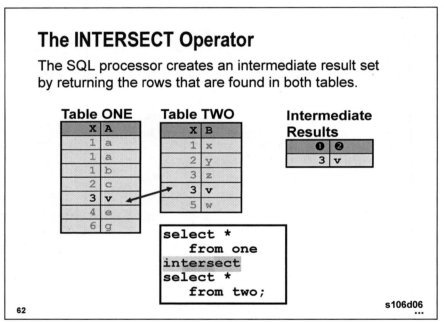

```
select *
   from one
intersect
select *
   from two;
```

62   s106d06
                                              ...

The INTERSECT Operator

The column names are determined by Table ONE in the final result set.

Table ONE

X	A
1	a
1	a
1	b
2	c
3	v
4	e
6	g

Table TWO

X	B
1	x
2	y
3	z
3	v
5	w

Final Results

X	A
3	v

```
select *
   from one
intersect
select *
   from two;
```

s106d06

63

6.05 Quiz

Submit the program **s106a03** and review the results. Add the ALL keyword to the second PROC SQL step and re-submit.

Will the addition of the ALL keyword have any effect on the output?

Table AAA

X	A
1	a
1	a
1	b
2	c
3	v
4	e
6	g

Table BBB

X	B
1	a
1	a
2	z
3	z
3	v
5	w

```
select *
   from aaa
intersect all
select *
   from bbb;
```

s106a03

65

The INTERSECT Operator with CORR

Display the unique rows common to Table ONE and
Table TWO, based on the same-named columns.

Table ONE

X	A
1	a
1	a
1	b
2	c
3	v
4	e
6	g

Table TWO

X	B
1	x
2	y
3	z
3	v
5	w

```
select *
   from one
intersect corr
select *
   from two;
```

67   s106d07
...

The INTERSECT Operator with CORR

The SQL processor eliminates any columns not found
in both tables.

Table ONE

X	A
1	a
1	a
1	b
2	c
3	v
4	e
6	g

Table TWO

X	B
1	x
2	y
3	z
3	v
5	w

```
select *
   from one
intersect corr
select *
   from two;
```

68   s106d07
...

The INTERSECT Operator with CORR

The SQL processor eliminates duplicate rows and rows that are not common to Table ONE and Table TWO.

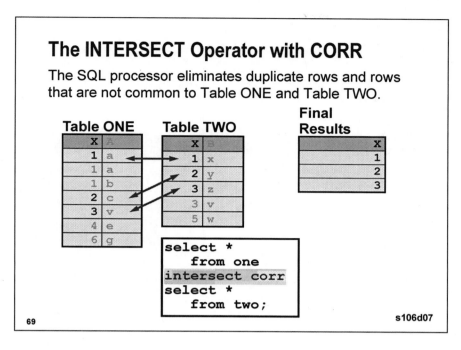

```
select *
    from one
intersect corr
select *
    from two;
```

69   s106d07

Business Scenario (Review)

Create a report that displays the employee identification number of current Level III and Level IV Sales staff hired in 2004, who made at least one sale by the end of 2005.

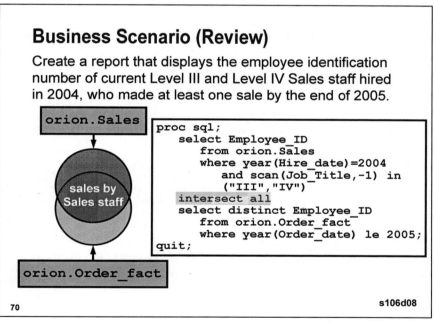

```
proc sql;
    select Employee_ID
        from orion.Sales
        where year(Hire_date)=2004
            and scan(Job_Title,-1) in
            ("III","IV")
intersect all
    select distinct Employee_ID
        from orion.Order_fact
        where year(Order_date) le 2005;
quit;
```

70   s106d08

The INTERSECT Operator

PROC SQL Output

Employee ID
120179

71

 **Exercises**

Level 1

1. Using the EXCEPT Operator

Create a report that displays the employee identification numbers of employees who have phone numbers, but do not appear to have address information. The `orion.Employee_phones` table contains `Employee_ID` and `Phone_Number`. If an employee's address is on file, the `orion.Employee_Addresses` table contains the `Employee_ID` value and address information. The query should:

- Use the column `Employee_ID` from `orion.Employee_phones`.
- Use the appropriate SET operator.
- Use the column `Employee_ ID` from `orion.Employee_Addresses`.

PROC SQL Output

Employee IDs with Phone Numbers But Not Address Information
Employee_ID
12099
20683
21149

2. Using the INTERSECT Operator

Create a report that shows the `Customer_ID` of all customers who placed orders. The `orion.Order_fact` table contains information about the orders that were placed by Orion Star customers, including `Customer_ID`. The `orion.Customer` table contains information about all Orion Star customers, including `Customer_ID`. The query should do the following:

- Use the column `Customer_ID` from `orion.Order_fact`.
- Use the appropriate SET operator.
- Use the column `Customer_ ID` from `orion.Customer`.

Partial PROC SQL Output

Customers Who Placed Orders
Customer ID
4
5
9
... ...

Level 2

3. Using the EXCEPT Operator to Count Rows

Create a report that displays the total count of employees who did not make any charitable donations. The **orion.Employee_organization** table contains a record for every employee in the Orion Star organization and includes the employee identification numbers. The **orion.Employee_donations** table contains records only for employees who made charitable donations, including the **Employee_ID** value.

PROC SQL Output

```
                                            No.
                                      Employees
                                          w/ No
                                      Charitable
                                       Donations
                                      ----------
                                            300
```

4. Using the INTERSECT Operator to Count Rows

Create a report that shows the total number of customers who placed orders. The **orion.Order_fact** table contains information about the orders that were placed by Orion Star customers, including **Customer_ID**. The **orion.Customer** table contains information on all Orion Star customers, including **Customer_ID**.

PROC SQL Output

```
                                            No.
                                      Customers
                                       w/ Orders
                                      ----------
                                            75
```

Level 3

5. Using the EXCEPT Operator with a Subquery

Create a report that displays the employee identification numbers and names of sales representatives who did not sell any products in 2007. The `orion.Sales` table contains the `Employee_ID` values of all sales representatives. The `orion.Order_fact` table contains the `Employee_ID` value of the salesperson, and other information about all sales that were made. The `orion.Employee_Addresses` table contains the `Employee_ID` and `Employee_Name` values of all Orion Star employees. Provide a title for the report as indicated in the sample output, and include the row number as part of the report.

Partial PROC SQL Output

```
                    Sales Reps Who Made No Sales in 2007


          Row   Employee_ID   Employee_Name
          _____

           1      121044      Abbott, Ray
           2      120145      Aisbitt, Sandy
           3      121038      Anstey, David
           4      121030      Areu, Jeryl
           5      121062      Armant, Debra
           6      120144      Barbis, Viney
           7      120168      Barcoe, Selina
                  ...  ...  ...
```

6. Using the INTERSECT Operator with a Subquery

Create a report that includes `Customer_ID` and `Customer_Name` for all customers who placed orders. The `orion.Order_fact` table contains information about the orders that were placed by Orion Star customers, including `Customer_ID`. The `orion.Customer` table contains information on all Orion Star customers, including `Customer_ID` and `Customer_Name`.

Partial PROC SQL Output

```
                    Name of Customers Who Placed Orders


       Customer ID  Customer Name
       _____

                 4  James Kvarniq
                 5  Sandrina Stephano
                 9  Cornelia Krahl
                10  Karen Ballinger
                11  Elke Wallstab
                12  David Black
                13  Markus Sepke
                16  Ulrich Heyde
                17  Jimmie Evans
                18  Tonie Asmussen
                19  Oliver S. Füßling
                20  Michael Dineley
                23  Tulio Devereaux
                24  Robyn Klem
                ...  ...  ...
```

6.4 The UNION Operator

Objectives
- Describe the SQL process when you use the UNION set operator and keywords.
- Use the UNION set operator.

75

UNION
Both result sets are combined, and then unique rows are selected with columns overlaid.

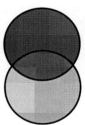

76

Business Scenario

The management team needs a payroll report for Level I, II, and III Orion Star employees. The UNION operator could be useful here. Below is a sketch of the desired report:

Payroll Report for Level I, II, and III Employees	
Total Paid to ALL Level I Staff	1,234,567
Total Paid to ALL Level II Staff	1,456,789
Total Paid to ALL Level III Staff	2,123,456

77

Flow Diagram: UNION Operator

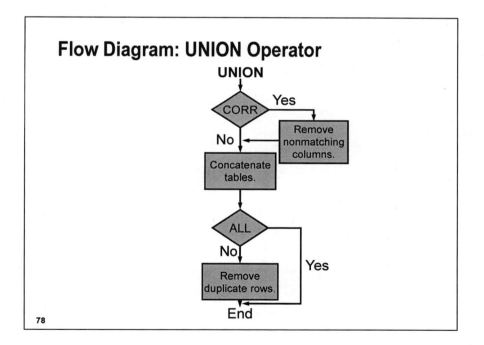

78

The UNION Operator

Display all of the unique rows from both Table ONE and Table TWO.

Table ONE

X	A
1	a
1	a
1	b
2	c
3	v
4	e
6	g

Table TWO

X	B
1	x
2	y
3	z
3	v
5	w

```
select *
   from one
union
select *
   from two;
```

79   s106d09
                                                ...

The UNION Operator

The SQL processor creates an intermediate result set by concatenating and sorting Table ONE and Table TWO.

Table ONE

X	A
1	a
1	a
1	b
2	c
3	v
4	e
6	g

Table TWO

X	B
1	x
2	y
3	z
3	v
5	w

Intermediate Results

❶	❷
1	a
1	a
1	b
1	x
2	c
2	y
3	v
3	v
3	z
4	e
5	w
6	g

```
select *
   from one
union
select *
   from two;
```

80   s106d09
                                                ...

The UNION Operator

The SQL processor removes duplicate rows from the intermediate result.

Table ONE

X	A
1	a
1	a
1	b
2	c
3	v
4	e
6	g

Table TWO

X	B
1	x
2	y
3	z
3	v
5	w

```
select *
    from one
union
select *
    from two;
```

Intermediate Results

❶	❷
1	a
1	a
1	b
1	x
2	c
2	y
3	v
3	v
3	z
4	e
5	w
6	g

81   s106d09 ...

The UNION Operator

Final Result Set

Table ONE

X	A
1	a
1	a
1	b
2	c
3	v
4	e
6	g

Table TWO

X	B
1	x
2	y
3	z
3	v
5	w

```
select *
    from one
union
select *
    from two;
```

Final Results

X	A
1	a
1	b
1	x
2	c
2	y
3	v
3	z
4	e
5	w
6	g

82   s106d09

The UNION Operator with CORR

Display all of the unique rows of same-named columns in Table ONE and Table TWO.

Table ONE

X	A
1	a
1	a
1	b
2	c
3	v
4	e
6	g

Table TWO

X	B
1	x
2	y
3	z
3	v
5	w

```
select *
    from one
union corr
select *
    from two;
```

83

s106d10
...

The UNION Operator with CORR

The SQL processor creates an intermediate result set by concatenating and sorting data from same-named columns.

Table ONE

X	A
1	a
1	a
1	b
2	c
3	v
4	e
6	g

Table TWO

X	B
1	x
2	y
3	z
3	v
5	w

Intermediate Results

X
1
1
1
1
2
2
3
3
3
4
5
6

```
select *
    from one
union corr
select *
    from two;
```

84

s106d10
...

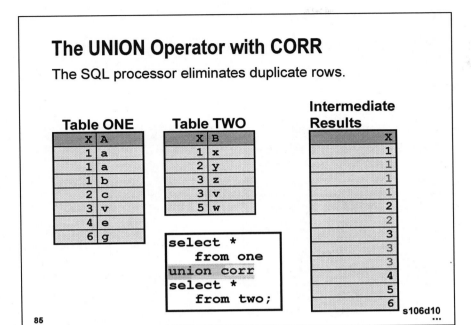

The UNION Operator with CORR

The SQL processor eliminates duplicate rows.

Table ONE	
X	A
1	a
1	a
1	b
2	c
3	v
4	e
6	g

Table TWO	
X	B
1	x
2	y
3	z
3	v
5	w

Intermediate Results

X
1
1
1
1
2
2
3
3
3
4
5
6

```
select *
   from one
union corr
select *
   from two;
```

85   s106d10 ...

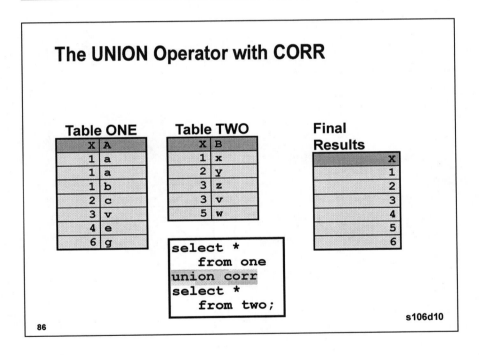

The UNION Operator with CORR

Table ONE	
X	A
1	a
1	a
1	b
2	c
3	v
4	e
6	g

Table TWO	
X	B
1	x
2	y
3	z
3	v
5	w

Final Results

X
1
2
3
4
5
6

```
select *
   from one
union corr
select *
   from two;
```

86   s106d10

Business Scenario (Review)

The management team needs a payroll report for the Level I, II, and III Orion Star employees.

- The `orion.Staff` table contains the job title and salary information for all Orion Star employees.
- Use the UNION set operator to combine the results from each query that calculates the total paid to **all** Level I, II, and III employees.

Payroll Report for Level I, II, and III Employees	
Total Paid to ALL Level I Staff	1,234,567
Total Paid to ALL Level II Staff	1,456,789
Total Paid to ALL Level III Staff	2,123,456

87

The UNION Operator

```
proc sql;
   select 'Total Paid to ALL Level I Staff',
          sum(Salary) format=comma12.
      from orion.Staff
      where scan(Job_Title,-1, ' ')='I'
   union
   select 'Total Paid to ALL Level II Staff',
          sum(Salary) format=comma12.
      from orion.Staff
      where scan(Job_Title,-1,' ')='II'
   union
   select 'Total Paid to ALL Level III Staff',
          sum(Salary) format=comma12.
      from orion.Staff
      where scan(Job_Title,-1,'  ')='III';
quit;
```

88   s106d11

The UNION Operator

PROC SQL Output

Payroll Report for Level I, II, and III Employees	
Total Paid to ALL Level I Staff	3,582,630
Total Paid to ALL Level II Staff	3,569,580
Total Paid to ALL Level III Staff	2,296,425

89

Set Operators and Keywords: Flow Diagrams

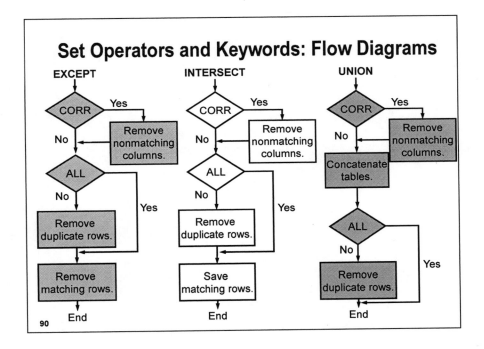

90

6.06 Poll

Is it more or less efficient to use the ALL keyword in a set operation?

○ More efficient

○ Less efficient

92

6.5 The OUTER UNION Operator

Objectives

- Describe SQL OUTER UNION set operators and keywords.
- Use the OUTER UNION set operators.
- Compare the SQL set operators to traditional SAS programming tools.

96

Business Scenario

Write a query to display the employee ID numbers, job titles, and salaries for all Administrative staff. The data that you need is in four separate data sets with identical structures. The OUTER UNION operator could be useful here.

97

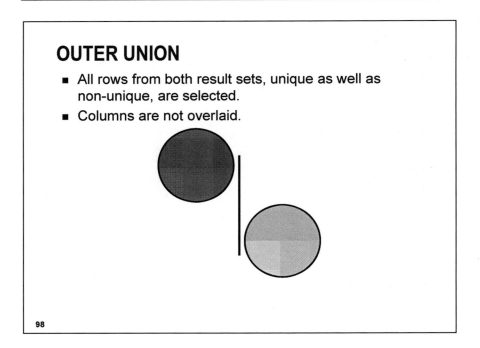

OUTER UNION CORR is useful when you have two or more source tables with some columns in common and extra columns that do not exist in all tables. You can use this technique if you want to include at least one of those extra columns in the output.

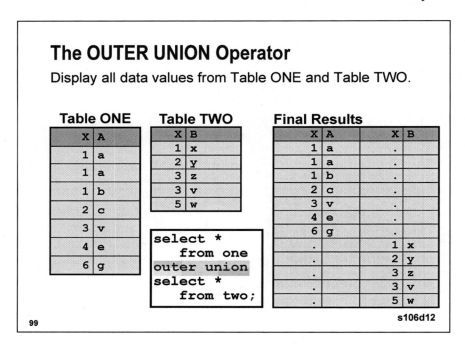

With the OUTER UNION operator, the ALL keyword is implied.

The OUTER UNION Operator with CORR

Display all data values from Table ONE and Table TWO, but overlay common columns.

Table ONE

X	A
1	a
1	a
1	b
2	c
3	v
4	e
6	g

Table TWO

X	B
1	x
2	y
3	z
3	v
5	w

```
select *
   from one
outer union corr
select *
   from two;
```

Final Results

X	A	B
1	a	
1	a	
1	b	
2	c	
3	v	
4	e	
6	g	
1		x
2		y
3		z
3		v
5		w

100

s106d13

Business Scenario (Review)

Write a query to display the employee ID numbers, job titles, and salaries for all Administrative staff.

Considerations:

The data that you need is in four separate data sets with identical structures:

- `work.Admin_I`
- `work.Admin_II`
- `work.Admin_III`
- `work.Admin_IV`

101

The OUTER UNION Operator with CORR

The OUTER UNION operator with the CORR keyword might be useful here.

```
proc sql;
    select *
        from work.Admin_I
    outer union corr
    select *
        from work.Admin_II
    outer union corr
    select *
        from work.Admin_III
    outer union corr
    select *
        from work.Admin_IV;
```

102   s106d14

The OUTER UNION Operator Results

PROC SQL Output

Employee ID	Employee Job Title	Employee Annual Salary
120105	Secretary I	$27,110
120992	Office Assistant I	$26,940
120993	Office Assistant I	$26,260
120994	Office Administrator I	$31,645
120106	Office Assistant II	$26,960
120662	Secretary II	$27,045
120749	Office Assistant II	$26,545
120995	Office Administrator II	$34,850
121147	Secretary II	$29,145
120107	Office Assistant III	$30,475
120267	Secretary III	$28,585
120667	Office Assistant III	$29,980
120799	Office Assistant III	$29,070
121146	Secretary III	$29,320
120266	Secretary IV	$31,750
120996	Office Assistant IV	$32,745

103

SQL versus Traditional SAS Programming

The following programs produce the same report:

```
data three;
    set one two;
run;
proc print data=three noobs;
run;
```

```
proc sql;
    select * from one
    outer union corr
    select * from two;
quit;
```

```
proc append base=one data=two;
run;
proc print data=one noobs;
run;
```

s105d15

104

6.07 Multiple Choice Poll

What DATA step statement yields the same results
as OUTER UNION CORR?

a. MERGE
b. APPEND
c. SET
d. STACK

106

SQL Set Operators versus the DATA Step

Key Points	SQL	DATA Step
Number of tables processed simultaneously	Limited to two tables	Not limited by SAS; limited only by system resources.
Column handling	Depends on the SET operator and keywords	All columns from all data sets are included in output data set(s), unless specified using data set options or program logic.
Duplicate row handling	Depends on the SET operator and keywords	All rows are output unless specified using data set options or program logic.

✎ Also consider PROC APPEND for vertical table combination.

108

 **Exercises**

Level 1

7. **Using the UNION Operator**

    Create a report that displays the total salary for female and male sales representatives and the total number of female and male sales representatives. The **orion.Salesstaff** table contains information on all the Orion Star sales representatives, including **Salary** and **Gender**. The query should do the following:

    -   Create the first row of the report. Use the constant text **Total Paid to ALL Female Sales Representatives**, **SUM(Salary)**, and the total number of rows using the COUNT(*) function. Summarize data in the **orion.Salesstaff** table for those rows that have **Gender** = **'F'** and **Job_Title** containing **'Rep'**.

    -   Use the appropriate SET operator.

    -   Create the second row of the report. Use the constant text **Total Paid to ALL Male Sales Representatives**, **SUM(Salary)**, and the total number of rows using the COUNT(*) function. Summarize data in the **orion.Salesstaff** table for those rows that have **Gender** = **'M'** and **Job_Title** containing **'Rep'**.

    -   Provide a title for the report as shown below.

    PROC SQL Output

Payroll Report for Sales Representatives		
		Total
Total Paid to ALL Female Sales Representatives	$1,898,804	68
Total Paid to ALL Male Sales Representatives	$2,655,678	95

8. **Using the OUTER UNION Operator with the CORR Keyword**

   Create a report that displays the sales data for the first and second quarters of 2007. The
   `orion.Qtr1_2007` table contains the sales data for the first quarter, and the `orion.Qtr2_2007`
   table contains the sales data for the second quarter.

   Partial PROC SQL Output

			First and Second Quarter 2007 Sales		

Order ID	Order Type	Customer ID	Date Order was placed by Customer	Date Order was Delivered	Employee ID
1241054779	3	24	02JAN2007	05JAN2007	.
1241063739	1	89	03JAN2007	04JAN2007	.
		... ...			
1241731828	1	31	18MAR2007	18MAR2007	.
1241789227	3	17023	25MAR2007	30MAR2007	.
1241895594	1	56	05APR2007	09APR2007	121051
1241909303	0	46966	07APR2007	08APR2007	99999999
		... ...			
1242647539	1	45	27JUN2007	27JUN2007	121109
1242657273	1	90	28JUN2007	28JUN2007	121037

Level 2

9. **Comparing UNION and OUTER UNION Operators**

   Stack the `orion.Qtr1_2007` and `orion.Qtr2_2007` tables to produce a single report.

   a. Use the UNION operator to stack the data in `orion.Qtr1_2007` and `orion.Qtr2_2007`.

   b. Use the OUTER UNION operator without the CORR keyword to stack the data in
       `orion.Qtr1_2007` and `orion.Qtr2_2007`. Set the LINESIZE system option to 140 to
       prevent wrapping of the SQL output.

   c. Were the final results the same? If not, how did they differ? _____

       _____

   d. Can the UNION operator and OUTER UNION operator yield the same results if you use the
       CORR keyword in this example? _____

       _____

6.6   Chapter Review

Chapter Review

1. How many **rows** will this query produce?

```
proc sql;
    select *
        from table1
    INTERSECT
    select *
        from table2
;
quit;
```

Table 1	
ID	Var
1	Abc
2	Def
3	Ghi

Table 2	
ID	Var
1	Abc
2	Zxy
3	Ghi

110

Chapter Review

2. How many **rows** will this query produce?

```
proc sql;
    select *
        from table1
    EXCEPT
    select *
        from table2
;
quit;
```

Table 1	
ID	Var
1	Abc
2	Def
3	Ghi

Table 2	
ID	Var
1	Abc
2	Zxy
3	Ghi

112

Chapter Review

3. Will the addition of the CORR and ALL keywords change the number of rows that this query produces?

```
proc sql;
    select *
        from table1
    EXCEPT CORR ALL
    select *
        from table2
;
quit;
```

Table 1

ID	Var
1	Abc
2	Def
3	Ghi

Table 2

ID	Var
1	Abc
2	Zxy
3	Ghi

114

Chapter Review

4. How many **columns** will this query produce?

```
proc sql;
    select *
        from table1
    OUTER UNION CORR
    select *
        from table2
;
quit;
```

Table 1

ID	Var1
1	Abc
2	Def
3	Ghi

Table 2

ID	Var2
1	Abc
2	Zxy
3	Ghi

116

6.7 Solutions

Solutions to Exercises

1. **Using the EXCEPT Operator**

```
*** s106s01 ***;


proc sql;
title "Employee IDs with Phone Numbers But Not Address Information";
   select Employee_ID
      from orion.Employee_phones
   except
   select Employee_ID
      from orion.Employee_Addresses;
quit;
title;


   /* Alternative Solution using the CORR keyword */
proc sql;
title "Employee IDs with Phone Numbers But Not Address Information";
   select *
      from orion.Employee_phones
   except corr
   select *
      from orion.Employee_Addresses;
quit;
title;
```

2. **Using the INTERSECT Operator**

```
*** s106s02 ***;


proc sql;
title 'Customers Who Placed Orders';
   select Customer_ID
      from orion.Order_fact
   intersect
   select Customer_ID
      from orion.Customer;
quit;
title;
```

3. Using the EXCEPT Operator to Count Rows

```
*** s106s03 ***;

proc sql;
   select count(*) label='No. Employees w/ No Charitable Donations'
      from (select Employee_ID
               from orion.Employee_organization
            except
            select Employee_ID
               from orion.Employee_donations);
quit;
```

4. Using the INTERSECT Operator to Count Rows

```
*** s106s04 ***;

proc sql;
   select count(*) label='No. Customers w/ Orders'
      from (select Customer_ID
               from orion.Order_fact
            intersect
            select Customer_ID
               from orion.Customer);
quit;
title;
```

5. Using the EXCEPT Operator with a Subquery

```
*** s106s05 ***;

proc sql number;
title 'Sales Reps Who Made No Sales in 2007';
   select Employee_ID, Employee_Name
      from orion.Employee_Addresses
      where Employee_ID in
         (select Employee_ID
             from orion.Sales
             where Job_Title like '%Rep%'
      except all
         select Employee_ID
             from orion.Order_fact
             where year(order_date)=2007);
quit;
title;
```

6. **Using the INTERSECT Operator with a Subquery**

```
*** s106s06 ***;

proc sql;
title 'Name of Customers Who Placed Orders';
   select Customer_ID, Customer_name
      from orion.Customer
      where Customer_ID in
         (select Customer_ID
             from orion.Order_fact
          intersect
          select Customer_ID
             from orion.Customer);
quit;
title;
```

7. **Using the UNION Operator**

```
*** s106s07 ***;

proc sql;
title 'Payroll Report for Sales Representatives';
   select 'Total Paid to ALL Female Sales Representatives',
             sum(Salary) format=dollar14., count(*) label='Total'
      from orion.Salesstaff
      where gender='F' and  Job_Title like '%Rep%'
   union
   select 'Total Paid to ALL Male Sales Representatives',
             sum(Salary) format=dollary14. , count(*) label='Total'
      from orion.Salesstaff
      where gender='M' and Job_Title like '%Rep%';
quit;
title;
```

8. **Using the OUTER UNION Operator with the CORR Keyword**

```
*** s106s08 ***;

proc sql;
title 'First and Second Quarter 2007 Sales ';
   select *
      from orion.Qtr1_2007
   outer union corr
   select *
      from orion.Qtr2_2007;
quit;
title;
```

9. Comparing UNION and OUTER UNION Operators

   a. The **Customer_ID** column contains some **Employee_ID** values because the columns are overlaid.

```
*** s106s09 ***;

  /* a */

proc sql;
title 'Results with UNION operator';
   select *
      from orion.Qtr1_2007
   union
   select *
      from orion.Qtr2_2007;
quit;
title;
```

Partial PROC SQL Output

			Results with UNION operator		

Order ID	Order Type	Customer ID	Date Order was placed by Customer	Date Order was Delivered	Date Order was Delivered
.	1	120127	20JUN1960	13MAY2007	13MAY2007
.	3	99999999	14NOV2151	11MAY2007	14MAY2007
1241054779	3	24	02JAN2007	05JAN2007	.
1241063739	1	89	03JAN2007	04JAN2007	.
1241066216	1	171	04JAN2007	04JAN2007	.
1241086052	3	53	06JAN2007	09JAN2007	.
1241147641	1	53	13JAN2007	13JAN2007	.
1241235281	1	171	23JAN2007	30JAN2007	.
1241244297	1	111	24JAN2007	24JAN2007	.
1241263172	3	3959	25JAN2007	26JAN2007	.
1241286432	3	27	28JAN2007	02FEB2007	.
1241298131	2	2806	29JAN2007	08FEB2007	.
1241359997	1	12	05FEB2007	05FEB2007	.
1241371145	1	171	07FEB2007	07FEB2007	.
1241390440	1	41	09FEB2007	09FEB2007	.
1241461856	1	18	16FEB2007	17FEB2007	.
1241561055	1	171	28FEB2007	28FEB2007	.
1241623505	3	24	06MAR2007	09MAR2007	.
1241645664	2	70100	09MAR2007	13MAR2007	.
1241652707	3	27	09MAR2007	14MAR2007	.
1241686210	1	10	13MAR2007	19MAR2007	.
1241715610	1	92	16MAR2007	16MAR2007	.
1241731828	1	31	18MAR2007	18MAR2007	.
1241789227	3	17023	25MAR2007	30MAR2007	.
1241895594	1	121051	26FEB1960	05APR2007	09APR2007
1241909303	0	99999999	02AUG2088	07APR2007	08APR2007
1241930625	3	99999999	28JAN1960	09APR2007	14APR2007
1241977403	1	120152	20JUN1960	15APR2007	15APR2007
1242012259	1	121040	11JAN1960	18APR2007	12APR2007
1242012269	1	121040	15FEB1960	18APR2007	18APR2007
1242035131	1	120132	02JUL1960	21APR2007	21APR2007
1242076538	3	99999999	01FEB1960	25APR2007	29APR2007
1242130888	1	121086	02APR1960	01MAY2007	01MAY2007
1242140006	4	99999999	06JAN1960	02MAY2007	07MAY2007
1242140009	2	99999999	31MAR1960	02MAY2007	04MAY2007
1242149082	1	121032	31MAR1960	03MAY2007	03MAY2007
1242159212	3	99999999	06JAN1960	04MAY2007	09MAY2007
1242161468	3	99999999	25DEC1966	04MAY2007	09MAY2007
1242162201	3	99999999	02AUG2088	05MAY2007	06MAY2007
1242173926	3	99999999	30OCT1962	06MAY2007	10MAY2007
1242185055	1	120136	11FEB1960	08MAY2007	08MAY2007
1242259863	2	99999999	01MAR2152	16MAY2007	21MAY2007

b. With the OUTER UNION operator, all rows from both tables are selected. This includes both unique and non-unique rows. The columns are not overlaid. Examine the column for `Employee_ID`.

```
/* b */
options ls=140;
proc sql;
title 'Results with OUTER UNION operator';
   select *
      from orion.Qtr1_2007
   outer union
   select *
      from orion.Qtr2_2007;
quit;
title;
```

Partial PROC SQL Output

					Results with OUTER UNION operator						
Order ID	Order Type	Customer ID	Date Order was placed by Customer	Date Order was Delivered	Order ID	Order Type	Employee ID	Customer ID	Date Order was placed by Customer	Date Order was Delivered
1241054779	3	24	02JAN2007	05JAN2007	.	.	.	.	.	.
1241063739	1	89	03JAN2007	04JAN2007	.	.	.	.	.	.
1241066216	1	171	04JAN2007	04JAN2007	.	.	.	.	.	.
1241086052	3	53	06JAN2007	09JAN2007	.	.	.	.	.	.
1241147641	1	53	13JAN2007	13JAN2007	.	.	.	.	.	.
1241235281	1	171	23JAN2007	30JAN2007	.	.	.	.	.	.
1241244297	1	111	24JAN2007	24JAN2007	.	.	.	.	.	.
1241263172	3	3959	25JAN2007	26JAN2007	.	.	.	.	.	.
1241286432	3	27	28JAN2007	02FEB2007	.	.	.	.	.	.
1241298131	2	2806	29JAN2007	08FEB2007	.	.	.	.	.	.
1241359997	1	12	05FEB2007	05FEB2007	.	.	.	.	.	.
1241371145	1	171	07FEB2007	07FEB2007	.	.	.	.	.	.
1241390440	1	41	09FEB2007	09FEB2007	.	.	.	.	.	.
1241461856	1	18	16FEB2007	17FEB2007	.	.	.	.	.	.
1241561055	1	171	28FEB2007	28FEB2007	.	.	.	.	.	.
1241623505	3	24	06MAR2007	09MAR2007	.	.	.	.	.	.
1241645664	2	70100	09MAR2007	13MAR2007	.	.	.	.	.	.
1241652707	3	27	09MAR2007	14MAR2007	.	.	.	.	.	.
1241686210	1	10	13MAR2007	19MAR2007	.	.	.	.	.	.
1241715610	1	92	16MAR2007	16MAR2007	.	.	.	.	.	.
1241731828	1	31	18MAR2007	18MAR2007	.	.	.	.	.	.
1241789227	3	17023	25MAR2007	30MAR2007	.	.	.	.	.	.
.	.	.	.	.	1241895594	1	121051	56	05APR2007	09APR2007
.	.	.	.	.	1241909303	0	99999999	46966	07APR2007	08APR2007
.	.	.	.	.	1241930625	3	99999999	27	09APR2007	14APR2007
.	.	.	.	.	1241977403	1	120152	171	15APR2007	15APR2007
.	.	.	.	.	1242012259	1	121040	10	18APR2007	12APR2007
.	.	.	.	.	1242012269	1	121040	45	18APR2007	18APR2007
.	.	.	.	.	1242035131	1	120132	183	21APR2007	21APR2007
.	.	.	.	.	1242076538	3	99999999	31	25APR2007	29APR2007
.	.	.	.	.	1242130888	1	121086	92	01MAY2007	01MAY2007
.	.	.	.	.	1242140006	4	99999999	5	02MAY2007	07MAY2007
.	.	.	.	.	1242140009	2	99999999	90	02MAY2007	04MAY2007
.	.	.	.	.	1242149082	1	121032	90	03MAY2007	03MAY2007
.	.	.	.	.	1242159212	3	99999999	5	04MAY2007	09MAY2007
.	.	.	.	.	1242161468	3	99999999	2550	04MAY2007	09MAY2007
.	.	.	.	.	1242162201	3	99999999	46966	05MAY2007	06MAY2007
.	.	.	.	.	1242173926	3	99999999	1033	06MAY2007	10MAY2007
.	.	.	.	.	1242185055	1	120136	41	08MAY2007	08MAY2007
.	.	.	.	.		3	99999999	70079	11MAY2007	14MAY2007
.	.	.	.	.		1	120127	171	13MAY2007	13MAY2007

c. Were the final results the same? If not, how did they differ? <u>No, the final results are different. When the UNION operator is used, the `Customer_ID` column contains some `Employee_ID` values because the columns are overlaid. When the OUTER UNION operator is used, all of the rows from both tables are selected. These rows include both unique and non-unique rows. Also notice that there is a separate column for `Employee_ID`, because the columns are not overlaid when you use the OUTER UNION operator.</u>

d. Can the UNION operator and OUTER UNION operator yield the same results if you use the CORR keyword in this example? <u>No, the UNION operator with the CORR keyword cannot yield the same results as the OUTER UNION operator with the CORR keyword for this example, because UNION CORR discards columns that do not have matching names, while OUTER UNION CORR retains all columns.</u>

```
/* d - NO*/
proc sql;
title 'Results with UNION operator and CORR modifier';
   select *
       from orion.Qtr1_2007
   union corr
   select *
       from orion.Qtr2_2007;
quit;
title;
```

Partial PROC SQL Output

```
          Results with  UNION  operator and CORR modifier

                                              Date
                                           Order was        Date
                          Order            placed by    Order was
          Order  ID       Type   Customer  ID  Customer   Delivered
                    .        1        171   13MAY2007   13MAY2007
                    .        3      70079   11MAY2007   14MAY2007
          1241054779        3         24   02JAN2007   05JAN2007
          1241063739        1         89   03JAN2007   04JAN2007
          1241066216        1        171   04JAN2007   04JAN2007
          1241086052        3         53   06JAN2007   09JAN2007
          1241147641        1         53   13JAN2007   13JAN2007
          1241235281        1        171   23JAN2007   30JAN2007
          1241244297        1        111   24JAN2007   24JAN2007
          1241263172        3       3959   25JAN2007   26JAN2007
          1241286432        3         27   28JAN2007   02FEB2007
          1241298131        2       2806   29JAN2007   08FEB2007
          1241359997        1         12   05FEB2007   05FEB2007
          1241371145        1        171   07FEB2007   07FEB2007
          1241390440        1         41   09FEB2007   09FEB2007
          1241461856        1         18   16FEB2007   17FEB2007
          1241561055        1        171   28FEB2007   28FEB2007
          1241623505        3         24   06MAR2007   09MAR2007
          1241645664        2      70100   09MAR2007   13MAR2007
          1241652707        3         27   09MAR2007   14MAR2007
          1241686210        1         10   13MAR2007   19MAR2007
          1241715610        1         92   16MAR2007   16MAR2007
          1241731828        1         31   18MAR2007   18MAR2007
          1241789227        3      17023   25MAR2007   30MAR2007
          1241895594        1         56   05APR2007   09APR2007
          1241909303        0      46966   07APR2007   08APR2007
          1241930625        3         27   09APR2007   14APR2007
          1241977403        1        171   15APR2007   15APR2007
          1242012259        1         10   18APR2007   12APR2007
          1242012269        1         45   18APR2007   18APR2007
          1242035131        1        183   21APR2007   21APR2007
          1242076538        3         31   25APR2007   29APR2007
          1242130888        1         92   01MAY2007   01MAY2007
          1242140006        4          5   02MAY2007   07MAY2007
          1242140009        2         90   02MAY2007   04MAY2007
          1242149082        1         90   03MAY2007   03MAY2007
          1242159212        3          5   04MAY2007   09MAY2007
          1242161468        3       2550   04MAY2007   09MAY2007
          1242162201        3      46966   05MAY2007   06MAY2007
          1242173926        3       1033   06MAY2007   10MAY2007
          1242185055        1         41   08MAY2007   08MAY2007
          1242259863        2      70187   16MAY2007   21MAY2007
```

```
proc sql;
title 'Results with OUTER UNION operator and CORR modifier';
   select *
       from orion.Qtr1_2007
   outer union corr
   select *
       from orion.Qtr2_2007;
quit;
title;
```

Partial PROC SQL Output

```
                  Results with  OUTER UNION  operator and CORR modifier

                                           Date
                                        Order was       Date
                           Order        placed by     Order was
          Order ID         Type     Customer ID  Customer    Delivered    Employee ID

          1241054779        3             24     02JAN2007   05JAN2007          .
          1241063739        1             89     03JAN2007   04JAN2007          .
          1241066216        1            171     04JAN2007   04JAN2007          .
          1241086052        3             53     06JAN2007   09JAN2007          .
          1241147641        1             53     13JAN2007   13JAN2007          .
          1241235281        1            171     23JAN2007   30JAN2007          .
          1241244297        1            111     24JAN2007   24JAN2007          .
          1241263172        3           3959     25JAN2007   26JAN2007          .
          1241286432        3             27     28JAN2007   02FEB2007          .
          1241298131        2           2806     29JAN2007   08FEB2007          .
          1241359997        1             12     05FEB2007   05FEB2007          .
          1241371145        1            171     07FEB2007   07FEB2007          .
          1241390440        1             41     09FEB2007   09FEB2007          .
          1241461856        1             18     16FEB2007   17FEB2007          .
          1241561055        1            171     28FEB2007   28FEB2007          .
          1241623505        3             24     06MAR2007   09MAR2007          .
          1241645664        2          70100     09MAR2007   13MAR2007          .
          1241652707        3             27     09MAR2007   14MAR2007          .
          1241686210        1             10     13MAR2007   19MAR2007          .
          1241715610        1             92     16MAR2007   16MAR2007          .
          1241731828        1             31     18MAR2007   18MAR2007          .
          1241789227        3          17023     25MAR2007   30MAR2007          .
          1241895594        1             56     05APR2007   09APR2007      121051
          1241909303        0          46966     07APR2007   08APR2007    99999999
          1241930625        3             27     09APR2007   14APR2007    99999999
          1241977403        1            171     15APR2007   15APR2007      120152
          1242012259        1             10     18APR2007   12APR2007      121040
          1242012269        1             45     18APR2007   18APR2007      121040
          1242035131        1            183     21APR2007   21APR2007      120132
          1242076538        3             31     25APR2007   29APR2007    99999999
          1242130888        1             92     01MAY2007   01MAY2007      121086
          1242140006        4              5     02MAY2007   07MAY2007    99999999
          1242140009        2             90     02MAY2007   04MAY2007    99999999
          1242149082        1             90     03MAY2007   03MAY2007      121032
          1242159212        3              5     04MAY2007   09MAY2007    99999999
          1242161468        3           2550     04MAY2007   09MAY2007    99999999
          1242162201        3          46966     05MAY2007   06MAY2007    99999999
          1242173926        3           1033     06MAY2007   10MAY2007    99999999
          1242185055        1             41     08MAY2007   08MAY2007      120136
                   .        3          70079     11MAY2007   14MAY2007    99999999
                   .        1            171     13MAY2007   13MAY2007      120127
          1242259863        2          70187     16MAY2007   21MAY2007    99999999
```

Solutions to Student Activities (Polls/Quizzes)

6.01 Poll – Correct Answer

By default the EXCEPT, INTERSECT, and UNION set operators remove duplicate rows from the query output.

⊙ True
○ False

16

6.02 Quiz – Correct Answer

What are the results when you combine ALL with CORR?

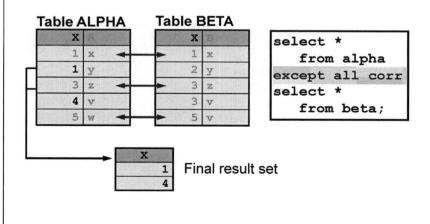

38

6.03 Quiz – Correct Answer

Answer the questions about the following program:

```
select Employee_ID, Job_Title
   from orion.Employee_organization
except all
select Employee_ID, Job_Title
   from orion.Sales;
```

1. Why is the CORR keyword not used in this example?

   **Both SELECT lists specify the same column names
   in the same order, so CORR is not necessary.**

45

6.04 Poll – Correct Answer

By default, the EXCEPT set operator selects **all** the rows
from the first result set that are not in the second result
set.

○ True

 False

**By default, the EXCEPT operator eliminates
duplicate rows first. It selects only *unique* rows from
the first result set that are not in the second result
set.**

52

6.05 Quiz – Correct Answer

Will the addition of the ALL keyword have any effect on the output?

Yes. There are duplicate rows common to both tables. The ALL keyword will include the duplicate rows.

Table AAA

X	A
1	a
1	a
1	b
2	c
3	v
4	e
6	g

Table BBB

X	B
1	a
1	a
2	z
3	z
3	v
5	w

```
select *
    from aaa
intersect all
select *
    from bbb;
```

Final Results

X	A
1	a
1	a
3	v

s106a03

66

6.06 Poll – Correct Answer

Is it more or less efficient to use the ALL keyword in a set operation?

◉ More efficient
○ Less efficient

No de-duplication is required.

93

6.07 Multiple Choice Poll – Correct Answer

What DATA step statement yields the same results
as OUTER UNION CORR?

- a. MERGE
- b. APPEND
- (c.) SET
- d. STACK

107

Solutions to Chapter Review

Chapter Review Answers

1. How many **rows** will this query produce?

   Two

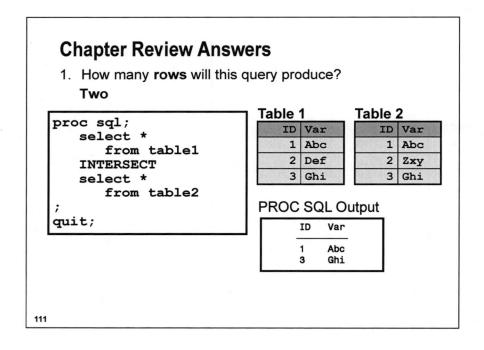

111

Chapter Review Answers

2. How many **rows** will this query produce?

One

```
proc sql;
    select *
        from table1
    EXCEPT
    select *
        from table2
;
quit;
```

Table 1

ID	Var
1	Abc
2	Def
3	Ghi

Table 2

ID	Var
1	Abc
2	Zxy
3	Ghi

PROC SQL Output

ID	Var
2	Def

113

Chapter Review Answers

3. Will the addition of the CORR and ALL keywords change the number of rows that this query produces?

No

```
proc sql;
    select *
        from table1
    EXCEPT CORR ALL
    select *
        from table2
;
quit;
```

Table 1

ID	Var
1	Abc
2	Def
3	Ghi

Table 2

ID	Var
1	Abc
2	Zxy
3	Ghi

PROC SQL Output

ID	Var
2	Def

115

Chapter Review Answers

4. How many **columns** will this query produce?

   Three

```
proc sql;
    select *
        from table1
    OUTER UNION CORR
    select *
        from table2
;
quit;
```

Table 1

ID	Var1
1	Abc
2	Def
3	Ghi

Table 2

ID	Var2
1	Abc
2	Zxy
3	Ghi

PROC SQL Output

ID	Var	Var2
1	Abc	
2	Def	
3	Ghi	
1		Abc
2		Xyz
3		Ghi

117

Chapter 7   Creating Tables and Views

7.1 Creating Views with the SQL Procedure

Objectives

- Create SQL views.
- Use SQL views in SQL queries.
- Use SQL views in other SAS processes.

3

PROC SQL Views

Sometimes referred to as virtual tables, views store query code that retrieves data stored elsewhere.

When the query is referenced, the stored query acts as your view to the ever-changing data.

4

What Is a PROC SQL View?

A *PROC SQL view*

- is a stored query
- contains no actual data
- can be derived from one or more tables, PROC SQL views, DATA step views, or SAS/ACCESS views
- extracts underlying data each time that it is used, and accesses the most current data
- can be referenced in SAS programs in the same way as a data table
- cannot have the same name as a data table stored in the same SAS library.

5

Views are sometimes referred to as *virtual tables* because they are referenced in SAS programs in the same manner as actual data tables, but they are not data tables. They contain no actual data but instead store the instructions required to retrieve and present the data to which they refer.

A copy of a data table performs in a manner similar to a snapshot. It is accurate as of the particular point in time that the copy was made. Subsequent changes to the source data table are not reflected in the copy.

A view's performance resembles the monitor for a security camera that is aimed at the source data. As the source data changes, the view on the monitor also changes. The data presented is always in synch with the data in the source data table, but no permanent "copy" is kept on the monitor.

Conceptually, the instructions in the view are executed each time that the view is referenced by a SAS procedure or DATA step, producing a virtual table. SAS then processes this virtual table's data as if it were in an actual, physical data table.

Creating a View

General form of the CREATE VIEW statement:

> **CREATE VIEW** *view-name* **AS**
> *query-expression*;

✏ The CREATE VIEW statement differs from the CREATE TABLE statement in that a view is **always** created from the results of a query. Methods that create empty tables without extracting data are not appropriate for creating views.

6

✏ Within any SAS library, a view cannot have the same name as an existing table, nor can a table be created with the same name as an existing view.

Business Scenario

Tom Zhou is a sales manager who frequently needs access to personnel information for his direct reports, including name, job title, salary, and years of service. He asked for access to personnel data so that he can generate reports.

7

Business Scenario

Considerations:

The data Tom needs can be obtained from these tables:

`orion.Employee_Addresses`

`orion.Employee_Payroll`

`orion.Employee_Organization`

Tom knows enough SAS to write simple PROC SQL queries and use basic SAS procedures, but cannot write complex joins.

Tom should not be allowed access to personnel data for any employee that is not his direct report.

8

Creating a View

A view containing personnel information for Tom Zhou's direct reports can provide the information that Tom needs and avoid inadvertent access to data for employees who do not report to him.

```
proc sql;
create view orion.Tom_Zhou as
   select Employee_Name as Name format=$25.0,
          Job_Title as Title format=$15.0,
          Salary 'Annual Salary' format=comma10.2,
          int((today()-Employee_Hire_Date)/365.25)
             as YOS 'Years of Service'
      from orion.Employee_Addresses as a,
           orion.Employee_Payroll as p,
           orion.Employee_Organization as o
      where a.Employee_ID=p.Employee_ID and
            o.Employee_ID=p.Employee_ID and
            Manager_ID=120102;
```

9   s107d10

In the example above, the view **orion.Tom_Zhou** creates a virtual table from the stored query (SELECT statement). The data and structure of the underlying tables **orion.Employee_Addresses**, **orion.Employee_Payroll**, and **orion.Employee_Organization** might change, but the instructions within the view about how to produce the virtual table remain the same. This view will always return **only** those employees managed by Tom Zhou because the WHERE clause filters for Tom's **Employee_ID** (120102) in the **Manager_ID** column.

When the PROC SQL step creating the view is executed, SAS does not actually **execute** the SELECT statement that follows the AS keyword. It partially compiles and stores the SELECT statement in a data file with a member type of VIEW.

SAS requires every column in a data table to have a unique name. If, in the above example, the alias **YOS** is omitted when you attempt to use the VIEW in standard SAS programming, SAS generates a sequentially suffixed variable name for any column (variable) for which you fail to provide an alias (name), and places a warning in the SAS log:

```
WARNING: The SQL View ORION.TOM_ZHOU contains un-named expressions in its select list. SQL will
         generate internal names using the template _TEMVnnn.
```

Using a View

Tom can use the view to produce simple reports.

```
proc sql;
title "Tom Zhou's Direct Reports";
title2 "By Title and Years of Service";
   select *
      from orion.Tom_Zhou
      order by Title desc, YOS desc;
```

Partial PROC SQL Output (executed 02FEB2008)

```
                Tom Zhou's Direct Reports
                By Title and Years of Service

                                      Annual   Years of
Name                  Title           Salary   Service

Nowd, Fadi            Sales Rep. IV   30,660.00      34
Hofmeister, Fong      Sales Rep. IV   32,040.00      28
Phoumirath, Lynelle   Sales Rep. IV   30,765.00      21
Platts, Alexei        Sales Rep. IV   32,490.00      10
```

10   s107d10

Using a View

Tom can also use the view to produce simple descriptive statistics to help him better manage his group.

```
title "Tom Zhou's Group - Salary Statistics";
proc means data=orion.Tom_Zhou min mean max;
   var salary;
   class title;
run;
```

Partial PROC MEANS Output

```
          Tom Zhou's Group - Salary Statistics
                   The MEANS Procedure
          Analysis Variable : Salary Annual Salary

Title            N Obs   Minimum      Mean    Maximum

Sales Rep. I        18  25185.00  26466.67  27260.00
Sales Rep. II       13  26165.00  27123.46  28100.00
Sales Rep. III      12  28135.00  29895.42  36605.00
Sales Rep. IV        5  30660.00  31369.00  32490.00
```

11   s107d10

There is no need for Tom to remember the names of the three tables underlying this view, nor does he have to worry about how to perform the join. From Tom's perspective, the complexity of accessing and using this data is greatly reduced.

Administering Views

After a view is created, you can use the DESCRIBE VIEW statement to investigate the view's contents.

```
proc sql;
    describe view orion.Tom_Zhou;
```

Partial SAS Log

```
NOTE: SQL view ORION.TOM_ZHOU is defined as:
select Employee_Name as Name format=$25.0,
       Job_Title as Title format=$15.0,
       Salary label='Annual Salary' format=COMMA10.2,
       INT((TODAY()-Employee_Hire_Date)/365.25) as YOS
          label='Years of Service'
   from ORION.EMPLOYEE_ADDRESSES a, ORION.EMPLOYEE_PAYROLL p,
        ORION.EMPLOYEE_ORGANIZATION o
   where (a.Employee_ID=p.Employee_ID) and
         (o.Employee_ID=p.Employee_ID) and
         (Manager_ID=120102);
```

12   s107d10

7.01 Quiz

What differences are there between the SQL code written to the SAS log by the DESCRIBE VIEW statement and the CREATE VIEW code, which actually created the view **orion.Tom_Zhou**?

14

7.02 Poll

Considering the differences discussed previously, if you submit the code produced by the DESCRIBE VIEW statement, would the view produced be identical to the original view?

○ Yes

○ No

20

Views: Advantages

You can use views to do the following:

- avoid storing copies of large data tables
- avoid a frequent refresh of data table copies. When the underlying data changes, a view surfaces the most current data
- pull together data from multiple database tables and multiple libraries or databases
- simplify complex queries
- prevent other users from inadvertently altering the query code

22

Views: Disadvantages

- Because views access the most current data in changing tables, the results might be different each time that you access the view.
- Views can require significant resources each time that they execute. With a view, you save disk storage space at the cost of extra CPU and memory usage.
- When accessing the same data several times in a program, use a table instead of a view. This ensures consistent results from one step to the next and can significantly reduce the resources that are required.

23

Business Scenario

You created an SQL view to provide Tom Zhou, a sales manager, access to personnel data for his direct reports. Tom was pleased and used his new view daily.

Later, to simplify reporting, Tom copied his view to the folder on his hard drive where he stores all of his personal, permanent SAS files. Now Tom reports that the view does not work anymore, and he asked for your help to resolve the problem.

24

Two-Level Table Names in Permanent Views

The following program creates a permanent view,
Level_II, in the default SAS library location, using
the libref **test** instead of **orion**:

```
libname test '.';
proc sql;
   create view test.Level_II as
      select Employee_ID, Gender,
             Job_Title as Title
         from test.Staff
         where scan(Job_Title,-1) ='II'
               and Emp_Term_Date is missing
;
```

25   s107d11

Two-Level Table Names in Permanent Views

Step 1: Assign a libref.

```
libname test '.';
```

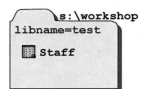

26   s107d11
                                                      ...

The pathnames assigned to the folders in the slides in this section are typical for Windows SAS classes (s:\workshop and others). Actual paths differ if your data is installed at another location, or if you are running a different operating system, such as UNIX or z/OS.

Two-Level Table Names in Permanent Views

Step 1: Assign a libref.

Step 2: Create the view.

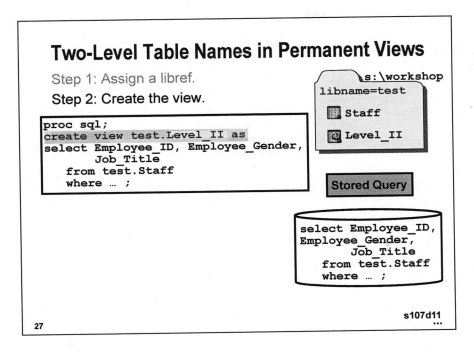

```
proc sql;
create view test.Level_II as
select Employee_ID, Employee_Gender,
       Job_Title
   from test.Staff
   where … ;
```

s:\workshop
libname=test
Staff
Level_II

Stored Query

```
select Employee_ID,
Employee_Gender,
       Job_Title
   from test.Staff
   where … ;
```

s107d11
...

27

Two-Level Table Names in Permanent Views

Step 1: Assign a libref.

Step 2: Create the view.

Step 3: Access the view.

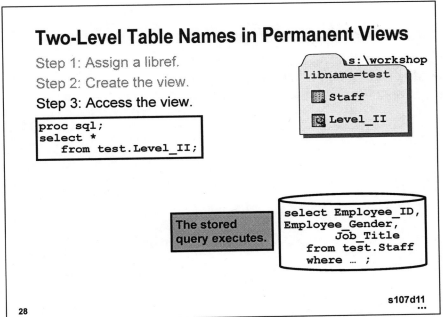

```
proc sql;
select *
   from test.Level_II;
```

s:\workshop
libname=test
Staff
Level_II

The stored query executes.

```
select Employee_ID,
Employee_Gender,
       Job_Title
   from test.Staff
   where … ;
```

s107d11
...

28

Two-Level Table Names in Permanent Views

Step 1: Assign a libref.

Step 2: Create the view.

Step 3: Access the view.

```
proc sql;
select *
   from test.Level_II;
```

Partial SQL Output

Employee ID	Employee Gender	Job Title
120121	F	Sales Rep. II
120122	F	Sales Rep. II
120126	M	Sales Rep. II
120127	F	Sales Rep. II

29   s107d11

Two-Level Table Names in Permanent Views

Several weeks later, you remember creating the **Level_II** view and decide that it is the perfect source to use for the current reporting project.

30

Two-Level Table Names in Permanent Views

Step 1: Assign a libref.

```
libname orion '.';
```

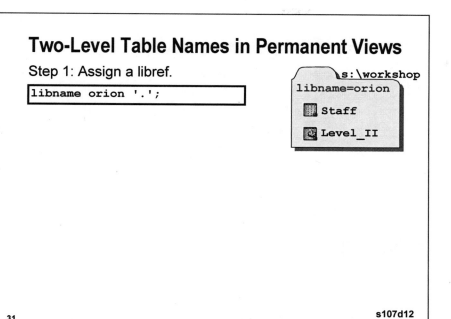

31   s107d12
                                                        ...

Two-Level Table Names in Permanent Views

Step 1: Assign a libref.

Step 2: Access the view.

```
proc sql;
select *
   from orion.Level_II;
```

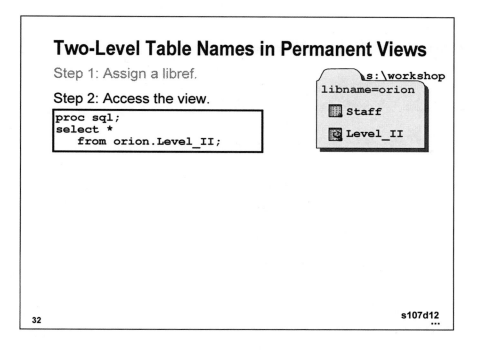

32   s107d12
                                                        ...

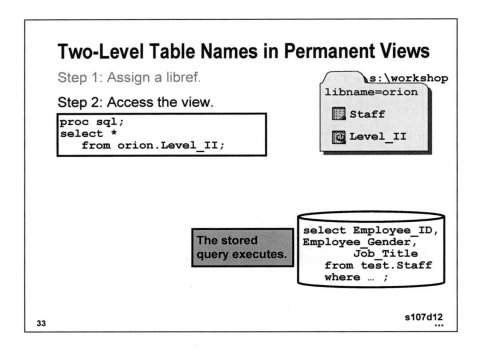

Two-Level Table Names in Permanent Views

Step 1: Assign a libref.

Step 2: Access the view.

```
proc sql;
select *
   from orion.Level_II;
```

`s:\workshop`
`libname=orion`
  Staff
  Level_II

The stored query executes.

```
select Employee_ID,
Employee_Gender,
       Job_Title
   from test.Staff
   where ... ;
```

33   s107d12
      ...

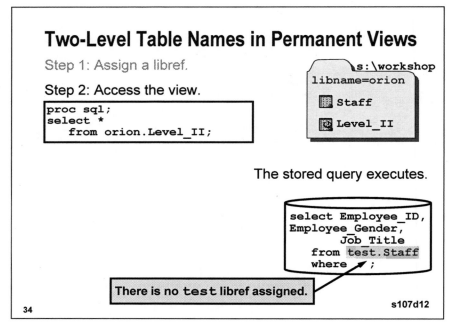

Two-Level Table Names in Permanent Views

Step 1: Assign a libref.

Step 2: Access the view.

```
proc sql;
select *
   from orion.Level_II;
```

`s:\workshop`
`libname=orion`
  Staff
  Level_II

The stored query executes.

```
select Employee_ID,
Employee_Gender,
       Job_Title
   from test.Staff
   where    ;
```

There is no test libref assigned.

34   s107d12

7.03 Multiple Choice Poll

What will be the result of executing the code on the previous slide?

a. The code executes properly and a report is produced. The SAS log contains only the expected messages.

b. The code executes properly and a report is produced. A special note is written to the SAS log about the VIEW libref.

c. The code does not execute and no report is produced. An error message is written to the SAS log.

36

Two-Level Table Names in Permanent Views

You can use two techniques to address the issues demonstrated when you reference permanent tables in views:

- ANSI method:
  Omit the libref; use a single-level table name.
- SAS enhancement:
  Embed the LIBNAME statement with a USING clause.

38

Two-Level Table Names in Permanent Views

ANSI Example: Omit the libref.

```
libname test '.';
proc sql;
create view test.Level_II as
   select Employee_ID, Gender,
          Job_Title as Title
      from Staff
      where scan(Job_Title,-1) ='II'
            and Emp_Term_Date is missing;
```

This method works as long as the view and table are stored in the same location.

When a view is not stored in the same location as its source tables (co-located), this method is not appropriate.

39   ...

Two-Level Table Names in Permanent Views

ANSI Example: Omit the libref.

```
libname test '.';
proc sql;
create view test.Level_II as
   select Employee_ID, Gender,
          Job_Title as Title
      from Staff
      where scan(Job_Title,-1) ='II'
            and Emp_Term_Date is missing;
```

A SAS programmer might interpret this as a reference to the table `work.Staff`.

40   ...

Two-Level Table Names in Permanent Views

ANSI Example: Omit the libref.

```
libname test '.';
proc sql;
create view test.Level_II as
   select Employee_ID, Gender,
          Job_Title as Title
      from Staff
      where scan(Job_Title,-1) ='II'
         and Emp_Term_Date is missing;
```

At view execution, PROC SQL interprets this as the following: "Look in the location where the Level_II view is stored for a table named Staff."

41

Two-Level Table Names in Permanent Views

Step 1: Assign a libref.

```
libname test '.';
```

s:\workshop
libname=test
Staff

42

s107d13a
...

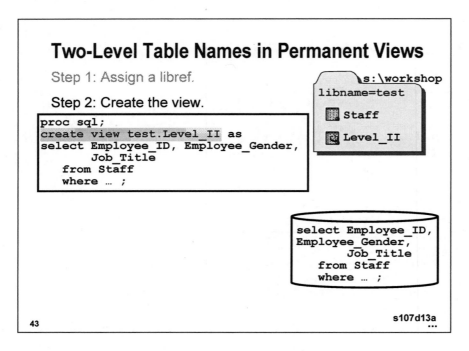

Two-Level Table Names in Permanent Views

Step 1: Assign a libref.

Step 2: Create the view.

```
proc sql;
create view test.Level_II as
select Employee_ID, Employee_Gender,
       Job_Title
   from Staff
   where … ;
```

s:\workshop
libname=test

Staff

Level_II

```
select Employee_ID,
Employee_Gender,
       Job_Title
   from Staff
   where … ;
```

43   s107d13a
                                      ...

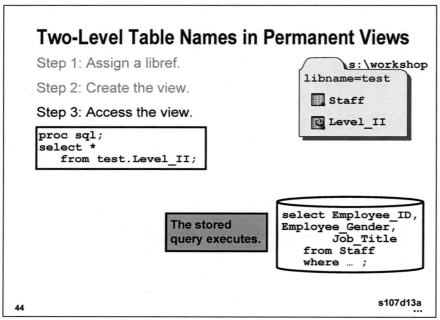

Two-Level Table Names in Permanent Views

Step 1: Assign a libref.

Step 2: Create the view.

Step 3: Access the view.

```
proc sql;
select *
   from test.Level_II;
```

s:\workshop
libname=test

Staff

Level_II

The stored
query executes.

```
select Employee_ID,
Employee_Gender,
       Job_Title
   from Staff
   where … ;
```

44   s107d13a
                                      ...

Two-Level Table Names in Permanent Views

Step 1: Assign a libref.

Step 2: Create the view.

Step 3: Access the view.

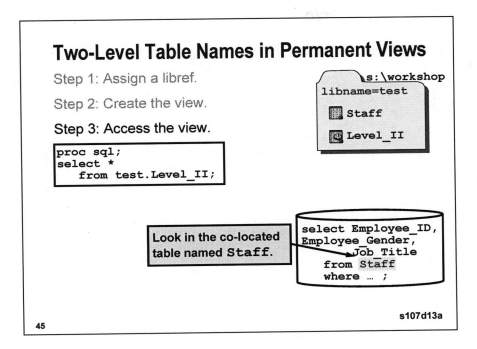

```
proc sql;
select *
   from test.Level_II;
```

s:\workshop

libname=test

Staff

Level_II

Look in the co-located table named **Staff**.

```
select Employee_ID,
Employee_Gender,
       Job_Title
   from Staff
   where … ;
```

s107d13a

45

7.04 Multiple Choice Poll

What will be the result of executing the code on the previous slide?

a. The code executes properly and a report is produced. The SAS log contains only the expected messages.

b. The code executes properly and a report is produced. A special note is written to the SAS log about the VIEW libref.

c. The code does not execute and no report is produced. An error message is written to the SAS log.

47

Two-Level Table Names in Permanent Views

Step 1: Assign a libref.

Step 2: Create the view.

Step 3: Access the view.

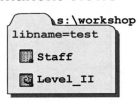

```
proc sql;
select *
    from test.Level_II;
```

Partial SQL Output

Employee ID	Employee Gender	Job Title
120121	F	Sales Rep. II
120122	F	Sales Rep. II
120126	M	Sales Rep. II
120127	F	Sales Rep. II

49   s107d13a

Two-Level Table Names in Permanent Views

You move the **Level_II** view file to your personal storage area, for example, **./test**. Then you attempt to use the view to create a report.

50

Two-Level Table Names in Permanent Views

Step 1: Assign the librefs.

```
libname orion '.';
libname test './test';
```

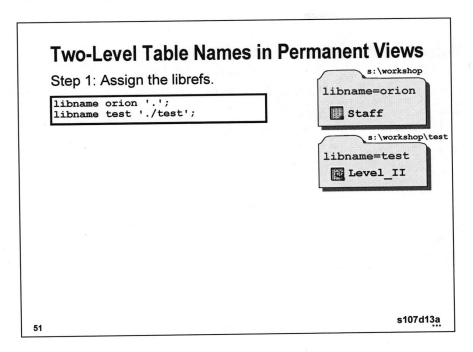

51   s107d13a

Two-Level Table Names in Permanent Views

Step 1: Assign the librefs.

Step 2: Access the view.

```
proc sql;
select *
   from test.Level_II;
```

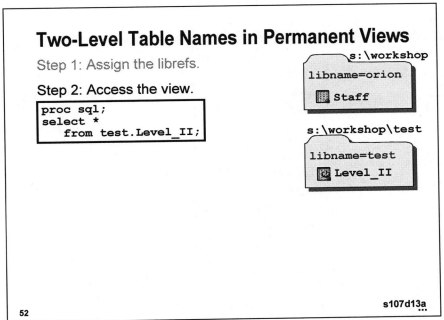

52   s107d13a

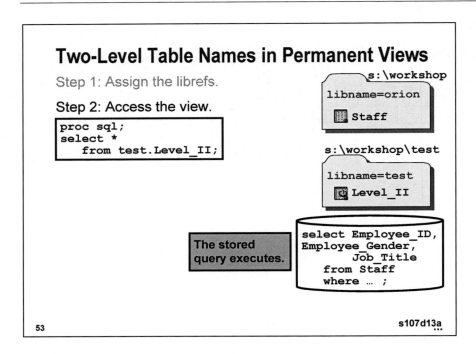

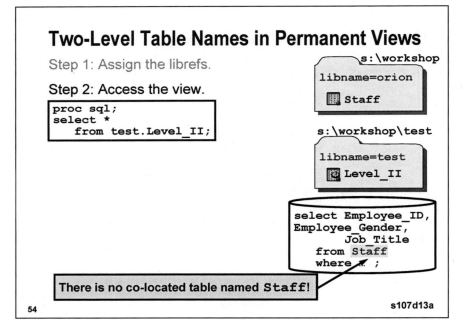

7.05 Multiple Choice Poll

What will be the result of executing the code on the previous slide?

a. The code executes properly and a report is produced. The SAS log contains only the expected messages.

b. The code executes properly and a report is produced. A special note is written to the SAS log about the VIEW libref.

c. The code does not execute and no report is produced. An error message is written to the SAS log.

56

Two-Level Table Names in Permanent Views

SAS Enhancement: Embed the LIBNAME statement with a USING clause.

CREATE VIEW *proc-sql-view* **AS** *query-expression*
    <USING *LIBNAME-clause<, ...LIBNAME-clause>>*;

The scope of the embedded libref is local to the view, and it will not conflict with an identically named libref in the SAS session.

58

Two-Level Table Names in Permanent Views

Example: Embed the LIBNAME statement with a USING
          clause.

```
libname test './test';
proc sql;
create view test.Level_II as
    select Employee_ID, Gender,
           Job_Title as Title
        from orion.Staff
        where scan(Job_Title,-1) ='II'
              and Emp_Term_Date is missing
        using libname orion 's:\workshop';
```

When the view `test.Level_II` executes, the libref `orion`
always refers to the location 's:\workshop'.

 The path defined in an embedded LIBNAME statement might not
be valid if the view is executed on a different operating system.

59

Two-Level Table Names in Permanent Views

Step 1: Assign some librefs.

```
libname orion   'c:\temp';
libname sasdata '.';
libname test    './test';
```

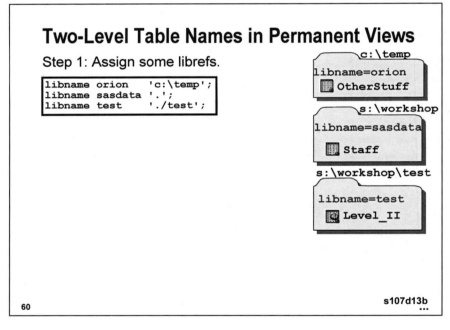

60   s107d13b
                                                ...

✎   The pathnames assigned to the folders in the slides in this section are typical for Windows
    SAS classes (s:\workshop and so on). Actual paths differ if your data is installed at another
    location, or if you are running a different operating system, such as UNIX or z/OS.

Two-Level Table Names in Permanent Views

Step 1: Assign some librefs.

Step 2: Access the view.

```
proc sql;
select *
   from test.Level_II;
```

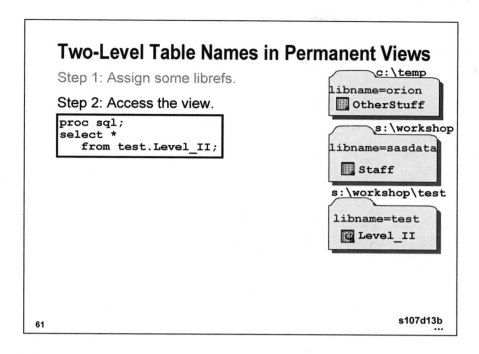

61

s107d13b
...

Two-Level Table Names in Permanent Views

Step 1: Assign some librefs.

Step 2: Access the view.

```
proc sql;
select *
   from test.Level_II;
```

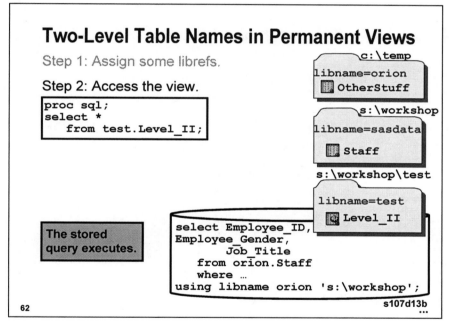

The stored
query executes.

```
select Employee_ID,
Employee_Gender,
        Job_Title
   from orion.Staff
   where ...
using libname orion 's:\workshop';
```

62

s107d13b
...

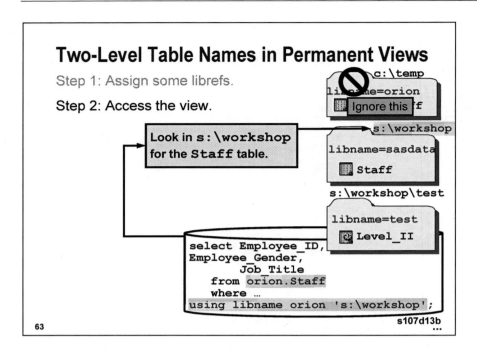

Two-Level Table Names in Permanent Views

Step 1: Assign some librefs.

Step 2: Access the view.

> Look in `s:\workshop` for the `Staff` table.

```
select Employee_ID,
Employee_Gender,
        Job_Title
    from orion.Staff
    where ...
using libname orion 's:\workshop';
```

63   s107d13b
                                                           ...

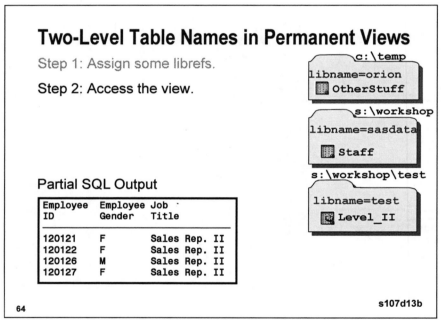

Two-Level Table Names in Permanent Views

Step 1: Assign some librefs.

Step 2: Access the view.

Partial SQL Output

Employee ID	Employee Gender	Job Title
120121	F	Sales Rep. II
120122	F	Sales Rep. II
120126	M	Sales Rep. II
120127	F	Sales Rep. II

64   s107d13b

✎   If tables referenced in the FROM clause reside in different libraries, multiple LIBNAME statements might be specified in the USING clause, separated by commas. For example:

```
create view xyz as
    select <...>
    from one.a, two.b
    where <...>
    using libname one 'c:\...',
          libname two 'd:\...'
;
```

Business Scenario

Re-create the view for Tom Zhou. Use an embedded LIBNAME statement to make it portable.

Tom can then copy the view to any location that he chooses and use it to create his reports.

65

Making a View Portable

```
proc sql;
create view orion.Tom_Zhou as
   select Employee_Name as Name format=$25.0,
          Job_Title as Title format=$15.0,
          Salary "Annual Salary" format=comma10.2,
          int((today()-Employee_Hire_Date)/365.25)
            as YOS 'Years of Service'
     from orion.Employee_Addresses as a,
          orion.Employee_Payroll as p,
          orion.Employee_Organization as o
     where a.Employee_ID=p.Employee_ID and
           o.Employee_ID=p.Employee_ID and
           Manager_ID=120102
     using libname orion 's:\workshop'
;
quit;
```

66   s107d14

Making a View Portable

Tom copied the new view to his hard drive and is happily using it to generate reports.

```
libname tom "./Test";
proc copy in=orion out=tom memtype=view;
   select Tom_Zhou;
run;

title "Tom Zhou's Group - Salary Statistics";
proc means data=tom.Tom_Zhou
           min mean max;
   var salary;
   class Level;
run;
title;
```

67   s107d14

Using Views to Enhance Security

PROC MEANS Output

```
          Tom Zhou's Group - Salary Statistics
                  The MEANS Procedure
        Analysis Variable : Salary Annual Salary

Title            N Obs   Minimum      Mean   Maximum

Sales Rep. I        18  25185.00  26466.67  27260.00

Sales Rep. II       13  26165.00  27123.46  28100.00

Sales Rep. III      12  28135.00  29895.42  36605.00

Sales Rep. IV        5  30660.00  31369.00  32490.00
```

68   s107d14

General Guidelines for Using Views

- Avoid ORDER BY clauses in view definitions, which force data sorting each time that the view is referenced.
- When you create a permanent view with permanent tables in the FROM clause, use a USING clause to specify the location of the libraries to make your view portable.

69

 **Exercises**

> If you restarted SAS since the last exercise, submit a LIBNAME statement to assign the libref **orion** to the SAS data library for this course.
>
>   libname orion '_____';

Level 1

1. **Creating and Using a View**

    a. Create a view named **orion.Phone_List** containing the following columns:
        - **Department (format=$25.)**
        - **Name (format=$25.)**
        - **Phone_Number (label='Home Phone'** and **format=$16.)**

        Use data found in the following tables: (Columns of interest are in parentheses.)
        - **orion.Employee_Addresses (Employee_ID, Employee_Name)**
        - **orion.Employee_Organization (Employee_ID, Department)**
        - **orion.Employee_Phones (Employee_ID, Phone_Number, Phone_Type)**

        Include only those phone number records where **Phone_Type="Home"**.

    b. Use the new **orion.Phone_List** view as the source for a query that produces the phone list for the Engineering Department, sorted by **Name**. Add this title to the report: **Engineering Department Home Phone Numbers**.

        PROC SQL Output

Engineering Department Home Phone Numbers	
Name	Home Phone
Arizmendi, Gilbert	+1(619)551-0293
Elleman, Lal	+61(2)5555-4127
Elmoslamy, Wilson	+1(619)551-0291
Hargrave, Seco	+1(215)551-0289
Hartshorn, Darshi	+61(2)5555-2265
Liguori, Donelle	+1(305)551-0290
Mccleary, Bill	+61(3)5555-9767
Peiris, Krishna	+61(2)5555-5585
Sullivan, Lutezenia	+1(305)551-0292

Level 2

2. Creating and Using a View to Provide Consolidated Information

a. Create a view named **orion.T_Shirts** containing the following columns:

- **Product_ID**
- **Supplier_Name** (formatted as $20.)
- **Product_Name**
- **Price** (Label it **Retail Price**.)

Use data from the following tables: (Columns of interest are in parentheses.)

- **orion.Product_Dim** (**Product_ID**, **Product_Name**, **Supplier_Name**)
- **orion.Price_list** (**Product_ID**, **Unit_Sales_Price**)

Select only those records where **Product_Name** includes the word **T-Shirt**.

b. Write a query to display the data from your new **orion.T_Shirts** view. Sort the report by **Supplier_Name** and **Product_ID**. Supply a useful title.

Partial PROC SQL Output

```
                              Available T-Shirts

     Product ID  Supplier Name      Product Name              Retail Price

     210201000050  3Top Sports       Kid Children's T-Shirt        $19.60
     240500200016  3Top Sports       T-Shirt                       $31.70
     220101300001  A Team Sports     T-Shirt, Short-sleeved,       $33.60
                                     Big Logo
     220101300012  A Team Sports     Men's T-Shirt Small Logo      $19.40
     220101300017  A Team Sports     Toncot Beefy-T                $16.60
                                     Emb T-Shirt
     220101300017  A Team Sports     Toncot Beefy-T                $16.60
                                     Emb T-Shirt
```

c. Write a query using your new **orion.T_Shirts** view to display **Product_ID**, **Product_Name**, and **Price** for all T-shirts priced less than $20.00. Sort the report by price. Supply a useful title.

PROC SQL Output

```
                              T-Shirts under $20

                                                              Retail
     Product ID  Product Name                                  Price

     220101300017  Toncot Beefy-T Emb T-Shirt                   $16.60
     220101300012  Men's T-Shirt Small Logo                     $19.40
     210201000050  Kid Children's T-Shirt                       $19.60
```

Level 3

3. Creating and Using a View That Updates Itself over Time

a. Create a view named **orion.Current_Catalog**. The view must contain all of the columns in **orion.Product_dim** and a new column named **Price** (labeled **Current Retail Price**). Use data found in the following tables:

- **orion.Product_dim**
- **orion.Price_list**

The value of the current price (**Price**) is determined by multiplying the original **Unit_Sales_Price** times the number of years since the product was first offered times the inflation **Factor**. Calculate the number of years that a product was offered by subtracting the year in which the product was first offered from the current year. The inflation **Factor** is a percentage of the original price. The formula is shown below:

```
Price=Unit_Sales_Price *
       (Factor**(year(Today())-year(Start_Date)))
```

Round the calculated **Price** to the nearest cent.

b. Write a query to display **Supplier_Name**, **Product_Name**, and **Price** from your new **orion.Current_Catalog** view for products with "Roller Skate" in the product name. Sort the output by supplier name and price. Supply a useful title for your report. If the current year is later than 2009 your results will differ, as prices will have increased.

Partial PROC SQL Output

		Current
Supplier Name	Product Name	Retail Price
Magnifico Sports	Children's Roller Skates	$102.40
Magnifico Sports	Pro-roll Lazer Roller Skates	$113.20
Magnifico Sports	Pro-roll Sabotage-Rp Roller Skates	$175.90

Current Roller Skate Prices

c. Write a query to display **Product_Name**, original **Unit_Sales_Price** (former **Price**), current **Price**, and the amount of **Increase** (calculated as **Price** − **Unit_Sales_Price**) for all products having an increase greater than $5.00. Sort the report by decreasing **Increase**. Supply a useful title. If the current year is later than 2009 your results will differ, as prices will have increased.

Partial PROC SQL Output

2009 prices > 5.00 higher than original price

Product Name	Old Price	New Price	Increase
Twain Ac7/Ft7 Men's Roller Skates	$181.30	$192.34	$11.04
Top R&D Long Jacket	$536.30	$547.08	$10.78
Perfect Fit Men's Roller Skates	$393.90	$401.82	$7.92

7.2 Creating Tables with the SQL Procedure (Self-Study)

Objectives

- Create a new table by defining the column structure.
- Create a new table by copying column structure from an existing table.
- Load data into a table.
- Create a new table and add data using a single query.

73

Creating Tables with SQL

Multiple techniques are used to create tables and insert data into tables with SQL.

Method	Syntax	Result
1	**CREATE TABLE** *table-name* (*column-name type(length)* <, *...column-name type(length)*>);	Create an empty table by manually specifying all column attributes.
2	**CREATE TABLE** *table-name* LIKE *old-table-name*;	Create an empty table by copying column attributes from an existing table using a LIKE clause.
3	**CREATE TABLE** *table-name* AS *query-expression*;	Create a table and add data all in one step, using a query.

74

   Method 3 is the method most commonly used to create tables. Methods 1 and 2 are described in the Self-Study sections of this chapter.

The CREATE TABLE statement does not produce output. A separate SELECT statement is required to produce a report based on the new table.

Creating Tables

Method 1: Define the columns.

General form of the CREATE TABLE statement:

CREATE TABLE *table-name*
    (*column-name type(length)*
    <, ...column-name type(length)>);

75

Method 1: Defining Columns

Method 1: Define the columns. You must add data later.

```
proc sql;
    create table Discounts
        (Product_ID num format=z12.,
         Start_Date date,
         End_Date date,
         Discount num format=percent.);
quit;
```

Name the new table.

Define the columns.

The table definition is enclosed in parentheses.
Individual column definitions are separated by commas.

76

s107d01

Method 1: Defining Columns

For ANSI compliance, PROC SQL accepts the following data types in table definitions:

ANSI Type	Resulting SAS Type	Default Length	Default Format
CHAR(n)	Character	8	$w.
VARCHAR	Character	8	$w.
INTEGER	Numeric	8	BEST.
SMALLINT	Numeric	8	BEST.
DECIMAL	Numeric	8	BEST.
NUMERIC	Numeric	8	BEST.
FLOAT	Numeric	8	BEST.
REAL	Numeric	8	BEST.
DOUBLE PRECISION	Numeric	8	BEST.
DATE	Numeric	8	DATE.

77

No matter what data type is in the table definition, SAS tables still only have two types of variables: character or numeric. It is possible to create other data types when you create tables to be stored in a DBMS other than SAS.

Method 1: Defining Columns

Example: Create the table structure for the
Testing_Types table using ANSI
standard terms to define the columns.

```
proc sql;
   create table Testing_Types
      (Char_Column char(4),
       Varchar_Column varchar,
       Int_Column int,
       SmallInt_Column smallint,
       Dec_Column dec,
       Num_Column num,
       Float_Column float,
       Real_Column real,
       Date_Column date,
       Double_Column double precision);
quit;
```

78   s107d02

The table created above does not contain any rows. Use this method when you create a table unlike any other existing table.

Method 1: Defining Columns

Partial SAS Log

```
NOTE:Table WORK.TESTING_TYPES created, with 0
rows and 10 columns.
```

Partial PROC CONTENTS Output

#	Variable	Type	Len	Format	Informat
1	Char_Column	Char	4		
2	Varchar_Column	Char	8		
3	Int_Column	Num	8		
4	SmallInt_Column	Num	8		
5	Dec_Column	Num	8		
6	Num_Column	Num	8		
7	Float_Column	Num	8		
8	Real_Column	Num	8		
9	Date_Column	Num	8	DATE.	DATE.
10	Double_Column	Num	8		

79

Setup for the Poll

Submit the program **s107d01** and review the SAS log.

```
proc sql;
   create table Discounts
     (Product_ID num format=z12.,
      Start_Date date,
      End_Date date,
      Discount num format=percent.);
   describe table Discounts;
quit;
```

81   s107d01

7.06 Multiple Choice Poll

Based on the query in program **s107d01**, which different data types does the **work.Discounts** table have?

a. All columns are NUMERIC type.

b. Some columns are DATE type and some are NUMERIC type.

c. Some columns are CHARACTER type and some are NUMERIC type.

d. Some columns are CHARACTER type, some are DATE type, and some are NUMERIC type.

82

Creating Tables

Method 2: Copy the table structure.

General form of the CREATE TABLE statement:

```
CREATE TABLE table-name-2
    LIKE table-name-1;
```

84

Method 2: Copying Table Structure

Copy the structure of **orion.Sales** to create the
work.New_Sales_Staff table.

```
proc sql;
    create table work.New_Sales_Staff
        like orion.Sales;
quit;
```

85   s107d02a

Use this method when the table that you want to create is similar or identical to an existing table.

Method 2: Copying Table Structure

Partial SAS Log

```
NOTE:Table WORK.NEW_SALES_STAFF created, with 0
rows and 9 columns.
```

Partial PROC CONTENTS Output

#	Variable	Type	Len	Format
1	Employee_ID	Num	8	12.
2	First_Name	Char	12	
3	Last_Name	Char	18	
4	Gender	Char	1	
5	Salary	Num	8	
6	Job_Title	Char	25	
7	Country	Char	2	
8	Birth_Date	Num	8	
9	Hire_Date	Num	8	

86

Creating Tables (Review)

Method 3: Create and populate a table with an SQL query.

General form of the CREATE TABLE statement:

CREATE TABLE *table-name* **AS**
      query-expression;

87

Method 3: Create and Populate a Table with an SQL Query (Review)

The SELECT list defines the structure of the **work.Melbourne** table, and the rows are populated with the data returned by the query.

Define table columns.

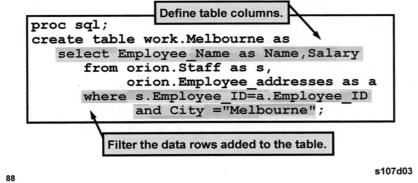

```
proc sql;
create table work.Melbourne as
    select Employee_Name as Name,Salary
        from orion.Staff as s,
            orion.Employee_addresses as a
        where s.Employee_ID=a.Employee_ID
            and City ="Melbourne";
```

Filter the data rows added to the table.

88   s107d03

This method is most often used to create subsets or supersets of tables. This is the only one of the three methods that **creates and populates** a table in one statement.

Method 3: Create and Populate a Table with an SQL Query (Review)

Partial SAS Log

```
NOTE: Table WORK.MELBOURNE created, with 41 rows
      and 2 columns.
```

Partial PROC CONTENTS Output

```
        Data Set Name   WORK.MELBOURNE          Observations   41
...

#    Variable    Type    Len    Format      Label
1    Name        Char     40
2    Salary      Num       8    DOLLAR12.   Employee Annual Salary
```

89

Method 3: Create and Populate a Table with an SQL Query (Review)

After you create a table, a separate query is required to display the data from the new table.

```
title "Melbourne Employees";
select *
    from work.Melbourne
    order by name;
title;
quit;
```

90   s107d03

Method 3: Create and Populate a Table with an SQL Query (Review)

Partial PROC SQL Output

```
                     Melbourne Employees

                                              Employee
                                                Annual
        Name                                    Salary

        Aisbitt, Sandy                         $26,060
        Barcoe, Selina                         $25,275
        Blanton, Brig                          $26,910
        Catenacci, Reyne                       $26,665
        Chantharasy, Judy                      $26,390
```

91

Adding Data to a Table

The INSERT statement can be used to add data to an empty table, or to append data to a table that already contains data, using one of three methods.

Method	Syntax	Description
A	**INSERT INTO** *table-name* **SET** *column-name=value,* *column-name=value,...;*	One clause per row using column-value pairs
B	**INSERT INTO** *table-name* *<(column list)>* **VALUES** *(value,value,...);*	One clause per row using positional values
C	**INSERT INTO** *table-name* *<(column list)>* **SELECT** *columns* **FROM** *table-name;*	A query returning multiple rows, and based on positional values

92

Method A: Adding Data with a SET Clause

The SET clause requires that you add data using column name–value pairs:

```
insert into Discounts
    set Product_ID=230100300006,
        Start_Date='01MAR2007'd,
        End_Date='15MAR2007'd,Discount=.33
    set Product_ID=230100600018,
        Start_Date='16MAR2007'd,
        End_Date='31MAR2007'd, Discount=.15
;
```

93   s107d04

You can nest a SELECT statement in a SET clause, as follows:

```
proc sql;
   insert into discounts
      set Product_ID=123456789012, Start_Date=(select max(Order_Date)
          from orion.Order_Fact);
```

Method B: Adding Data with a VALUES Clause

The VALUES clause adds data to the columns in a single row of data.

```
insert into Discounts
    values (230100300006,'01MAR2007'd,
           '15MAR2007'd,.33)
    values (230100600018,'16MAR2007'd,
           '31MAR2007'd,.15);
```

 The VALUES clause must produce values in the same order as the INSERT INTO statement column list.

94   s107d05

Method B: Adding Data with a VALUES Clause

Optionally, the INSERT statement can list the columns into which data is to be inserted, in the order in which the VALUES clause will provide the data.

```
insert into Discounts
(Start_Date,End_Date, Product_ID, Discount)
   values ('01MAR2007'd,'15MAR2007'd,
           230100300006,.33)
   values ('16MAR2007'd,'31MAR2007'd,
           230100600018,.15);
```

95   s107d05

Method B: Adding Data with a VALUES Clause

Example: Load the **Discounts** table created
          earlier using the INSERT statement.

```
insert into Discounts
  (Product_ID,Start_Date,End_Date,Discount)
   values (220200200022,'01Mar2007'd,
          '31Mar2007'd,.35)
   values (220200200024,'01Mar2007'd,
          '31Mar2007'd,.35)
;
```

96   s107d06

Method B: Adding Data with a VALUES Clause

```
select *
    from Discounts;
```

PROC SQL Output

Product_ID	Start_Date	End_Date	Discount
220200200022	01MAR07	31MAR07	35%
220200200024	01MAR07	31MAR07	35%

97   s107d06

Method C: Adding Data with a Query

Rows returned by the query are appended to the table.

```
proc sql;
    insert into Discounts
        (Product_ID,Discount,Start_Date,End_Date)
        select distinct Product_ID,.35,
                '01MAR2007'd,'31mar2007'd
            from orion.Product_Dim
            where Supplier_Name contains
                'Pro Sportswear Inc';
quit;
```

 Query results are inserted positionally. The query
must produce values in the same order as the
INSERT statement column list.

98   s107d07

7.07 Quiz

Locate three syntax errors in the following code:

```
proc sql;
   create table Discounts
     (Product_ID num format=z12.,
      Start_Date date, End_Date date,
      Discount num format=percent.)
   insert into discounts
     (Product_ID,Start_Date,End_Date Discount)
      values (220200200022,'01Mar2007'd,
             '31Mar2007'd,.35)
      values (220200200024,'01Mar2007'd,
             '31Mar2007'd, '.35');
```

100

 **Exercises**

If you restarted SAS since the last exercise, submit a LIBNAME statement to assign the libref **orion** to the SAS data library for this course.

```
libname orion '_____';
```

Level 1

4. **Creating a Table and Adding Data Using a Query**

   a. Create a table containing the following columns and name it **orion.Employees**:

      - **Employee_ID**
      - **Hire_Date**
      - **Salary**
      - **Birth_Date**
      - **Gender**
      - **Country**
      - **City**

      Format all date columns with **MMDDYYYY10.** and **Salary** with **COMMA10.2**. Only include current employees (rows where **Employee_Term_Date** is missing). Order the output by year (**Employee_Hire_Date**) and then by descending **Salary**. The data that you need can be obtained from these tables:

      - **orion.Employee_Addresses**
      - **orion.Employee_Payroll**

      Column Sourcing Information

Employees	Employee_Addresses	orion.Employee_Payroll
Employee_ID	Employee_ID	Employee_ID
Hire_Date	–	Employee_Hire_Date
Salary	–	Salary
Birth_Date	–	Birth_Date
Gender	–	Employee_Gender
Country	Country	–
City	City	–

b. Query the new table **orion.Employees** to produce the following report:

Partial PROC SQL Output

```
Employee_
      ID  Hire_Date       Salary  Birth_Date  Gender  Country  City

  121141  01/01/1974  194,885.00  06/19/1944  M       US       Philadelphia
  120659  01/01/1974  161,290.00  07/16/1949  M       US       Philadelphia
  120103  01/01/1974   87,975.00  01/22/1949  M       AU       Sydney
  120712  01/01/1974   63,640.00  06/12/1949  F       US       Miami-Dade
  120804  01/01/1974   55,400.00  02/11/1944  M       US       Miami-Dade
```

Level 2

5. Creating a Table by Defining Its Structure and Adding Data

a. Create a table named **orion.Rewards** with four columns:

- **Purchased** – a numeric column, formatted to be nine characters wide, including commas and two decimal places
- **Year** – a numeric column, formatted to be four characters wide with no decimal places
- **Level** – a character column, which holds the value Silver, Gold, or Platinum
- **Award** – a character column (maximum of 50 characters)

b. Add six rows of data to the **orion.Rewards** table, and then write a query to display the contents of the **Rewards** table. The results should resemble the following:

PROC SQL Output

```
Purchased  Year  Level     Award

   200.00  2006  Silver    25% Discount on one item over $25
   300.00  2006  Gold      15% Discount on one order over $50
   500.00  2006  Platinum  10% Discount on all 2007 purchases
   225.00  2007  Silver    25% Discount on one item over $50
   350.00  2007  Gold      15% Discount on one order over $100
   600.00  2007  Platinum  10% Discount on all 2008 purchases
```

Level 3

6. Creating a Table and Inserting Data Using a Complex Query

Create a table named **Direct_Compensation** in the Work library. The table should contain the following information for all **non-managerial** Sales staff (those with a level listed in their titles), formatted as indicated:

Employee_ID	Name	Level	Salary	Commission	Direct_Compensation
12345	First Last	(I, II, III or IV)	12,345.00	1,234.00	13,579.00

- Sales information is available in **orion.Order_fact**.
- The table **orion.Sales** contains **Employee_ID**, **First_Name**, **Last_Name**, **Job_Title**, and **Salary** information for all Sales staff.
- **Job_Title** contains level information for each employee.
- To calculate **Commission**, add the **Total_Retail_Price** values for all sales made by an employee with an **Order_Date** in 2007, and take 15% of that total value as commission.
- To calculate **Direct_Compensation**, add **Commission** plus **Salary**.

Partial PROC SQL Output

Employee_ID	Name	Level	Salary	Commission	Direct_Compensation
121029	Kuo-Chung Mcelwee	I	27,225.00	3.53	27,228.53
121135	Tammy Ruta	I	27,010.00	24.12	27,034.12
120131	Marinus Surawski	I	26,910.00	59.82	26,969.82
120130	Kevin Lyon	I	26,955.00	11.10	26,966.10
121086	John-Michael Plybon	I	26,820.00	24.08	26,844.08
120136	Atul Leyden	I	26,605.00	13.88	26,618.88
120124	Lucian Daymond	I	26,480.00	132.02	26,612.02
121028	William Smades	I	26,585.00	10.41	26,595.41
120152	Sean Dives	I	26,515.00	2.87	26,517.87
121109	Harold Boulus	I	26,035.00	18.25	26,053.25
121051	Glorina Myers	I	26,025.00	18.76	26,043.77
121106	James Hilburger	I	25,880.00	2.54	25,882.54

7.3 Integrity Constraints (Self-Study)

Objectives

- Define integrity constraints.
- Apply integrity constraints to a table.
- Identify and correct integrity constraint violations.

107

Integrity Constraints

- *Integrity constraints* are rules enforced when data is added to a table to guarantee data validity.
- To preserve the consistency and correctness of your data, specify integrity constraints for the SAS data file.
- SAS uses integrity constraints to validate data values when you insert or update columns for which you defined integrity constraints.

108

Integrity Constraints

Integrity constraints

- were added to Base SAS software in SAS 8
- follow ANSI standards
- cannot be defined for views
- can be specified when a table is created
- can be added to a table that already contains data
- are commonly found in large database management systems (DBMS) with frequently updated tables.

109

7.08 Poll

Have you ever written data into tables that contain integrity constraints?

- ○ Yes
- ○ No

111

Five Integrity Constraints

General:

- NOT NULL
- CHECK
- UNIQUE

Referential:

- PRIMARY KEY
- FOREIGN KEY

112

NOT NULL	requires data in this column; missing values are not allowed.
CHECK	specifies rules to check when values are entered in this column. Attempting to insert or update data in this column that violates these rules causes the update or insertion to be rejected.
UNIQUE	ensures that every value in a column is unique. Data might be missing, but if one row has a missing value in this column, no other row can have a missing value. All rows must have unique values for this column.
PRIMARY KEY	identifies a column or columns in a table as the table's primary key. A unique, non-missing value is required for the primary key. The effect emulates specifying both NOT NULL and UNIQUE constraints.
FOREIGN KEY	limits the values entered into one or more columns in this table to a list of values provided by the PRIMARY KEY columns(s) found in **another** table. A column with a FOREIGN KEY constraint might have a missing value, but any non-missing values entered must be one of the values found in the PRIMARY KEY columns of the related table.

Creating Integrity Constraints with PROC SQL

General form of PROC SQL using integrity constraints:

```
PROC SQL;
    CREATE TABLE table
            (column-specification,…
            <constraint-specification,…>);
```

Integrity constraints are assigned as part of the table definition.

113

 Constraints might be applied to existing tables ("back fitted") using PROC SQL and the ALTER TABLE statement, or PROC DATASETS and the IC CREATE statement.

Creating Integrity Constraints with PROC SQL

Example: Re-create the **Discounts** table with an integrity constraint limiting discounts to 50%.

```
proc sql;
create table Discounts
   (Product_ID num format=z12.,
    Start_Date date,
    End_Date date,
    Discount num format=percent.,
    constraint ok_discount
    check (Discount le .5))
;
```

s107d08

114

Integrity constraints must have unique names. Use variable naming conventions when you name an integrity constraint.

- Names consist of 1 to 32 characters.
- Names must begin with a letter or an underscore character. The remaining characters must be a combination of letters, underscores, and numbers.

Integrity Constraint Violations

Example: Insert three rows of data.

```
insert into Discounts
   values (240500200009,'01Mar2007'd,
           '31Mar2007'd,.45)
   values (220200200036,'01Mar2007'd,
           '31Mar2007'd, .54)
   values (220200200038,'01Mar2007'd,
           '31Mar2007'd,.25)
;
```

This could be a costly typo!

115   s107d08

Integrity Constraint Violations

Partial Log

```
ERROR: Add/Update failed for data set WORK.DISCOUNTS because data
       value(s) do not comply with integrity constraint ok_discount.
NOTE: This insert failed while attempting to add data from VALUES
      clause 2 to the data set.
NOTE: Deleting the successful inserts before error noted above to
      restore table to a consistent state.
```

A constraint violation invokes an UNDO process.

- PROC SQL deletes **all** rows inserted or modified by the errant INSERT INTO or UPDATE statement.
- The table returns to a consistent state, that is, to the condition existing before the statement executed.

116

Controlling the UNDO_POLICY Option

Changing the UNDO_POLICY option in PROC SQL gives you control over how UNDO is performed when integrity constrains are violated.

You can choose to enable rows that do not violate integrity constraints to remain in the table, while you reject only the rows that contain bad data.

117

Controlling the UNDO_POLICY Option

- UNDO_POLICY=REQUIRED (default)

  undoes all inserts or updates up to the point of the error. Sometimes the UNDO operation cannot be accomplished reliably.

- UNDO_POLICY=NONE

  rejects only rows that violate constraints. Rows that do not violate constraints are inserted.

- UNDO_POLICY=OPTIONAL

  operates in a manner similar to REQUIRED when the UNDO operation can be accomplished reliably; otherwise, operates similar to NONE.

118

 The COMMIT and ROLLBACK statements are ANSI standards not currently supported by PROC SQL. In PROC SQL, insertions and updates are immediately committed.

UNDO_POLICY=REQUIRED (This is the default.)

PROC SQL reverses all previous row inserts or updates up to the point of the error. Sometimes the UNDO operation cannot be performed reliably. Examples of conditions where changes cannot reliably be reversed include the following:

- When you update or insert data using a SAS/ACCESS view, PROC SQL might not be able to reverse the effects of the statement without also reversing the effects of other changes that were made at the same time.

- When you update or insert data in a SAS data set opened with row-level locking (CNTLLEV=RECORD) through a SAS/SHARE server, other users can edit any row except the one you are currently updating, including rows previously updated by your current INSERT or UPDATE statement.

UNDO_POLICY=NONE

PROC SQL keeps any compliant updates or inserts, and skips updates or inserts that were not compliant.

UNDO_POLICY=OPTIONAL

PROC SQL reverses any updates or inserts that it can reverse reliably. Otherwise PROC SQL keeps any compliant updates or inserts, and skips updates or inserts that were not compliant.

This option enables PROC SQL to decide which of the first two options to apply, based on current conditions. PROC SQL proceeds as if UNDO_POLICY=REQUIRED were in effect if the UNDO can be reliably performed. Otherwise, PROC SQL proceeds as if UNDO_POLICY=NONE were specified.

Setup for the Poll

Program **s107a01** re-creates the table **Discounts** with integrity constraints and attempts to insert three rows of data, using UNDO_POLICY=NONE.

- Submit the program **s107a01**.
- Review the SAS log.

```
proc sql undo_policy=none;
   insert into Discounts
      values (240500200009,'01Mar2007'd,
             '31Mar2007'd,.45)
      values (220200200036,'01Mar2007'd,
             '31Mar2007'd,.54)
      values (220200200038,'01Mar2007'd,
             '31Mar2007'd,.25);
quit;
```

120   s107a01

7.09 Poll

Were the rows containing good data rejected along with the rows containing bad data when you used the PROC SQL option UNDO_POLICY=NONE?

○ Yes

○ No

121

Troubleshooting Integrity Constraint Violations

When an integrity constraint is violated, the SAS log identifies which VALUES clause contained the error, and names the violated integrity constraint.

To correct the problem, you need more information about the violated integrity constraint.

123

Troubleshooting Integrity Constraint Violations

The DESCRIBE statement can display column attributes of a table as well as information about indexes and integrity constraints.

General form of the DESCRIBE statement:

```
PROC SQL;
    DESCRIBE TABLE table-name<, ...table-name>;
    DESCRIBE VIEW proc-sql-view <, ...proc-sql-view>;
    DESCRIBE TABLE CONSTRAINTS table-name
                    <, ...table-name>;
```

DESCRIBE statements produce output in the SAS log.

124

The DESCRIBE TABLE statement (without the CONSTRAINTS keyword) writes a CREATE TABLE statement to the SAS log for the specified table regardless of how the table was originally created (for example, with a DATA step).

If the table contains an index, CREATE INDEX statements for those indexes are also written to the SAS log.

Troubleshooting Integrity Constraint Violations

Statement	Results Produced in the SAS Log
DESCRIBE VIEW	SQL code that would create a view identical to the view being described
DESCRIBE TABLE	SQL code that would create a table identical to the table being described (including indexes) and a description of the table's integrity constraints
DESCRIBE TABLE CONSTRAINTS	A description of the table's integrity constraints

125

Troubleshooting Integrity Constraint Violations

Example: Show the column attributes and integrity constraints for the **Discounts** table.

```
proc sql;
   describe table constraints Discounts;
quit;
```

126   s107d09

Troubleshooting Integrity Constraint Violations

Partial SAS Log

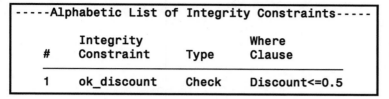

```
-----Alphabetic List of Integrity Constraints-----

         Integrity              Where
  #      Constraint    Type     Clause
  ─────────────────────────────────────────────
  1      ok_discount   Check    Discount<=0.5
```

127

Setup for the Poll

The program **s107a02** re-creates the table **Discounts** with integrity constraints and attempts to insert three rows of data, using UNDO_POLICY=NONE.

- Submit the program **s107a02**.
- Review the SAS log.
- Correct the second VALUES clause to provide a discount of 0.45.
- Resubmit **only** the INSERT INTO PROC SQL step.
- Review the SAS log.

129   s107a02

7.10 Multiple Choice Poll

After you correct and resubmit only the INSERT INTO query using UNDO_POLICY=NONE, how many rows are in the **Discounts** table?

a. 5

b. 3

c. 2

130

7.4 Chapter Review

Chapter Review

True or False:

1. A view requires less disk storage space than a table.

2. An SQL view can be used as input for PROC FREQ

3. If an SQL query requires 30 minutes to execute, creating a view from that query will greatly reduce the time required to access the results.

132

7.5 Solutions

Solutions to Exercises

1. **Creating and Using a View**

    a.

    ```
    *** s107s01 ***;
      /* a. */
    proc sql;
       create view orion.Phone_List as
          select Department format=$25.,
                 Employee_Name as Name format=$25.0,
                 Phone_Number 'Home Phone' format=$16.
            from orion.Employee_addresses as a,
                 orion.Employee_phones as p,
                 orion.Employee_organization as o
          where a.Employee_ID=p.Employee_ID and
                o.Employee_ID=p.Employee_ID and
                Phone_Type="Home"
       ;
    quit;
    ```

    b.

    ```
      /* b. */
    proc sql;
    title "Engineering Department Home Phone Numbers";
    select Name, Phone_Number
       from orion.Phone_List
       where Department="Engineering"
       order by Name
       ;
    quit;
    title;
    ```

2. Creating and Using a View to Provide Consolidated Information

    a.

```
** s107s02 ***;
 /* a. */
proc sql;
   create view orion.T_Shirts as
      select d.Product_ID, Supplier_Name format=$20.,
               Product_Name,
               Unit_Sales_Price as Price 'Retail Price'
         from orion.Product_dim as d, orion.Price_list as l
         where d.Product_ID=l.Product_ID
            and lowcase(Product_Name) like '%t-shirt%'
   ;
quit;
```

    b.

```
   /* b. */
proc sql flow=6 35;
title "Available T-Shirts";
   select *
      from orion.T_Shirts
      order by Supplier_Name, Product_ID
   ;
quit;
title;
```

    c.

```
   /* c. */
proc sql;
title "T-Shirts under $20";
   select Product_ID, Product_Name, Price format=dollar6.2
      from orion.T_Shirts
      where Price < 20
      order by Price
   ;
quit;
title;
```

3. Creating and Using a View That Updates Itself over Time

    a.

```
*** s107s03 ***;
 /* a. */
proc sql;
   create view orion.Current_Catalog as
      /*orion.Product_Dim includes duplicate records*/
      select distinct d.*
         , round((l.Unit_Sales_Price *
                  factor**(year( Today() )-year( Start_Date )))
               ,.01) 'Current Retail Price' format=dollar13.2
            as Price
```

```
      from orion.Product_dim as d,
           orion.Price_list as l
      where d.Product_ID=l.Product_ID
;
quit;
```

b.

```
   /* b. */
proc sql flow=5 35;
title "Current Roller Skate Prices";
   select Supplier_Name, Product_Name, Price
       from orion.Current_Catalog
       where lowcase(Product_Name) like '%roller skate%'
       order by Supplier_Name, Price
   ;
quit;
title;
```

c.

```
   /* c. */
proc sql flow=5 35;
title "2009 prices > 5.00 higher than original price";
   select c.Product_Name, Unit_Sales_Price 'Old Price',
           Price 'New Price',
           Price-Unit_Sales_Price as Increase format=dollar9.2
       from orion.Current_Catalog as c,
            orion.Price_list as p
       where c.Product_ID=p.Product_id
             and calculated Increase gt 5
       order by Increase Desc
   ;
quit;title;
```

4. Creating a Table and Adding Data Using a Query

a.

```
   *** s107s04 ***;
   /* a. */
proc sql;
   create table orion.Employees as
       select a.Employee_ID,
               Employee_Hire_Date as Hire_Date
               format=mmddyy10.,
               Salary format=comma12.2,
               Birth_Date format=mmddyy10.,
               Employee_Gender as Gender,
               Country, City
         from orion.Employee_addresses as a,
              orion.Employee_payroll as p
         where a.Employee_ID=p.Employee_ID
```

```
                    and Employee_Term_Date is missing
             order by year(Employee_Hire_Date), salary desc
;
quit;
```

b.

```
   /* b. */
title;
proc sql;
   select *
      from orion.Employees
;
quit;
```

5. Creating a Table by Defining Its Structure and Adding Data

a.

```
   *** s107s05 ***;
   /* a. */
proc sql;
   create table orion.Rewards
      (Purchased num format=comma9.2,
       Year num format=4., Level char(9),
       Award char(50))
;
quit;
```

b.

```
   /* b. */
proc sql;
   insert into orion.Rewards (Year,Level,Purchased,Award)
      values (2006,'Silver',200,'25% Discount on one item over $25')
      values (2006,'Gold',300,'15% Discount on one order over $50')
      values (2006,'Platinum',500,'10% Discount on all 2007
              purchases')
      values (2007,'Silver',225,'25% Discount on one item over $50')
      values (2007,'Gold',350,'15% Discount on one order over $100')
      values (2007,'Platinum',600,'10% Discount on all 2008
              purchases')
;
quit;
proc sql;
  select *
     from orion.Rewards;
quit;
   /****************************************************
   Alternate method - add the data using set clauses
proc sql;
   insert into orion.Rewards
      set year=2006,Level='Silver',Purchased=200,
          Award='25% Discount on one item over $25'
      set year=2006,Level='Gold',Purchased=300,
```

```
              Award='15% Discount on one order over $50'
        set year=2006,Level='Platinum',Purchased=500,
              Award='10% Discount on all 2007 purchases'
        set year=2007,Level='Silver',Purchased=225,
              Award='25% Discount on one item over $50'
        set year=2007,Level='Gold',Purchased=350,
              Award='15% Discount on one order over $100'
        set year=2007,Level='Platinum',Purchased=600,
              Award='10% Discount on all 2008 purchases'
    ;
quit;
    ************************************************/
```

6. **Creating a Table and Inserting Data Using a Complex Query**

```
    *** s107s06 ***;
proc sql;
    create table work.Direct_Compensation as
        select hr.Employee_ID,
                catx(' ',First_Name,Last_Name) as Name,
                scan(Job_Title,-1) format=$3. as Level,
                Salary format=comma12.2,
                Sales*0.15  format=comma7.2 as Commission,
                Salary+calculated Commission format=comma12.2
                  as Direct_Compensation
            from orion.Sales as hr,
                (select Employee_ID,
                        sum(Total_Retail_Price) as Sales
                    from orion.Order_fact
                    where year(Order_Date)=2007
                    group by Employee_ID) as sales
            where hr.Employee_ID=sales.Employee_ID
                and Job_Title like ( '%Rep%')
    ;
    select *
        from work.Direct_Compensation
        order by Level, Direct_Compensation desc
    ;
quit;
```

Solutions to Student Activities (Polls/Quizzes)

7.01 Quiz – Correct Answer

Differences between the SQL code produced by the DESCRIBE VIEW statement and the actual CREATE VIEW code, which created **orion.Tom_Zhou**:

Original
```
select Employee_Name as Name format=$25.0,
       Job_Title as Title format=$15.0,
       Salary 'Annual Salary' format=comma10.2,
       int((today()-Employee_Hire_Date)/365.25)
       as YOS 'Years of Service'
  from ORION.Employee_Addresses as a,ORION.Employee_Payroll as p,
       ORION.Employee_Organization as o
 where a.Employee_ID=p.Employee_ID and
       o.Employee_ID=p.Employee_ID and
       Manager_ID=120102;
```

DESCRIBE VIEW
```
select Employee_Name as Name format=$25.0,
       Job_Title as Title format=$15.0,
       Salary label='Annual Salary' format=COMMA10.2,
       int((today()-Employee_Hire_Date)/365.25)
           as YOS label='Years of Service'
  from ORION.EMPLOYEE_ADDRESSES a, ORION.EMPLOYEE_PAYROLL p,
       ORION.EMPLOYEE_ORGANIZATION o
 where (a.Employee_ID=p.Employee_ID) and
       (o.Employee_ID=p.Employee_ID) and
       (Manager_ID=120102);
```

7.01 Quiz – Correct Answer

Differences between the SQL code produced by the DESCRIBE VIEW statement and the actual CREATE VIEW code, which created **orion.Tom_Zhou**:

Original
```
select Employee_Name as Name format=$25.0,
       Job_Title as Title format=$15.0,
       Salary 'Annual Salary' format=c
       int((today()-Employee_Hire_Date
       as YOS 'Years of Service'
  from ORION.Employee_Addresses as a,
       ORION.Employee_Organization as
 where a.Employee_ID=p.Employee_ID a
       o.Employee_ID=p.Employee_ID a
       Manager_ID=120102;
```

1. You used ANSI labels in the CREATE VIEW code. DESCRIBE VIEW produced SAS (LABEL=) syntax.

DESCRIBE VIEW
```
select Employee_Name as Name format=$25.0,
       Job_Title as Title format=$15.0,
       Salary label='Annual Salary' format=COMMA10.2,
       int((today()-Employee_Hire_Date)/365.25)
           as YOS label='Years of Service'
  from ORION.EMPLOYEE_ADDRESSES a, ORION.EMPLOYEE_PAYROLL p,
       ORION.EMPLOYEE_ORGANIZATION o
 where (a.Employee_ID=p.Employee_ID) and
       (o.Employee_ID=p.Employee_ID) and
       (Manager_ID=120102);
```

7.01 Quiz – Correct Answer

Differences between the SQL code produced by the DESCRIBE VIEW statement and the actual CREATE VIEW code, which created `orion.Tom_Zhou`:

Original
```
select Employee_Name as Name format=$25.0,
       Job_Title as Title format=$15.0,
       Salary 'Annual Salary' format=comma10.2,
       int((today()-Employee_Hire_Date)/365.25)
           as YOS 'Years of Service'
  from ORION.Employee_Addresses as a,ORION.Employee_Payroll as p,
       ORION.Employee_Organization as o
 where a.Employee_ID=p.Employee_ID and
       o.Employee_ID=p.Employee_ID and
```

DESCRIBE VIEW
```
select E
       J
       S
       int((today()-Employee_Hire_Date)/365.25)
           as YOS label='Years of Service'
  from ORION.EMPLOYEE_ADDRESSES a, ORION.EMPLOYEE_PAYROLL p,
       ORION.EMPLOYEE_ORGANIZATION o
 where (a.Employee_ID=p.Employee_ID) and
       (o.Employee_ID=p.Employee_ID) and
       (Manager_ID=120102);
```

> 2. You used the keyword AS to assign table aliases. DESCRIBE VIEW omitted the keyword AS when assigning table aliases.

7.01 Quiz – Correct Answer

Differences between the SQL code produced by the DESCRIBE VIEW statement and the actual CREATE VIEW code, which created `orion.Tom_Zhou`:

Original
```
select Employee_Name as Name format=$25.0,
       Job_Title as Title format=$15.0,
       Salary 'Annual Salary' format=comma10.2,
       int((today()-Employee_Hire_Date)/365.25)
           as YOS 'Years of Service'
  from ORION.Employee_Addresses as a,ORION.Employee_Payroll as p,
       ORION.Employee_Organization as o
 where a.Employee_ID=p.Employee_ID and
       o.Employee_ID=p.Employee_ID and
       Manager_ID=120102;
```

DESCRIBE VIEW
```
select Employee_Name as Name format=$25.0
       
       
  from ORION.EMPLOYEE_ADDRESSES a, ORION.EMPLOYEE_PAYROLL p,
       ORION.EMPLOYEE_ORGANIZATION o
 where (a.Employee_ID=p.Employee_ID) and
       (o.Employee_ID=p.Employee_ID) and
       (Manager_ID=120102);
```

> 3. DESCRIBE VIEW inserted parentheses around the expressions between each AND operator.

7.02 Poll – Correct Answer

Considering the differences discussed previously, if you submit the code produced by the DESCRIBE VIEW statement, would the view produced be identical to the original view?

 Yes

○ No

21

7.03 Multiple Choice Poll – Correct Answer

What will be the result of executing the code on the previous slide?

a. The code executes properly and a report is produced. The SAS log contains only the expected messages.

b. The code executes properly and a report is produced. A special note is written to the SAS log about the VIEW libref.

c. The code does not execute and no report is produced. An error message is written to the SAS log.

Partial SAS Log:

```
ERROR: File TEST.STAFF.DATA does not exist.
NOTE: The SAS System stopped processing this step because of errors.
```

37

7.04 Multiple Choice Poll – Correct Answer

What will be the result of executing the code on the previous slide?

a. The code executes properly and a report is produced. The SAS log contains only the expected messages.

b. The code executes properly and a report is produced. A special note is written to the SAS log about the VIEW libref.

c. The code does not execute and no report is produced. An error message is written to the SAS log.

48

7.05 Multiple Choice Poll – Correct Answer

What will be the result of executing the code on the previous slide?

a. The code executes properly and a report is produced. The SAS log contains only the expected messages.

b. The code executes properly and a report is produced. A special note is written to the SAS log about the VIEW libref.

c. The code does not execute and no report is produced. An error message is written to the SAS log.

Partial SAS Log

```
ERROR: Libname TEST is not assigned.
NOTE: The SAS System stopped processing this step because of errors.
```

57

7.06 Multiple Choice Poll – Correct Answer

Based on the query in program **s107d01**, which different data types does the **work.Discounts** table have?

a. All columns are NUMERIC type.

  b. Some columns are DATE type and some are NUMERIC type.

  c. Some columns are CHARACTER type and some are NUMERIC type.

  d. Some columns are CHARACTER type, some are DATE type, and some are NUMERIC type.

SAS has only two data types: character and numeric.

In PROC SQL, if you specify the ANSI data type DATE when you create a table, the actual data type in the underlying SAS data set is numeric.

83

7.07 Quiz – Correct Answer

Locate three syntax errors in the following code:

1. **Missing semicolon in the CREATE TABLE statement**
2. **Missing comma in the column name list**
3. **Quotation marks around numeric value in second VALUES clause**

```
proc sql;
   create table Discounts
     (Product_ID num format=z12.,
      Start_Date date, End_Date date,
      Discount num format=percent. ;
   insert into discounts
     (Product_ID,Start_Date,End_Date,Discount)
       values (220200200022,'01Mar2007'd,
             '31Mar2007'd,.35)
       values (220200200024,'01Mar2007'd,
             '31Mar2007'd, .35) ;
```

103

7.09 Poll – Correct Answer

Were the rows containing good data rejected along
with the rows containing bad data when you used
the PROC SQL option UNDO_POLICY=NONE?

○ Yes

◉ No

Partial Log

```
ERROR: Add/Update failed for data set WORK.DISCOUNTS because data
       value(s) do not comply with integrity constraint ok_discount.
NOTE: This insert failed while attempting to add data from VALUES
      clause 2 to the data set.
NOTE: 3 rows were inserted into WORK.DISCOUNTS --
      of these 1 row was rejected as an ERROR,
      leaving 2 rows that were inserted successfully.
```

122

7.10 Multiple Choice Poll – Correct Answer

After you correct and resubmit only the INSERT INTO
query using UNDO_POLICY=NONE, how many rows
are in the **Discounts** table?

(a.) 5

b. 3

c. 2

 If you specify UNDO_POLICY=NONE when
correcting for constraint violations, ensure that
you re-submit only the corrected data rows, or
you might inadvertently add unwanted duplicates
of the original non-rejected rows to the table.

131

Solutions to Chapter Review

Chapter Review Answers

True or False:

1. A view requires less disk storage space than a table.
   True

2. An SQL view can be used as input for PROC FREQ
   True

3. If an SQL query requires 30 minutes to execute, creating a view from that query will greatly reduce the time required to access the results.
   False

133

Chapter 8 Additional PROC SQL Features

8.1 Setting SQL Procedure Options

Objectives
- Use SQL procedure options to control processing details.

3

Controlling Processing
PROC SQL options give you finer control over your SQL processes by providing the following features:
- syntax checking without executing your code
- expanding SQL statements to their fully-qualified values
- restricting the number of rows processed
- providing system utilization statistics for query tuning

General form of the PROC SQL statement:

PROC SQL *options*;

4

8.01 Multiple Answer Poll

Review: Specifying the NOEXEC option in a PROC SQL statement does which of the following?

a. Prevents statement execution for the current invocation of PROC SQL
b. Applies only to the SELECT statement
c. Checks SQL query syntax without actually executing the statements
d. Displays rewritten PROC SQL statements after references are expanded and certain other transformations are made

6

Controlling Processing

Selected options:

Option	Effect
INOBS=n	sets a limit of *n* rows from each source table that contributes to a query.
OUTOBS=n	restricts the number of rows that a query outputs (displays or writes to a table).
NOSTIMER|STIMER	controls whether or not PROC SQL writes resource utilization statistics to the SAS log.

8

continued...

Controlling Processing

Option	Effect
PRINT|NOPRINT	controls whether the results of a SELECT statement are displayed in the OUTPUT window.
NONUMBER|NUMBER	controls whether the row number is displayed as the first column in query output.
NODOUBLE|DOUBLE	controls whether the report is double-spaced.

9

continued...

Controlling Processing

Option	Effect
NOFLOW|FLOW|FLOW=n|FLOW=n <m>	controls the appearance of wide character columns. The FLOW option causes text to flow in its column rather than wrapping an entire row. Specifying n determines the width of the flowed column. Specifying n and m floats the width of the column between the limits to achieve a balanced layout.

10

 The default value appears first in the slides.

The NONUMBER\|NUMBER option only affects PROC SQL results written to the Output window. It cannot be used to add observation numbers to data tables created using PROC SQL.

Resetting Options

Use the RESET statement to add or change PROC SQL options without re-invoking the procedure.

General form of the RESET statement:

> **RESET** *option(s)*;

11

An option specified in the PROC SQL statement remains in effect until you re-invoke PROC SQL or until you issue a RESET statement.

Controlling Processing

If you attempt to display all of the columns in the `orion.Employee_Organization` table in a typical 80-column Output window, there is not enough room on one line to display an entire row. By default, PROC SQL wraps the output, and places the remaining information for the row on the next line.

```
options ls=80;
proc sql;
title "Default Output";
   select *
      from orion.Employee_Organization
;
quit;
```

12

s108d01

Controlling Processing

Partial PROC SQL Output

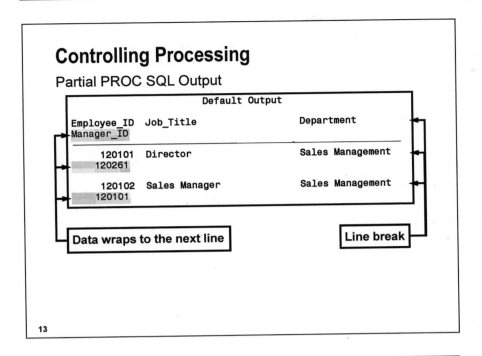

Controlling Processing

You can override this default behavior in PROC SQL with
the FLOW option. The FLOW option wraps text within a
column instead of at the end of the line.

```
proc sql flow=15;
title "Flow=15 Option";
    select *
        from orion.Employee_Organization
;
quit;
```

s108d01

14

Controlling Processing

Partial PROC SQL Output

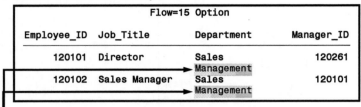

```
                    Flow=15 Option

Employee_ID  Job_Title      Department      Manager_ID

    120101   Director       Sales              120261
                            Management
    120102   Sales Manager  Sales              120101
                            Management
```

Data wraps within the column at a maximum width of 15 characters.

15

Controlling Processing

When text wraps in columns, providing some white space between rows can improve legibility.

The PROC SQL DOUBLE option produces output with a blank line between each row.

```
proc sql flow=15 double;
title "Flow=15 and Double Options";
   select *
       from orion.Employee_Organization
;
quit;
```

16   s108d01

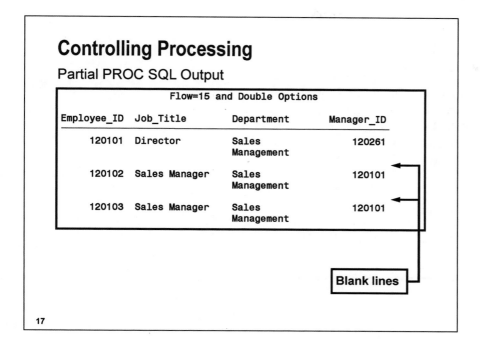

Controlling Processing

Partial PROC SQL Output

```
                Flow=15 and Double Options

Employee_ID  Job_Title       Department      Manager_ID

     120101  Director        Sales               120261
                             Management

     120102  Sales Manager   Sales               120101
                             Management

     120103  Sales Manager   Sales               120101
                             Management
```

Blank lines

17

Controlling Processing

Columns often have varying widths, and a one-size-fits-all approach does not produce well-balanced output. Providing the FLOW option with upper and lower boundaries enables PROC SQL to automatically adjust column sizes within the boundaries to produce a well-balanced report.

```
proc sql flow=6 25;
title "Flow=6 25 Option";
   select *
       from orion.Employee_Organization
;
quit;
```

18   s108d01

Choosing flow boundaries:

You can use code to help you estimate the lower and upper boundaries for the FLOW= option. The code shown below provides an example:

```
proc sql;
   select "Flow=", min (A,B,C,D),max (A,B,C,D)
       from (select max(length(put(Employee_ID,z6.))) as A,
                    max(length(Job_Title)) as B,
                    max(Length(Department)) as C,
                    max(length(put(Manager_ID,z6.)))as D
                from orion.Employee_Organization)
;
quit;
```

PROC SQL Output

Flow=	6	25

Controlling Processing

In this case, PROC SQL managed to get the entire row on a single line without wrapping text by adjusting individual column widths within the specified boundaries to produce well-balanced output.

Partial PROC SQL Output

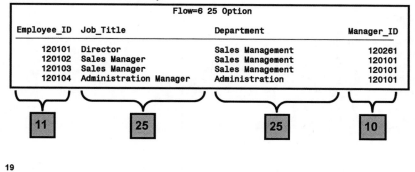

```
                              Flow=6 25 Option

Employee_ID  Job_Title                     Department                Manager_ID

     120101  Director                      Sales Management              120261
     120102  Sales Manager                 Sales Management              120101
     120103  Sales Manager                 Sales Management              120101
     120104  Administration Manager        Administration                120101
```

```
   11              25                         25                10
```

19

Controlling Processing

Example: Read ten rows from `orion.Price_List`.

```
proc sql inobs=10;
title "orion.Price_List - INOBS=10";
   select Product_ID,
           Unit_Cost_Price format=comma8.2,
           Unit_Sales_Price format=comma8.2,
           Unit_Sales_Price-Unit_Cost_Price
           as Margin format=comma8.2
      from orion.Price_List
;
quit;
```

20   s108d02

Controlling Processing

PROC SQL Output

```
                ORION.Price_List - INOBS=10

                                 Unit      Unit
                                 Cost     Sales
        Product ID      Price    Price   Margin

        210200100009    15.50    34.70    19.20
        210200100017    17.80    40.00    22.20
        210200200023     8.25    19.80    11.55
        210200600067    28.90    67.00    38.10
        210200600085    17.85    39.40    21.55
        210200600112     9.25    21.80    12.55
        210200900033     6.45    14.20     7.75
        210200900038     9.30    20.30    11.00
        210201000050     9.00    19.60    10.60
        210201000126     2.30     6.50     4.20
```

21

Controlling Processing

Example: Join all rows, but limit output to the 10 most
          profitable customers.

```
proc sql outobs=10;
title "10 Most Profitable Customers";
   select Customer_ID,
          sum(Unit_Sales_Price-Unit_Cost_Price)
          as Profit_2007 format=comma8.2
      from orion.Price_List as p,
           orion.Order_Fact as o
      where p.Product_ID=o.Product_id
            and year(Order_date) =2007
      group by Customer_ID
      order by Profit_2007 desc;
```

s108d02

22

Controlling Processing

PROC SQL Output

```
                10 Most Profitable Customers

           Customer ID   Profit_2007

                   10       634.10
                70100       372.70
                  908       266.10
                   31       225.35
                  171       207.50
                   27       204.95
                70201       197.85
                 2806       177.95
                   34       142.65
                46966       138.80
```

23

8.02 Quiz

Open the program **s108a01**. This SQL query joins
`orion.Employee_addresses` and
`orion.Employee_Donations` to calculate each
employee's total charitable contribution for 2007. Output
rows are numbered, and limited to 10 observations.

Without re-invoking PROC SQL, add a statement before
the second query that does the following:
- displays output rows without row numbers
- ensures that only nine rows are output

25

8.2 Dictionary Tables and Views

Objectives

- Use dictionary tables and views to obtain information about SAS files.

29

Dictionary Tables: Overview

Dictionary tables are read-only SAS views that contain session metadata, such as information about SAS libraries, data sets, and external files in use or available in the current SAS session.

Dictionary tables are

- created at SAS session initialization
- updated automatically by SAS
- limited to read-only access.

You can query dictionary tables with PROC SQL.

30

Metadata is data that provides information about other data.

Dictionary Tables: Overview

The metadata available in dictionary tables includes information about the following:

- SAS data sets and other SAS files available in SAS libraries
- any allocated external files
- SAS session metadata, including these items:
  - system option names and settings
  - macro variable names and values
  - title text
  - footnote text

31

Overview of Dictionary Tables

You can obtain information about dictionary tables
by querying `dictionary.Dictionaries`.

```
proc sql flow=6 25;
   select memname as Table,
          name as Column, type
       from dictionary.Dictionaries;
```

Partial PROC SQL Output

Table	Column	type
MEMBERS	LIBNAME	char
MEMBERS	MEMNAME	char
MEMBERS	MEMTYPE	char
MEMBERS	DBMS_MEMTYPE	char
MEMBERS	ENGINE	char
MEMBERS	INDEX	char
MEMBERS	PATH	char
TABLES	LIBNAME	char
TABLES	MEMNAME	char

32   s108d03

You can use the DESCRIBE TABLE statement in PROC SQL to become familiar with the various
columns that are in dictionary tables.

```
proc sql;
   describe table dictionary.Dictionaries;
quit;
```

SAS Log

```
proc sql;
   describe table dictionary.Dictionaries;
NOTE: SQL table DICTIONARY.DICTIONARIES was created like:

create table DICTIONARY.DICTIONARIES
  (
   memname char(32) label='Member Name',
   memlabel char(256) label='Dataset Label',
   name char(32) label='Column Name',
   type char(4) label='Column Type',
   length num label='Column Length',
   npos num label='Column Position',
   varnum num label='Column Number in Table',
   label char(256) label='Column Label',
   format char(49) label='Column Format',
   informat char(49) label='Column Informat'
  );

47   quit;
```

Metadata about SAS Libraries

DICTIONARY.LIBNAMES
- general information about SAS libraries

DICTIONARY.MEMBERS
- general information about SAS library members

DICTIONARY.TABLES
- detailed information about tables

DICTIONARY.VIEWS
- detailed information about all data views

DICTIONARY.CATALOGS
- information about catalog entries

DICTIONARY.COLUMNS
- detailed information about all columns in all tables

continued...

33

Metadata about Indexes and Constraints

DICTIONARY.INDEXES
- indexes defined for tables

DICTIONARY.TABLE_CONSTRAINTS
- integrity constraints in all tables

DICTIONARY.CHECK_CONSTRAINTS
- check constraints in all tables

DICTIONARY.REFERENTIAL_CONSTRAINTS
- referential constraints in all tables

DICTIONARY.CONSTRAINT_COLUMN_USAGE
- columns that are referenced by integrity constraints

DICTIONARY.CONSTRAINT_TABLE_USAGE
- tables that use integrity constraints

continued...

34

Metadata about the SAS Session

DICTIONARY.MACROS
- macro variables names and values

DICTIONARY.OPTIONS
- current settings of SAS system options

DICTIONARY.TITLES
- text currently assigned to titles and footnotes

DICTIONARY.EXTFILES
- currently assigned filerefs

35

SAS librefs are limited to eight characters. The libref **dictionary** is an automatically assigned, reserved libref that is accessible only from within PROC SQL.

Exploring Dictionary Tables

You can use a DESCRIBE statement to explore the structure of dictionary tables:

```
describe table dictionary.tables;
```

Partial Log

```
NOTE: SQL table DICTIONARY.TABLES was created like:

create table DICTIONARY.TABLES
  (
  libname char(8) label='Library Name',
  memname char(32) label='Member Name',
  ...
  crdate num format=DATETIME informat=DATETIME label='Date Created',
  modate num format=DATETIME informat=DATETIME label='Date Modified',
  nobs num label='Number of Observations',
  obslen num label='Observation Length',
  nvar num label='Number of Variables', ...);
```

36   s108d03

The DESCRIBE TABLE statement is a good tool for exploring dictionary tables. The complete log notes from the DESCRIBE statement are shown below:

```
create table DICTIONARY.TABLES
  (
  libname char(8) label='Library Name',
  memname char(32) label='Member Name',
  memtype char(8) label='Member Type',
  dbms_memtype char(32) label='DBMS Member Type',
  memlabel char(256) label='Dataset Label',
  typemem char(8) label='Dataset Type',
  crdate num format=DATETIME informat=DATETIME label='Date Created',
  modate num format=DATETIME informat=DATETIME label='Date Modified',
  nobs num label='Number of Physical Observations',
  obslen num label='Observation Length',
  nvar num label='Number of Variables',
  protect char(3) label='Type of Password Protection',
  compress char(8) label='Compression Routine',
  encrypt char(8) label='Encryption',
  npage num label='Number of Pages',
  filesize num label='Size of File',
  pcompress num label='Percent Compression',
  reuse char(3) label='Reuse Space',
  bufsize num label='Bufsize',
  delobs num label='Number of Deleted Observations',
  nlobs num label='Number of Logical Observations',
  maxvar num label='Longest variable name',
  maxlabel num label='Longest label',
  maxgen num label='Maximum number of generations',
  gen num label='Generation number',
  attr char(3) label='Dataset Attributes',
  indxtype char(9) label='Type of Indexes',
  datarep char(32) label='Data Representation',
  sortname char(8) label='Name of Collating Sequence',
  sorttype char(4) label='Sorting Type',
  sortchar char(8) label='Charset Sorted By',
  reqvector char(24) format=$HEX48 informat=$HEX48 label='Requirements Vector',
  datarepname char(170) label='Data Representation Name',
  encoding char(256) label='Data Encoding',
  audit char(3) label='Audit Trail Active?',
  audit_before char(3) label='Audit Before Image?',
  audit_admin char(3) label='Audit Admin Image?',
  audit_error char(3) label='Audit Error Image?',
  audit_data char(3) label='Audit Data Image?'
  );
```

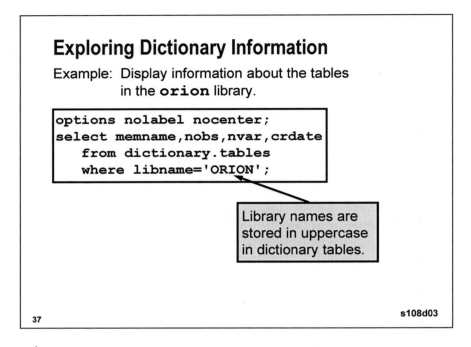

SAS library and table names are stored in uppercase in the dictionary tables. Using SAS functions, such as UPCASE() or LOWCASE(), when querying dictionary tables dramatically degrades query performance, because this prevents the PROC SQL Query Optimizer from seeing many conditions that could be optimized. This is especially apparent when librefs are assigned to a DBMS using a SAS/ACCESS engine.

When you query dictionary tables, you supply values to the WHERE clause in the appropriate case, and match the known case for library and table names (uppercase) and for column names (mixed case). (Know your data!)

The PRESERVE_TAB_NAMES=YES and PRESERVE_COL_NAMES=YES options change the way that some table and column names are seen by SAS in the dictionary tables. These options might require further investigation to maximize the efficiency of your queries.

Exploring Dictionary Information

Example: Display information about the tables
in the **orion** library.

Partial PROC SQL Output

memname	nobs	nvar	crdate
CUSTOMER	77	12	14DEC07:08:05:44
EMPLOYEE_ADDRESSES	424	9	23OCT07:10:12:23
EMPLOYEE_DONATIONS	124	7	14JAN08:10:34:21
EMPLOYEE_ORGANIZATION	424	4	12OCT07:14:06:32
Employee_payroll	424	8	14DEC07:08:08:06
EMPLOYEE_PHONES	923	3	12OCT07:16:45:19
GEOGRAPHY_DIM	632	11	14DEC07:08:05:47
ORDER_FACT	617	12	14DEC07:08:05:44
PRICE_LIST	259	6	14DEC07:08:05:45
PRODUCT_DIM	732	8	12OCT07:14:34:27
SALES	165	9	22JAN08:10:15:58
STAFF	424	10	14DEC07:08:05:44

38

Exploring Dictionary Information

Example: Display information about the columns
in **orion.Employee_addresses**.

```
proc sql;
   select Name,Type,Length
      from dictionary.columns
      where libname='ORION'
         and memname='EMPLOYEE_ADDRESSES'
;
```

Table names (**memnames**)
are also stored in uppercase
in dictionary tables.

s108d03

39

Exploring Dictionary Information

Example: Display information about the columns
in `orion.Employee_addresses`.

PROC SQL Output

Column names are stored in mixed case.

name	type	length
Employee_ID	num	8
Employee_Name	char	40
Street_ID	num	8
Street_Number	num	8
Street_Name	char	40
City	char	30
State	char	2
Postal_Code	char	10
Country	char	2

40

Using Dictionary Information

Example: Which tables contain the `Employee_ID`
column?

```
select memname, name
   from dictionary.columns
   where libname='ORION' and
         upcase(name)='EMPLOYEE_ID';
```

Because different tables might use different cases
for same-named columns, you can use the UPCASE
function for comparisons, but this significantly degrades
the performance of the query.

41   s108d03

Using Dictionary Information

PROC SQL Output

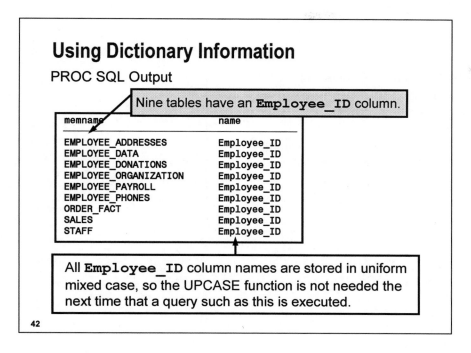

All **Employee_ID** column names are stored in uniform mixed case, so the UPCASE function is not needed the next time that a query such as this is executed.

42

Dictionary Information in Other SAS Processes

To use dictionary table metadata in other procedures or in a DATA step, you can do the following:

- use the SAS-provided views based on the dictionary tables in the Sashelp library
- create a PROC SQL view based on a dictionary table

Most of the Sashelp library metadata view names are similar to dictionary table names, but are shortened to eight characters or less. They begin with the letter **v** and do not end in **s**. For example:

```
dictionary.tables = sashelp.vtable
```

43

8.03 Quiz

In your SAS session's SAS Explorer window, navigate to the Sashelp library by selecting **libraries** ⇨ **SASHELP**. Scroll down to examine the Sashelp views.

Which view shows the names and data types of all the columns in every table available in the SAS session?

45

Using Dictionary Information

Example: Use **sashelp.vmember** to extract information from **dictionary.members** in a PROC TABULATE step.

```
proc tabulate data=sashelp.vmember format=8.;
   class libname memtype;
   keylabel N=' ';
   table libname, memtype/rts=10
         misstext='None';
run;
```

47   s108d04

Using Dictionary Information

PROC TABULATE Output

libname	memtype				
	CATALOG	DATA	ITEMSTOR	MDDB	VIEW
ORION	None	15	None	None	2
SASHELP	287	217	3	2	31
SASUSER	11	131	2	1	1
WORK	None	2	None	None	1

48

The numbers on this report might vary depending on the files that were created in your SAS session.

 **Exercises**

Level 1

1. Using PROC SQL Options and Displaying the Contents of a Dictionary Table

a. Write a query that retrieves **Memname** (table name) and **Memlabel** (description of the table) from **dictionary.Dictionaries**. Include only a single row per table name displayed. Use the FLOW= option to ensure that columns wrap between 6 – 35 characters. Title the report **Dictionary Tables**.

Partial PROC SQL Output

```
                              Dictionary Tables

 Member Name                     Data Set Label
 _____

 CATALOGS                        Catalogs and catalog-specific
                                 information
 CHECK_CONSTRAINTS               Check constraints
 COLUMNS                         Columns from every table
 CONSTRAINT_COLUMN_USAGE         Constraint column usage
 CONSTRAINT_TABLE_USAGE          Constraint table usage
 DATAITEMS                       Information Map Data Items
 DESTINATIONS                    Open ODS Destinations
 DICTIONARIES                    DICTIONARY tables and their columns
 ENGINES                         Available engines
 EXTFILES                        Files defined in FILENAME
                                 statements, or implicitly
```

b. Use the columns **memname**, **type**, and **length** from **dictionary.Columns** where **libname="ORION"** and the table contains a column (**Name**) named **Customer_ID** (**upcase(Name)='CUSTOMER_ID'**). Title the report **Tables containing Customer_ID**.

PROC SQL Output

```
                        Tables containing Customer_ID

                                         Column      Column
                   Member Name           Type        Length
                   _____

                   CUSTOMER              num              8
                   ORDER_FACT            num              8
                   QTR1_2007             num              8
                   QTR2_2007             num              8
```

Level 2

2. Using PROC SQL Options and Displaying Dictionary Table Information

a. Produce a report that includes **memname** (table name), **memlabel** (table description), and a count of the number of columns in each table, by querying **dictionary.Dictionaries**. Display only one row per table name. Use the FLOW= option to wrap columns between 6 – 35 characters. Title the report **Dictionary Tables**.

Partial PROC SQL Output

```
                              Dictionary Tables

      Member Name               Data Set Label                    Columns

      CATALOGS                  Catalogs and catalog-specific        10
                                information
      CHECK_CONSTRAINTS         Check constraints                     4
      COLUMNS                   Columns from every table             18
      CONSTRAINT_COLUMN_USAGE   Constraint column usage               7
```

b. List the table name (**memname**), number of rows (**nobs**), number of columns (**nvar**), file size (**filesize**), length of the widest column (**maxvar**), and length of the widest column label (**maxlabel**) by querying **dictionary.Tables**. Limit the list to tables in the **orion** library (**libname="ORION"**) and exclude views (**memtype ne 'VIEW'**) from your report. Order the report by table name. Give the columns labels as indicated by the sample output. Name the report **Orion Library Tables**. If you wrote additional tables to the **orion** library, your output might differ from the sample PROC SQL output.

PROC SQL Output

```
                         Orion Library Tables

                                              File      Widest     Widest
      Table                   Rows   Columns  Size      Column     Label

      CUSTOMER                  77      12     49152      18         19
      EMPLOYEE_ADDRESSES       424       9     86016      13          0
      EMPLOYEE_DONATIONS       124       7     36864      11         11
      EMPLOYEE_ORGANIZATION    424       4     49152      11          0
      EMPLOYEE_PAYROLL         424       8     40960      18          0
      EMPLOYEE_PHONES          923       3    229376      12         11
      ORDER_FACT               617      12     73728      18         48
      PRICE_LIST               259       6     24576      16         24
      PRODUCT_DIM              481       8    131072      16         16
      QTR1_2007                 22       5      8192      13         33
      QTR2_2007                 36       6      8192      13         33
      SALES                    165       9     32768      11          0
      SALESSTAFF               163      10     36864      13         25
      STAFF                    424      10     57344      13         25
```

Level 3

3. Using PROC SQL Options, SAS System Options, and Dictionary Tables to Document Data Tables in the Orion Star Library

a. Use PROC SQL options, SAS system options, and `dictionary.Tables` to document the data tables in the `orion` library. In the report, exclude views and output only one row per table. For each numeric column, the query should place an asterisk beside each of the maximum values. (See the sample output below.) If you created tables in the `orion` library during this class, your output might have additional entries. Give yourself bonus points for creating the report as a PDF file that is ready to e-mail to the rest of your project team!

Partial PROC SQL Output:

Table	Rows	Columns	File Size (Bytes)	Widest Column
CUSTOMER	77	12*	49152	18*
EMPLOYEE_ ADDRESSES	424	9	86016	13
EMPLOYEE_ ...	124	7	36864	11
SALESSTAFF	163	10	36864	13
STAFF	424	10	65536	13

ORION Library Table Information

* Largest in the Library

Hint: Consider using a CASE statement to generate the asterisks in the report. The JOURNAL style can make a report more readable when it is output to a PDF file.

PDF Output

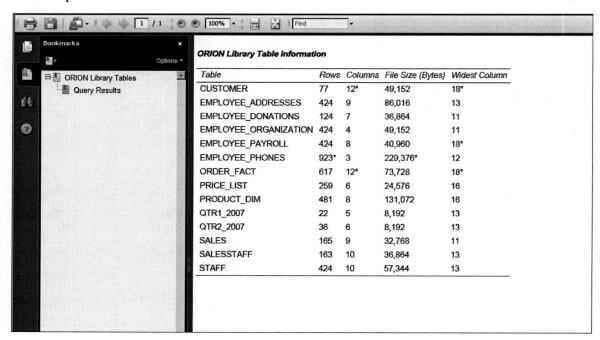

Copyright © 2011, SAS Institute Inc., Cary, North Carolina, USA. ALL RIGHTS RESERVED.

8.3 Interfacing PROC SQL with the Macro Language

Objectives

- State the purpose of the SAS macro language.
- Create and use SAS macro variables in PROC SQL.
- Insert information from dictionary tables into SAS macro variables to create a self-modifying SQL query.

52

The SAS Macro Language Overview

The SAS macro language

- is a programmable system for producing text
- uses syntax similar to Base SAS
- uses the percent sign (%) preceding most key words within macro statements, for example:

```
%put This is a test;
```

53

The SAS Macro Language Overview

Using the SAS macro language, you can write
SAS programs that are dynamic, that is, capable
of self-modification.

The SAS macro facility enables you to do the following:

- create macro variables that contain text, and resolve
  them (replace the variable name with the text stored
  in the variable) anywhere in a SAS program
- write special programs (macros) that generate
  tailored SAS code

54

Macro Variables

SAS macro variables are stored in an area of memory
referred to as the *global symbol table*.

SAS uses automatic macro variables to "remember"
important information about the SAS session. Macro
variables in SAS are classified as either automatic
(created and updated by SAS) or user-defined.

When SAS is invoked, the global symbol table is created
and several automatic macro variables values are
initialized by SAS.

Global Symbol Table

**Partial Listing of
Automatic
Variables
in the Global
Symbol Table**

Name	Value
...	...
SYSLAST	_NULL_
SYSSCP	WIN
SYSTIME	09:00
SYSVER	8.1
...	...

55

User-Defined Macro Variables

Executing a PROC SQL statement automatically creates and populates the following user-defined (global scope) macro variable values:

SQLOBS   records the number of rows (observations) that are output or deleted by the SQL statement.

SQLRC   contains the return code from each SQL statement, which can be decoded as follows:

Value	Meaning
0	The statement completed successfully with no errors.
4	A warning was issued, but execution continued.
> 4	An error that stopped execution was encountered.

56

User-Defined Macro Variables

You can create your own user-defined macro variables to "remember" values that are important to you in your programs. One method is to use the %LET statement to create and assign values to user-defined macro variables.

General form of the %LET statement:

> **%LET** *variable* = *value*;

where *variable* is any valid SAS variable name and *value* is any text string.

✎ Quotation marks included in *value* are treated as normal text, and become part of the text stored in the macro variable.

57

 Value can be any string.
- Maximum length is 64K characters.
- Minimum length is 0 characters *(null value)*.
- Numeric tokens are stored as character strings.
- Mathematical expressions are not evaluated.
- The case of *value* is preserved.
- Quotation marks are stored as part of *value*.
- Leading and trailing blanks are removed from *value* before the assignment is made.

User-Defined Macro Variables

The %LET macro statement
- is a global statement. You can use it anywhere in your programs.
- creates a user-defined macro variable and assigns it a value if the macro variable does not exist.
- changes the value of the macro variable if the macro variable already exists.

58

Resolving Symbolic References

A user-defined macro variable's name and value are also stored in the global symbol table.

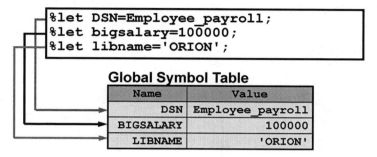

```
%let DSN=Employee_payroll;
%let bigsalary=100000;
%let libname='ORION';
```

Global Symbol Table

Name	Value
DSN	Employee_payroll
BIGSALARY	100000
LIBNAME	'ORION'

✎ Names are stored as uppercase; references to them are not case sensitive. All values are stored as mixed-case text.

59

Resolving Symbolic References

When the code is submitted, the macro variable is resolved. The value is obtained from the symbol table and substituted in the program before the syntax is evaluated.

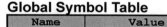

Global Symbol Table

Name	Value
DSN	Employee_payroll
BIGSALARY	100000

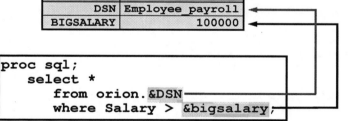

```
proc sql;
    select *
        from orion.&DSN
        where Salary > &bigsalary;
```

64

Resolving Symbolic References

When the code is submitted, the macro variable is resolved. The value is obtained from the symbol table and substituted in the program before the syntax is evaluated.

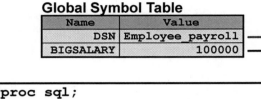

Global Symbol Table

Name	Value
DSN	Employee_payroll
BIGSALARY	100000

```
proc sql;
   select *
      from orion.Employee_payroll
      where Salary > 100000;
```

65

Displaying Macro Variable Values

Use the %PUT statement to display the resolved macro variable value along with descriptive text in the SAS log.

General form of the %PUT statement:

%PUT *text*;

Example

```
%put The value of bigsalary is &bigsalary;
```

Partial SAS Log

```
The value of bigsalary is 100000
```

66

Resolving Symbolic References

When you submit code containing macro variable references, use the SYMBOLGEN system option to see the value that was substituted in the code echoed in the SAS log.

General form of the SYMBOLGEN system option:

OPTIONS SYMBOLGEN;

67

NOSYMBOLGEN is the default system option setting.

Resolving Symbolic References

Display the results of a resolved macro variable reference in the SAS log with the SYMBOLGEN system option.

```
%let datasetname=Employee_Payroll;
%let bigsalary=100000;
options symbolgen;
proc sql;
title "Salaries > &bigsalary";
   select  Employee_ID, Salary
       from orion.&datasetname
       where Salary > &bigsalary
;
quit;
title;
```

68

s108d05

Resolving Symbolic References

Partial Log

```
 proc sql;
SYMBOLGEN:  Macro variable BIGSALARY resolves to 100000
  title "Salaries > &bigsalary";
  select  Employee_ID, Salary
    from orion.&datasetname
SYMBOLGEN:  Macro variable DATASETNAME resolves to Employee_Payroll
    where Salary > &bigsalary
SYMBOLGEN:  Macro variable BIGSALARY resolves to 100000
  ;
  quit;
```

69

Resolving Symbolic References

PROC SQL Output

```
              Salaries > 100000

        Employee_ID     Salary

            120101      163040
            120102      108255
            120259      433800
            120260      207885
            120261      243190
            120262      268455
            120659      161290
            121141      194885
            121142      156065
```

70

PROC SQL and Macro Variables

- The ANSI specification requires SQL to provide a mechanism for passing data values returned by a query to the host system. In PROC SQL, the host (SAS) receives data from a query as macro variable values.
- PROC SQL creates or updates macro variables using an INTO clause.
- The INTO clause has three syntaxes, and each produces a different result.

71

The INTO clause occurs between the SELECT statement and the FROM clause. It cannot be used in a CREATE TABLE or CREATE VIEW statement. Use the NOPRINT option if you do not want to display the query result.

PROC SQL and Macro Variables: Syntax 1

Syntax 1 places values from the **first row** returned by an SQL query into macro variable(s). Data from additional rows returned by the query is ignored.

General form of the SELECT statement with an INTO clause:

```
SELECT column-1<, ...column-n>
    INTO :macvar_1<, ... :macvar_n>
    FROM table|view ...
```

The value from the first column in the SELECT list is placed in the first macro variable listed in the INTO clause, and so on.

72

This method is most often used with queries that return only one row.

PROC SQL and Macro Variables: Syntax 1

Example: Create a single macro variable containing
         the average salary for the entire company,
         and use the INTO clause.

```
proc sql noprint;
   select avg(Salary)        Macro variable names are
      into :MeanSalary        preceded by a colon (:).
      from orion.Employee_payroll;
%put The average salary is &MeanSalary;
```

Partial SAS Log

```
The average salary is 38041.51
```

73   s108d06

PROC SQL and Macro Variables: Syntax 1

Example: Using the INTO clause, create multiple macro
         variables that contain the minimum, average,
         and maximum salary for the entire company.

```
select avg(Salary),min(Salary),max(Salary)
   into :MeanSalary, :MinSalary, :MaxSalary
   from orion.Employee_payroll;
%put Mean: &meansalary Min: &minsalary
     Max: &maxsalary;
```

Partial SAS Log

```
Mean: 38041.51 Min:     22710     Max:     433800
```

74   s108d06

Referencing a Macro Variable in Quotation Marks

To reference a macro variable within a quoted text string, enclose the reference in **double** quotation marks.

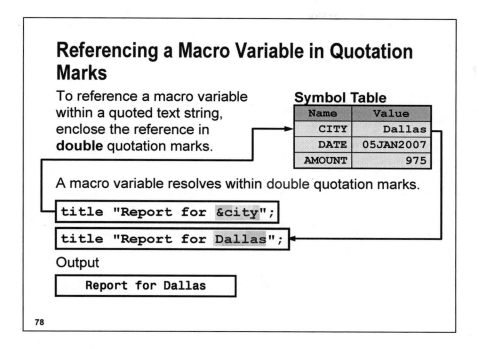

Symbol Table

Name	Value
CITY	Dallas
DATE	05JAN2007
AMOUNT	975

A macro variable resolves within double quotation marks.

```
title "Report for &city";
```

```
title "Report for Dallas";
```

Output

```
    Report for Dallas
```

78

Referencing a Macro Variable in Quotation Marks

A macro variable within **single** quotation marks will not resolve. The text is treated as literal, and no attempt is made to reference the global symbol table.

```
title 'Report for &city';
```

Output

```
    Report for &city
```

80

Business Scenario

Create a report listing all employees in the Sales Department with salaries above the department average. Include the average salary for the department in the report title.

Consideration:

If the average salary value were stored in a macro variable, it would be easier to include this information in the TITLE statement.

81

PROC SQL and Macro Variables: Syntax 1

Step 1 Calculate the average Sales Department salary and store the value in a macro variable.

```
%let Dept=Sales;
proc sql noprint;
   select avg(Salary)
       into :MeanSalary
       from orion.Employee_payroll as p,
            orion.Employee_Organization as o
       where p.Employee_ID=o.Employee_ID
            and Department=propcase("&Dept")
;
```

82   s108d07

PROC SQL and Macro Variables: Syntax 1

Step 2 List employees in the Sales Department with salaries greater than the average. Include the average salary in the title.

```
reset print number;
title "&Dept Department Employees Earning";
title2 "More Than The Department Average "
       "Of &meansalary";
select p.Employee_ID, Salary
   from orion.Employee_payroll as p,
        orion.Employee_Organization as o
   where p.Employee_ID=O.Employee_ID
      and Department=Propcase("&Dept")
      and Salary > &meansalary
;
```

s108d07

83

PROC SQL and Macro Variables: Syntax 1

Partial PROC SQL Output (Rows 57-69)

```
          Sales Department Employees Earning
     More Than The Department Average Of 27503.06

          Row    Employee_ID    Salary

          57      121081        30235
          58      121082        28510
          59      121085        32235
          60      121087        28325
          61      121089        28095
          62      121095        28010
          63      121099        32725
          64      121100        28135
          65      121104        28315
          66      121105        29545
          67      121107        31380
          68      121129        30945
          69      121139        27700
```

In the Sales Department, 69 employees earn above-average salaries.

84

8.04 Quiz

How many changes must be made to the program
to generate a report showing how many Engineering
Department employees earn above-average salaries?

```
%let Dept=Sales;
proc sql noprint;
   select avg(Salary)
       into :MeanSalary
       from orion.Employee_Payroll as p,
            orion.Employee_Organization as o
       where p.Employee_ID=O.Employee_ID
           and Department=Propcase("&Dept")
;
reset print number;
title   "&Dept Department Employees Earning";
title2 "More Than The Department Average "
       "Of &meansalary";
   select p.Employee_ID, Salary
       from orion.Employee_Payroll as p,
            orion.Employee_Organization as o
       where p.Employee_ID=O.Employee_ID
           and Department=Propcase("&Dept")
           and Salary > &meansalary;
quit;
title;
```

86

Using Macro Variables to Make Your Program Dynamic

s108d07

1. Retrieve the program **s108d07**.

2. Change the value assigned to the macro variable **Dept** in the %LET statement to **Engineering** and submit the program.

```
%let Dept=Engineering;
proc sql noprint;
   select avg(Salary)
      into :MeanSalary
      from orion.Employee_Payroll as p,
           orion.Employee_Organization as o
      where p.Employee_ID=O.Employee_ID
            and Department=propcase("&Dept")
;
reset print number;
title  "&Dept Department Employees Earning";
title2 "More Than The Department Average "
      "Of &meansalary";
   select p.Employee_ID, Salary
      from orion.Employee_Payroll as p,
           orion.Employee_Organization as o
      where p.Employee_ID=O.Employee_ID
            and Department=Propcase("&Dept")
            and Salary > &meansalary;
quit;
title;
```

3. Examine the results in the Output window.

PROC SQL OUTPUT

	Engineering Department Employees Earning	
	More Than The Department Average Of 30698.33	

Row	Employee_ID	Salary
1	120117	31670
2	121016	48075

The average and the results from the query are populated dynamically by making one simple change from **Sales** to **Engineering** for the value of **Dept**. To generate another report with different values, simply make one change to the value of **Dept** and the program is capable of making the substitutions dynamically at the appropriate places within the code.

Business Scenario

In the `orion.Customer` table, the first digit of the `Customer_Type_ID` column indicates a customer's tier. Customers with higher tier numbers are more valuable to the company.

Create a program that determines how many levels of tiers exist and produce separate reports for each tier.

The reports should include customer name and country. Include the actual tier number and the total number of customers in the tier in the report title.

89

PROC SQL and Macro Variables: Syntax 2

Syntax 2 extracts values from the first *n* rows of the query result and inserts these values into a series of *n* macro variables. Values for rows 1-*n* in the first column in the SELECT list are placed in a numbered series of macro variables *a1-an*, and so on.

General form of the SELECT statement to create a series of macro variables:

```
SELECT a, b, ...
    INTO :a1-:an, :b1-:bn
    FROM table|view ...
```

90

The PUT Function

The PUT function returns a value using a specified format. It is commonly used to convert numeric values to character.

General form of the PUT function:

PUT(*source,format.*)

source the SAS variable or constant whose value you want to reformat

format. the SAS format to be applied to *source*

91

PROC SQL and Macro Variables: Syntax 2

Step 1 Determine tier levels.

```
proc sql;
    select substr(put(Customer_Type_ID,4.),1,1)
           as Tier, count(*)
       from orion.Customer
       group by Tier;
%let Rows=&SQLOBS;
%put NOTE:  There are &Rows Tiers;
```

✎ After the first query, SQLOBS contains the number of rows (tiers).

92

s108d08
continued...

PROC SQL and Macro Variables: Syntax 2

PROC SQL Output

Tier	
1	48
2	21
3	8

Partial Log

```
%put NOTE:  There are &Rows Tiers;
NOTE:  There are 3 Tiers
```

93

PROC SQL and Macro Variables: Syntax 2

Step 2 Create macro variables to capture tier values.

```
reset noprint;
   select substr(put(Customer_Type_ID,4.),1,1)
          as Tier, count(*)
      into :Tier1-:Tier&Rows,:Count1-:Count&Rows
      from orion.Customer
      group by Tier;
%put NOTE: Tier1 is &tier1  Count1 is: &count1;
%put NOTE: Tier2 is &tier2  Count2 is: &count2;
%put NOTE: Tier3 is &tier3  Count3 is: &count3;
```

The second query adds an INTO clause using the value of &Rows
to determine the number of macro variables required for the series.

Partial Log

```
NOTE: Tier1 is 1  Count1 is: 48
NOTE: Tier2 is 2  Count2 is: 21
NOTE: Tier3 is 3  Count3 is: 8
```

94   s108d08

Setup for the Poll

The first query in the program produced output,
but the second query produced no output.

```
proc sql;
select substr(put(Customer_Type_ID,4.),1,1)
       as Tier, count(*)
  from orion.Customer
  group by Tier;
%let Rows=&SQLOBS;
%put NOTE:  There are &Rows Tiers;
reset noprint;
select substr(put(Customer_Type_ID,4.),1,1)
       as Tier, count(*)
  into :Tier1-:Tier&Rows,:Count1-:Count&Rows
  from orion.Customer
  group by Tier;
```

96   s108d08

8.05 Multiple Choice Poll

Why did the first query in the program produce output,
while the second query did not?

a. The INTO clause suppressed output during the
   execution of the second query.

b. The RESET NOPRINT statement suppressed output
   for subsequent queries in this PROC SQL invocation.

c. The %PUT statement redirected the query results to
   the SAS log.

97

PROC SQL and Macro Variables: Syntax 2

Step 3 Use the macro variables to generate reports for each tier.

```
reset print;
title "Tier &Tier1 Customers (&Count1 total)";
   select Customer_Name, Country
      from orion.Customer
      where substr(put(Customer_Type_ID,4.),1,1)
           ="&Tier1"
      order by country, Customer_Name
;
```

The query above is copied three times and modified as follows:
Change &Tier1 to &Tier2 and &Count1 to &Count2 in the second copy.
Change &Tier1 to &Tier3 and &Count1 to &Count3 in the third copy.

99   s108d08

PROC SQL and Macro Variables: Syntax 2

Partial PROC SQL Output

```
           Tier 1 Customers (48 total)

Customer_Name                         Country

Cosi Rimmington                       AU
Dericka Pockran                       AU
...
              Tier 2 Customers (21 total)

   Customer_Name                        Country

   Ramesh Trentholme                    AU
   Angel Borwick                        CA
   ...
                 Tier 3 Customers (8 total)

      Customer_Name                      Country

      Candy Kinsey                       AU
      Lauren Marx                        CA
      ...
```

100

Business Scenario

You are responsible for the program that produces a report containing **Employee_ID** and all associated date columns from the **orion.Employee_Payroll** table. The database administrators sometimes add or delete date fields from this table, which forces you to update your query with each change.

You want to rewrite your program to be self-modifying, and automate the entire process.

101

PROC SQL and Macro Variables: Syntax 3

Syntax 3 extracts values from all rows of the query result and puts them into a single macro variable, separated by the specified delimiter.

General form of the SELECT statement to create a macro variable:

```
SELECT column-1<, ... column-2>
    INTO :macvar_1 SEPARATED BY 'delimiter'
        <, ... :macvar_2 SEPARATED BY 'delimiter'>
    FROM table|view ...
```

102

PROC SQL and Macro Variables: Syntax 3

Make a temporary table named **work.Payroll** to use for testing your new programming concept by submitting the program **s108d09a**.

```
proc sql;
   create table Payroll as
      select Employee_ID, Employee_Gender, Salary,
             Birth_Date format=date9.,
             Employee_Hire_Date as Hire_Date
             format=date9.,
             Employee_Term_Date as Term_Date
             format=date9.
         from orion.Employee_Payroll
         order by Employee_ID;
quit;
```

103   s108d09a

PROC SQL and Macro Variables: Syntax 3

Step 1   Submit the program **s108d09b**, which queries **dictionary.Columns** to list **Employee_ID** and all date columns in **work.Payroll**.

```
proc sql noprint;
select Name
   into :Column_Names separated by ","
   from Dictionary.Columns
   where libname ="WORK"
   and memname="PAYROLL"
   and upcase(Name) like '%DATE%';
reset print;
title "Dates of Interest by Employee_ID";
select Employee_ID, &Column_Names
   from work.Payroll
   order by Employee_ID;
quit;
```

104   s108d09b

PROC SQL and Macro Variables: Syntax 3

Step 1 Examine the **s108d09b** program output.

Partial PROC SQL Output

```
           Dates of Interest by Employee_ID

Employee_ID  Birth_Date  Hire_Date  Term_Date

     120101   18AUG1976   01JUL2003       .
     120102   11AUG1969   01JUN1989       .
     120103   22JAN1949   01JAN1974       .
     120104   11MAY1954   01JAN1981       .
     120105   21DEC1974   01MAY1999       .
     120106   23DEC1944   01JAN1974       .
```

105

PROC SQL and Macro Variables: Syntax 3

Step 2 Submit the program **s108d09c** to add two new date columns to **work.Payroll**.

```
proc sql;
alter table Payroll
    add Date_Last_Raise date,
        Promotion_Date date;
update Payroll
    set Promotion_Date=Hire_Date+180
    where Term_Date is missing
        and today()-180 ge Hire_Date;
update Payroll
    set Date_Last_Raise=Promotion_Date+180
    where Term_Date is missing
        and today()-180 ge Promotion_Date;
quit;
```

s108d09c

106

The ALTER TABLE and UPDATE statements are discussed in more detail later in this course.

PROC SQL and Macro Variables: Syntax 3

Step 3 Test the solution by re-submitting the program **s108d09b.**

```
proc sql noprint;
select Name
    into :Column_Names separated by ","
    from Dictionary.Columns
    where libname ="WORK"
    and memname="PAYROLL"
    and upcase(Name) like '%DATE%';
reset print;
title "Dates of Interest by Employee_ID";
select Employee_ID, &Column_Names
    from Payroll
    order by Employee_ID;
quit;
```

107

s108d09b

PROC SQL and Macro Variables: Syntax 3

The report shows all the date columns, including the one that you added, without code modifications.

Partial PROC SQL Output

Employee_ID	Birth_Date	Hire_Date	Term_Date	Date_Last_Raise	Promotion_Date
120101	18AUG1976	01JUL2003	.	25JUN04	28DEC03
120102	11AUG1969	01JUN1989	.	27MAY90	28NOV89
120103	22JAN1949	01JAN1974	.	27DEC74	30JUN74
120104	11MAY1954	01JAN1981	.	27DEC81	30JUN81
120105	21DEC1974	01MAY1999	.	25APR00	28OCT99
120106	23DEC1944	01JAN1974	.	27DEC74	30JUN74
120107	21JAN1949	01FEB1974	.	27JAN75	31JUL74
120108	23FEB1984	01AUG2006	.	27JUL07	28JAN07

Dates of Interest by Employee_ID

108

PROC SQL and Macro Variables: Syntax 3

 Step 4 Modify your program to use the permanent table instead of your temporary table, and your program is ready to deploy!

```
proc sql noprint;
select Name
   into :Column_Names separated by ","
   from Dictionary.Columns
   where libname ="ORION"
   and memname="EMPLOYEE_PAYROLL"
   and upcase(Name) like '%DATE%';
reset print;
title "Dates of Interest by Employee_ID";
select Employee_ID, &Column_Names
   from orion.Employee_Payroll
   order by Employee_ID;
quit;
```

109   s108d09d

 **Exercises**

Level 1

4. **Creating and Using Macro Variables**

   a. Write a query for the **Employee_payroll** table that returns the highest value of **Salary** (**max(Salary)**). Title the report as indicated in the sample output.

      PROC SQL Output

Highest Salary in Employee_payroll
_____
433800

   b. Use %LET statements to create and assign values to two macro variables:
      DataSet = Employee_payroll
      VariableName = Salary

      Use a %PUT statement to write their values back to the SAS log in this context:

      SAS Log

      ```
      NOTE:  DataSet=Employee_payroll, VariableName=Salary
      ```

   c. Modify the query you wrote in step **4.a**, and replace each hardcoded (typed) reference to **Employee_payroll** (once in the title and once in the query) with a reference to the macro variable **DataSet** (**&DataSet**), and each hardcoded (typed) reference to **Salary** (once in the title and once in the query) with a reference to the macro variable **VariableName** (**&VariableName**). Resubmit the query, and verify that the results are identical to the results obtained in step **a.** above.

   d. Use the %LET statements to change the values of your macro variables:

      DataSet = Price_List
      VariableName = Unit_Sales_Price

      Run the report again. The results appear below:

      PROC SQL Output

Highest Unit_Sales_Price in Price_List
_____
630.4

Level 2

5.   Creating a Macro Variable from an SQL Query

   a.   Produce a report of **Country** and a new column named **Purchases** (**SUM (Total_Retail_Price)**). Group the report by **Country**. Include only orders placed in 2007. Order the report so that the highest values of **Purchases** sums are at the top. The data is in the following tables (columns of interest in parenthesis):

   • **Order_fact** (**Customer_ID**, **Total_Retail_Price**)
   • **Customer** (**Customer_ID**, **Country**)

   Name the report **2007 Purchases by Country**. Label the columns as indicated in the sample report:

   PROC SQL Output

```
                       2007 Purchases by Country

                           Customer
                           Country    Purchases
                           ─────────────────────
                           US         $10,655.97
                           CA          $5,210.5
                           AU          $3,902.49
                           ZA          $1,954.1
                           TR            $961.4
                           DE            $429.6
                           IL            $194.6
```

   b.   Write a query similar to the first but modified to produce a report of **Purchases** by **Customer_Name** for the year 2007. (Keep a copy of your first query for use in step **5.c.**) Subset the query so that only customers from the top-buying country (the one listed at the top of the last report; in this case, **US**) are included. Order the report so that customers with the highest purchases are at the top. The data is in the following tables:

   • **Order_fact** (**Customer_ID**, **Total_Retail_Price**)
   • **Customer** (**Customer_ID**, **Customer_Name**, **Country**)

   Name the report **2007 US Customer Purchases** with a second title line of **Total US Purchases: $10,655.97** as indicated by the previous query. When you run the report, it should produce the following results:

   Partial PROC SQL Output

```
                    2007 US Customer Purchases
                  Total US Purchases: $10,655.97

           Customer Name                      Purchases
           ────────────────────────────────────────────
           Karen Ballinger                    $3,479.09
           Cynthia Martinez                   $1,777.60
           Cynthia Mccluney                   $1,093.60
           Wynella Lewis                        $736.60
           Alvan Goheen                         $728.80
```

c. Automate the report that you wrote in step **5.b.**

1) Modify the query from step **5.a.** so that instead of producing output, it merely writes the values for **Country** and **Purchases** for the first returned row into macro variables called **Country** and **Country_Purchases**, respectively.

2) Modify the query that you wrote in step **5.b.** by substituting the macro variable reference **&Country** for each instance where you typed the value **US** in the query, and the macro reference **&Country_Purchases** in the second title line in place of the **$10,655.97** value that you typed previously. When you are finished, run the modified queries. The results should be exactly as produced in step **5.b.**

Hint: Do not forget to use double quotation marks around macro variable references! Review Syntax 1 for inserting values into macro variables, if necessary.

d. Starting with the code from step **5.c.**, modify the first query so that the country with the lowest total purchases is read into the macro variable instead of the highest. Then rerun both queries. The queries should produce the following results without further modification:

PROC SQL Output:

```
                       2007 IL Customer Purchases
                    Total IL Purchases:    $194.60


        Customer Name                             Purchases
        ─────────────────────────────────────────────────────
        Avinoam Zweig                               $194.60
```

Level 3

6. Using Dictionary Tables and Macro Variables to Build Low-Maintenance Code

Create a program which, when provided with a libref and the name of a table column, locates in the specified library all of the tables that contain the named column, and writes a custom SQL query that joins them all, producing an output table.

Use the program **s108e06** as a starting point. This is a partially completed utility program that will, when completed, identify all of the tables in any user-specified library. Then join them based on a user-specified common key column to produce a single output table. Your job is to complete the first three steps of the program, which create and populate the macro variables required by the fourth (already completed) section of the program. The fourth section of the program demonstrates SAS macro programming techniques that are outside the scope of an SQL class. Do not modify this section until you successfully completed the exercise.

In step **6.a.**, you write a query to create a macro variable and store the number of tables in the specified library that contains the common key column. In step **6.b.**, you write a second query that creates a series of macro variables storing the names of the individual tables. In step **6.c.**, you write a third query that creates a single macro variable containing a comma-delimited list of all the tables that contain the common key column.

The two %LET statements near the top of the program assign values to two macro variables: **Library** and **JoinVar**. When you write your portion of the program, reference those values (**&Library**, **&JoinVar**) wherever you type the SAS library libref or the column name in your program code.

Following the %LET statements, there are three sections reserved to write each of the three queries necessary to complete the program. They are clearly labeled with comments: **Query 1:**, **Query 2:**, and **Query 3:**. Remember not to edit the already completed macro program code that follows these sections.

a. In the section reserved for Query 1, write a PROC SQL query that counts the number of tables in **Library** that contains the column **JoinVar**. Write that value to a macro variable named **Rows**.

b. In the section reserved for Query 2, write a PROC SQL query that creates a series of macro variables called **Table1, Table2,... TableN**, that is, one for each of the tables in **Library** that contains the column **JoinVar**. You should use the macro variable **Rows**, created in the previous query, to determine the number of macro variables that you need (*N*).

c. In the section reserved for Query 3, write a PROC SQL query that creates a macro variable named **SourceTables**. **SourceTables** must contain a list of the fully-qualified names of all of the tables in **Library** that contain the column **JoinVar**. The names should be separated by commas. The contents should resemble the following: **LIBRARY.Table1, LIBRARY.Tables,... LIBRARY.TableN**.

d. After you create your queries, run the entire program. Review the SAS log. There should be only one error message located near the bottom of the SAS log.

Partial SAS Log

```
ERROR: ************* JoinTheTables Macro ********************
ERROR:  Column Some_Column_Name not found in any of the ORION tables
ERROR: ************* JoinTheTables Macro ********************
```

e. Near the top of the code, change the value assigned to **JoinVar** in the %LET statement to **Customer_ID** and rerun the program. Review the SAS log and explore the table produced by the program to answer the following questions:

   1) What is the name of the table produced? _____

   2) How many columns does the table contain? _____

   3) How many tables contain the column **Customer_ID**? _____

f. Change the value assigned to **JoinVar** in the %LET statement to **Product_ID** and rerun the program. Review the SAS log and explore the table produced by the program to answer the following questions:

   1) What is the name of the table produced? _____

   2) How many columns does the table contain? _____

   3) How many tables contain the column **Product_ID**? _____

8.4 Program Testing and Performance

Objectives

- Use PROC SQL and SAS system options to test and evaluate SQL performance.

113

Testing and Performance Options

PROC SQL statement options are available to aid in testing programs and evaluating performance.

Selected options include the following:

Option	Effect
EXEC|NOEXEC	controls whether or not submitted SQL statements are executed.
NOSTIMER|STIMER	reports performance statistics in the SAS log for each SQL statement.
NOERRORSTOP| ERRORSTOP	makes PROC SQL enter syntax-check mode after an error occurs; usually used in batch and non-interactive submissions.

114

To use the STIMER SQL option, the system option STIMER or FULLSTIMER must also be in effect.

Other PROC SQL statement options that are useful in testing include the following:

- INOBS=n
- OUTOBS=n

Testing and Performance Options

Display the columns that are retrieved when you use
SELECT * in a query, and display any macro variable
resolutions, but do not execute the query.

```
proc sql feedback noexec;
   select *
      from orion.Employee_payroll;
quit;
```

115   s108d10

Testing and Performance Options

Partial Log

```
NOTE: Statement transforms to:
        select EMPLOYEE_PAYROLL.Employee_ID,
EMPLOYEE_PAYROLL.Employee_Gender,
EMPLOYEE_PAYROLL.Salary, EMPLOYEE_PAYROLL.Birth_Date,
EMPLOYEE_PAYROLL.Employee_Hire_Date,
EMPLOYEE_PAYROLL.Employee_Term_Date,
EMPLOYEE_PAYROLL.Marital_Status, EMPLOYEE_PAYROLL.Dependents
         from orion.EMPLOYEE_PAYROLL;
NOTE: Statement not executed due to NOEXEC option.
```

116

Performance Benchmarking

System performance issues are usually caused by bottlenecks in one of three major resources:

- CPU
- Memory
- Input/Output (I/O)

An overload of any one of these resources can significantly increase the elapsed time required to execute your program.

117

Performance Benchmarking

You can use the STIMER or FULLSTIMER options to gather information on how your SAS programs use CPU, memory, and I/O.

General form of the OPTIONS statements:

OPTIONS STIMER;   **OPTIONS** FULLSTIMER;

The STIMER SAS system option causes SAS to print performance statistics in the SAS log for each DATA or PROC step executed. The FULLSTIMER option provides greater detail in performance reporting.

Not all statistics are available on all operating systems, so the results might differ between operating environments.

118

Performance Benchmarking

The STIMER option can also be specified as a PROC SQL option:

```
proc sql stimer;
```

When used in conjunction with the STIMER or FULLSTIMER SAS system option, the PROC SQL STIMER option provides CPU, memory, and I/O performance information for each individual statement executed by PROC SQL during a single invocation. This enables a more granular analysis of resource utilization.

119

Testing and Performance Options

Example: Capture performance statistics for a complex query.

```
options fullstimer;
proc sql stimer;
   select distinct catx(' ',scan(Employee_Name,2,','),
          scan(Employee_Name,1,',')) format=$25.
          as Manager,City
      from orion.Order_Fact as of,
           orion.Product_Dim as pd,
           orion.Employee_Organization as eo,
           orion.Employee_Addresses as ea
      where of.Product_ID=pd.Product_ID
            and of.Employee_ID=eo.Employee_ID
            and ea.Employee_ID=eo.Manager_ID
            and Product_Name contains 'Expedition Zero'
            and year(Order_Date)=2003
            and eo.Employee_ID ne 99999999
   ;
```

120   s108d10a

Testing and Performance Options

The statistics provided can vary with the operating system.

Partial SAS Logs from Selected Systems
Windows XP

```
NOTE: SQL Statement used (Total process time):
      real time          0.09 seconds
      user cpu time      0.00 seconds
      system cpu time    0.03 seconds
      Memory                          1606k
```

z/OS

```
NOTE: The SQL Statement used the following resources:
      CPU     time -        00:00:00.34
      Elapsed time -        00:00:04.23
      EXCP count   - 403
      Task  memory - 7250K (0K data, 7250K program)
      Total memory - 16564K (4000K data, 12564K program)
NOTE: The address space has used a maximum of 672K below the
      line and 18004K above the line.
```

121

If you want to gather your performance statistics into a SAS data set for analysis, you can download a set of SAS macros to help with that task from http://support.sas.com/rnd/scalability/tools/fullstim/logparse.zip.

The reported statistics can vary from operating system (O/S) to operating system, and might include the following:

Real Time	The elapsed time or "wall clock" time spent to execute a job or step. This is the time that the user waits for the job/step to complete. Utilization of shared host system resources by others can increase this metric significantly.
User CPU Time	The time spent by the processor executing user-written code. This includes all SAS code required to execute the SAS program you submit.
System CPU Time	The time spent by the processor executing O/S tasks to support user-written code (all CPU tasks required by your job that were **not** included in User CPU Time).
EXCP	A measure of I/O for IBM mainframe systems. Under z/OS, I/O is handled by the "**EX**ecute **C**hannel **P**rogram" system macro. The EXCP statistic reported is a count of the number of times the EXCP macro was called by your program.
Task Memory	The amount of memory allocated to a job/step, not including the memory required for SAS System overhead (SAS Manager and others).
Total Memory	The total amount of memory allocated to a SAS job, including that required to perform the job/step and the memory allocated to the SAS System for overhead tasks (SAS Manager and others).
Page Faults	A count of the number of data pages that required an I/O to retrieve. (A read was done to the I/O subsystem.)
Page Reclaims	A count of the data pages retrieved from system page memory. No I/O activity was required to access this data.
Page Swaps	The number of times a process was swapped out of main memory.
Voluntary Context Switches	Represents the number of times a process releases its CPU time-slice voluntarily before its time-slice allocation is expired. This usually happens when waiting for the return from an external resource, such as an I/O call for more data.
Involuntary Context Switches	The number of times that a process releases its CPU time-slice involuntarily. This usually happens when a CPU time-slice expires before the task was finished, or a higher priority task preempts the time-slice.
Block Input Operations	A count of the number of bufsize reads (I/O operations to read data from a mass storage device into memory). If the page requested is still cached in memory from a previous read, the data can be obtained without an additional I/O operation. (See **Page Reclaims**.)
Block Output Operations	A count of the number of bufsize writes (I/O operations to write data back to mass storage). Similar to block input operations, not all block outputs require I/O due to memory caching.

Benchmarking Guidelines

- Elapsed time is affected by concurrent tasks and should not normally be used for benchmarking.
- Always benchmark your programs in separate SAS sessions. If benchmarking is done on different methods within a single SAS session, statistics for the second method can be misleading. SAS might retain modules loaded into memory or the operating system might cache data read from a disk that was used in prior steps.

122

continued...

Benchmarking Guidelines

- Run each program multiple times and average the performance statistics.
- Use realistic data for tests. Method A could be much more efficient than Method B when applied to small tables, but much less efficient on large tables.

123

8.5 Chapter Review

Chapter Review

Name the PROC SQL option:

Option	Effect
	syntax-checks SQL statements without attempting execution.
	limits the number of rows a query outputs.
	causes wide text columns to wrap in its own column rather than wrapping an entire row.

124

Chapter Review

Consider the following program:

```
proc sql noprint;
   select avg(Salary)
      into :MeanSalary
      from orion.Employee_payroll;
   title 'Those with Salaries > $&MeanSalary';
   reset print;
   select Employee_ID, Salary
      from orion.Employee_payroll
   where Salary > &MeanSalary;
```

1. What is the effect of the SELECT... INTO statement?

2. Will the first query produce results in the Output window?

126

Chapter Review

Consider the following program:

```
proc sql noprint;
   select avg(Salary)
      into :MeanSalary
      from orion.Employee_payroll;
   title 'Those with Salaries > $&MeanSalary';
   reset print;
   select Employee_ID, Salary
      from orion.Employee_payroll
   where Salary > &MeanSalary;
```

3. If `avg(Salary)` = 38041.51, what will be the title on
    the final report?

    a. **Those with Salaries > $&MeanSalary**

    b. **Those with Salaries > $38041.51**

    c. None. No results are written to the Output window.

128

8.6 Solutions

Solutions to Exercises

1. **Using PROC SQL Options and Displaying the Contents of a Dictionary Table**

   a.

```
*** s108s01 ***;
proc sql flow=6 35;
title "Dictionary Tables";
   select distinct memname,memlabel
      from dictionary.Dictionaries
;
quit;
title;
```

   b.

```
proc sql;
   select Memname, type, length
      from dictionary.Columns
      where libname="ORION"
            and upcase(Name)="CUSTOMER_ID"
;
quit;
```

2. **Using PROC SQL Options and Displaying Dictionary Table Information**

   a.

```
*** s108s02 ***;
proc sql flow=6 35;
title "Dictionary Tables";
   select memname as Table, memlabel as Contents,
          count(*) as Columns
      from dictionary.Dictionaries
      group by Table, Contents
;
quit;
title;
```

   b.

```
proc sql flow=6 35;
   select memname "Table",
          nobs "Rows",
          nvar "Columns",
          filesize "File Size",
          maxvar 'Widest Column',
          maxlabel 'Widest Label'
      from dictionary.tables
      where libname='ORION'
            and memtype ne 'VIEW'
;
quit;
```

3. **Using PROC SQL Options, SAS System Options, and Dictionary Tables to Document Data Tables in the Orion Star Library**

```
*** s108s03 ***;
  /**************************************************
    This query remerges summary data and will not work
    if OPTIONS SQLREMERGE=NO is in effect.
  **************************************************/

options ls=85 ps=20;
ods listing close;
ods pdf file="ORION Library Table Documentation.PDF" style=journal;
ods proclabel "ORION Library Tables";

proc  sql flow=2 25;
title "ORION Library Table Information";
footnote "* Largest in the Library";
   select memname "Table",
          cats(nobs,
               case
                  when nobs=max(nobs) then "*"
                  else ""
                end) "Rows",
          cats(nvar,
               case
                  when nvar=max(nvar) then "*"
                  else ""
               end) "Columns",
          cats(put(filesize,comma12.),
               case
                  when filesize=max(filesize) then "*"
                   else ""
               end) "File Size (Bytes)",
          cats(maxvar,
               case
                  when maxvar=max(maxvar) then "*"
                  else ""
               end) 'Widest Column'
     from dictionary.tables
     where libname='ORION'
          and memtype ne 'VIEW'
;
quit;
title;
ods pdf close;
ods listing;
footnote;
```

4. Creating and Using Macro Variables

a.

```
*** s108s04 ***;

proc sql;
title "Highest Salary in Employee_payroll";
   select max(Salary)
       from orion.Employee_Payroll
;
quit;
title;
```

b.

```
%let DataSet=Employee_Payroll;
%let VariableName=Salary;
%put NOTE:  DataSet=&DataSet, VariableName=&VariableName;
```

c.

```
proc sql;
title "Highest &VariableName in &DataSet";
   select max(&VariableName)
       from orion.&DataSet
;
quit;
title;
```

d.

```
%let DataSet=Price_List;
%let VariableName=Unit_Sales_Price;
proc sql;
title "Highest &VariableName in &DataSet";
   select max(&VariableName)
       from orion.&DataSet
;
quit;
title;
```

5. Creating a Macro Variable from an SQL Query

a.

```
*** s108s05 ***;
proc sql;
title "2007 Purchases by Country";
   select Country,
          sum(Total_Retail_Price) format=dollar10.2 as Purchases
   from orion.Customer as c,
        orion.Order_fact as o
   where c.Customer_ID=o.Customer_ID
     and year(Order_Date)=2007
   group by Country
   order by Purchases desc
;
quit;
title;
```

b.

```
proc sql;
title   "2007 US Customer Purchases";
title2 "Total US Purchases: $10,655.97" ;
   select Customer_Name,
          sum(Total_Retail_Price) format=dollar10.2 as Purchases
      from orion.Customer as c,
           orion.Order_fact as o
      where c.Customer_ID=o.Customer_ID
        and year(Order_Date)=2007
        and Country="US"
      group by Customer_Name
      order by Purchases desc
;
quit;
title;
```

c.

```
proc sql noprint;
   select Country,
          sum(Total_Retail_Price) format=dollar10.2 as Purchases
          into :Country, :Country_Purchases
      from orion.Customer as c,
           orion.Order_fact as o
      where c.Customer_ID=o.Customer_ID
        and year(Order_Date)=2007
      group by Country
      order by Purchases desc
;
reset print;

title   "2007 &Country Customer Purchases";
title2 "Total &Country Purchases: &Country_Purchases";
```

```
    select Customer_Name,
           sum(Total_Retail_Price) format=dollar10.2 as Purchases
      from orion.Customer as c,
           orion.Order_fact as o
      where c.Customer_ID=o.Customer_ID
        and year(Order_Date)=2007
        and Country="&Country"
      group by Customer_Name
      order by Purchases desc
   ;
quit;
title;
```

d.

```
proc sql noprint;
   select Country,
          sum(Total_Retail_Price) format=dollar10.2 as Purchases
          into :Country, :Country_Purchases
     from orion.Customer as c,
          orion.Order_fact as o
     where c.Customer_ID=o.Customer_ID
       and year(Order_Date)=2007
     group by Country
     order by Purchases /* ascending requires no keyword */
   ;
reset print;
title  "2007 &Country Customer Purchases";
title2 "Total &Country Purchases: &Country_Purchases" ;
select Customer_Name,
       sum(Total_Retail_Price) As Purchases
       format=dollar10.2
  from orion.Customer as c,
       orion.Order_fact as o
  where c.Customer_ID=o.Customer_ID
    and year(Order_Date)=2007
    and Country="&Country"
  group by Customer_Name
  order by Purchases desc
   ;
quit;
title;
```

6. Using Dictionary Tables and Macro Variables to Build Low-Maintenance Code

a.

```
*** s108s06 ***;
  /* Warning: Case sensitive! */
%let JoinVar=Some_Column_Name;
%let Library=%upcase(ORION);
proc sql noprint;
   select strip(put(count(*),5.))
          into :Rows
```

```
        from dictionary.columns
        where libname="&Library"
                and name="&JoinVar"
;
quit;
```

b.

```
proc sql noprint;
    select memname
        into :Table1-:Table&Rows
    from dictionary.columns
    where libname="&Library"
        and name="&JoinVar"
;
quit;
```

c.

```
proc sql noprint;
    select catx('.',libname,memname)
        into :SourceTables separated by ','
        from dictionary.columns
        where libname="&Library"
                and NAME="&JoinVar"
;
quit;

    /***************************************************
        For the exercise, do not edit below this line!
    ***************************************************/

    /***************************************************
    This macro program joins all the tables in Library
    which contain the column JoinVar by JoinVar, producing
    a table called Joined_By_JoinVar. By default, the table
    is created in the work library. For example, if
        JoinVar = Employee_ID
    then the table produced is
        work.Joined_by_employee_id
    ***************************************************/

options mprint;
%Macro JoinTheTables(OutLib);
%if &OutLib= %then %let OutLib=work;
%if &Rows gt 1 %then %do;
    %do i=1 %to &rows;
        proc sql noprint;
            select catx('.',"&&Table&i",Name)
                into :&&Table&i.._Columns separated by ","
                from Dictionary.Columns
                where libname="&Library"
                        and MEMNAME="&&Table&i"
                        and Name ne "&JoinVar"
```

```
        ;
        quit;
        %end;
    %put _user_;
```

(Continued on the next page.)

```
    proc sql;
    create table &OutLib..Joined_by_&JoinVar AS
        select &&Table1..&JoinVar
    %do i=1 %to &Rows;
        %let ThisColumn=&&&Table&i.._Columns;
        , &&&ThisColumn
    %end;
        from &SourceTables
        where &Table1..&JoinVar=&Table2..&JoinVar
    %do i=2 %to %eval(&Rows-1);
        %let j=%eval(&i+1);
        and &&Table&i...&JoinVar=&&Table&j...&JoinVar
    %end;
    ;
    quit;
        %put NOTE: ************* JoinTheTables Macro *************;
        %put NOTE: Column &JoinVar found was found in &Rows tables;
        %put NOTE: ************* JoinTheTables Macro *************;
    %end;
    %else %if &Rows=1 %then %do;
        %put NOTE: ************* JoinTheTables Macro *************;
        %put NOTE: Column &JoinVar found only in               ;
        %put NOTE: &Library..&Table1 table                     ;
        %put NOTE: No join could be performed                  ;
        %put NOTE: ************* JoinTheTables Macro *************;
    %end;
    %else %do;
        %put ERROR: ************* JoinTheTables Macro *************;
        %put ERROR: Column &JoinVar not found in any            ;
        %put ERROR: of the &Library tables                      ;
        %put ERROR: ************* JoinTheTables Macro *************;
    %end;
%mend;

%JoinTheTables;
```

d. No solution is required.

e. For the **Customer_ID** column:

1) What is the name of the table produced? **work.Joined_by_Customer_ID**

2) How many columns does the table contain? **22**

3) How many tables contained the column **Customer_ID**? **2**

f. For the **Product_ID** column:

1) What is the name of the table produced? <u>**work.Joined_by_Product_ID**</u>

2) How many columns does the table contain? <u>**24**</u>

3) How many tables contained the column **Product_ID**? <u>**3**</u>

Solutions to Student Activities (Polls/Quizzes)

8.01 Multiple Answer Poll – Correct Answer

Review: Specifying the NOEXEC option in a PROC SQL statement does which of the following?

(a.) Prevents statement execution for the current invocation of PROC SQL

b. Applies only to the SELECT statement

(c.) Checks SQL query syntax without actually executing the statements

d. Displays rewritten PROC SQL statements after references are expanded and certain other transformations are made

7

8.02 Quiz – Correct Answer

Without re-invoking PROC SQL, add a statement before the second query that does the following:

- displays output rows without row numbers
- ensures that only nine rows are output

```
reset nonumber outobs=9;
```

This statement displays output rows without row numbers and ensures that only nine rows are output without re-invoking PROC SQL.

26

8.03 Quiz – Correct Answer

In your SAS session's SAS Explorer window, navigate to the Sashelp library by selecting **libraries** ⇨ **SASHELP**. Scroll down to examine the Sashelp views.

Which view shows the names and data types of all the columns in every table available in the SAS session?

SASHELP.vcolumn

46

8.04 Quiz – Correct Answer

How many changes must be made to the program to generate a report showing how many Engineering Department employees earn above-average salaries?

One. Modify the value assigned to the macro variable Dept in the %LET statement.

```
%let Dept=Engineering;
```

87

8.05 Multiple Choice Poll – Correct Answer

Why did the first query in the program produce output, while the second query did not?

a. The INTO clause suppressed output during the execution of the second query.

b. The RESET NOPRINT statement suppressed output for subsequent queries in this PROC SQL invocation.

c. The %PUT statement redirected the query results to the SAS log.

98

Solutions to Chapter Review

Chapter Review Answers

Name the PROC SQL option:

Option	Effect
NOEXEC	syntax-checks SQL statements without attempting execution.
OUTOBS=	limits the number of rows a query outputs.
FLOW=	causes wide text columns to wrap in its own column rather than wrapping an entire row.

125

Chapter Review Answers

Consider the following program:

```
proc sql noprint;
   select avg(Salary)
      into :MeanSalary
      from orion.Employee_payroll;
   title 'Those with Salaries > $&MeanSalary';
   reset print;
   select Employee_ID, Salary
      from orion.Employee_payroll
   where Salary > &MeanSalary;
```

1. What is the effect of the SELECT... INTO statement?
   The results are written into the macro variable MeanSalary.

2. Will the first query produce results in the Output window?
   No, the NOPRINT option is in effect.

127

Chapter Review Answers

Consider the following program:

```
proc sql noprint;
   select avg(Salary)
      into :MeanSalary
      from orion.Employee_payroll;
   title 'Those with Salaries > $&MeanSalary';
   reset print;
   select Employee_ID, Salary
      from orion.Employee_payroll
   where Salary > &MeanSalary;
```

3. If `avg(Salary)` = 38041.51, what will be the title on the final report?

   a.) **Those with Salaries > $&MeanSalary**

   The RESET PRINT statement restores SQL procedure output, but the single quotation marks in the TITLE statement prevent the macro variable from resolving.

129

Chapter 9   Managing Tables

9.1   Introduction to Indexes

Objectives

- Describe the functions of an index.
- Determine if the SQL optimizer elected to use an index to process an SQL query.
- Take explicit control of index usage in an SQL query.

3

What Is an Index?

An *index* is an auxiliary data structure that stores information about the location of indexed table rows, based on the values in one or more **key** columns.

You can index both character and numeric columns.

4

The index can boost program performance by serving as a logical pointer to a physical location of a given value.

What Is an Index?

Indexed SAS Data Table

Obs	ID	Loc	Level
1	1001	US	I
2	1002	AU	II
3	1003	AU	III
4	1004	US	III
5	1005	US	II

Index File - Key=Level

Key Value	Location of Obs Page(obs,obs,…)	
I	1(1,…)	2(…) …
II	1(2,5,…)	2(…) …
III	1(3,4…)	2(…) …

Query Code

```
proc sql;
   select *
      from Table
      where Level='II';
```

Data Processed

Obs	ID	Loc	Level
2	1002	AU	II
5	1005	US	II

5

Why Use Indexes?

The SQL procedure can use available indexes to optimize data subsetting or joining tasks.

6

Why Use Indexes?

Indexes can provide fast access to small subsets of data.

```
proc sql;
   select *
      from orion.Staff
      where Job_Title='Sales Rep. I';
```

'Sales Rep. I' is one of many distinct values of the variable Job_Title.

7

A small subset is ≤ 15%.

Why Use Indexes?

Indexes can enhance join performance, especially equijoins.

```
proc sql;
   select *
      from orion.Employee_payroll,
           orion.Employee_addresses
      where Employee_payroll.Employee_ID=
            Employee_addresses.Employee_ID;
```

Performance of this equijoin on Employee_ID could be improved by using an index.

8

An index selected by the SQL Optimizer can improve the performance of WHERE clauses, even when using TRIM or SUBSTR functions and CONTAINS or LIKE operators.

Index Terminology

Two types of indexes are as follows:

- Simple
  - based on values of only one column
- Composite
  - based on values of more than one column, concatenated to form a single value, for example, `Product_ID` and `Order_ID`
  - can include mixed variable types, that is, a composite index might contain both character and numeric variables

✎ A table can have multiple simple and composite indexes.

9

Using an Index

If an index is available, the SQL Optimizer first estimates both the effects of using and not using the index, and then chooses the most efficient method to process a query.

You can use the MSGLEVEL system option to increase the detail level of SAS log messages, alerting you to when an index was used.

```
OPTIONS MSGLEVEL = N | I;
```

N = prints notes, warnings, and error messages only. N is the default.

I = prints additional notes pertaining to index usage, merge processing, and sort utilities.

10

Using an Index

Example: The compound index **Locale** was created on
the **City**, **State**, and **Country** columns
of **work.Employee_addresses**.

Use the MSGLEVEL=I system option to
determine which queries used the index.

Partial SAS Log

> The INFO message applies only
> to the preceding WHERE clause.

```
options msglevel = i;
proc sql;
   select *
      from work.Employee_addresses
      where State in ('CA','PA');
INFO:Index Locale selected for WHERE clause optimization.

   select *
      from work.Employee_addresses
      where Postal_Code ='33135';
```

11   s109d01a

Using an Index

Example: The compound index **Locale** was created on
the **City**, **State**, and **Country** columns
of **work.Employee_addresses**.

Use the MSGLEVEL=I system option to
determine which queries used the index.

Partial SAS Log

```
options msglevel = i;
proc sql;
   select *
      from work.Employee_addresses
      where State in ('CA','PA');
INFO:Index Locale selected for WHERE clause optimization.

   select *
      from work.Employee_addresses
      where Postal_Code ='33135';
```

> No index for
> **Postal_Code**

12   s109d01a

Using an Index

Example: The compound index **Locale** was created on
the **City**, **State**, and **Country** columns
of **work.Employee_addresses**.

Use the MSGLEVEL=I system option to
determine which queries used the index.

Partial SAS Log

The INFO message applies only
to the preceding WHERE clause.

```
options msglevel = i;
proc sql;
   select *
      from work.Employee_addresses
      where State in ('CA','PA');
INFO:Index Locale selected for WHERE clause optimization.

   select *
      from work.Employee_addresses
      where Postal_Code ='33135';
```

No index for
Postal_Code

13   s109d01a

Setup for the Poll

Submit the program **s109a01** to do the following:

- Create the table **work.Employee_addresses**.
- Add a composite index named **Locale** based on the
  columns **City**, **State**, and **Country**.
- Run three queries against the table.

Review your SAS log.

15

9.01 Multiple Choice Poll

Which query (or queries) used the **Locale** index?

a. Query 1 (State)
b. Query 2 (State and City)
c. Query 3 (City)
d. Queries 1 and 2
e. Queries 1 and 3
f. All queries used the index
g. None of the above

16

Controlling Index Usage

Two data set options can be used to explicitly control the use of indexes in WHERE expressions:

- IDXWHERE=YES | NO
- IDXNAME=*<name>*

18   ...

Controlling Index Usage

Two data set options can be used to explicitly control
the use of indexes in WHERE expressions:

```
Forces index usage
```

- IDXWHERE=YES | NO
- IDXNAME=<name>

These two options are not used in combination. Using
the IDXNAME= option implies IDXWHERE=YES.

19

Controlling Index Usage

Two data set options can be used to explicitly control
the use of indexes in WHERE expressions:

- IDXWHERE=YES | NO ← Prevents index usage
- IDXNAME=<name>

These two options are not used in combination. Using
the IDXNAME= option implies IDXWHERE=YES.

20

Controlling Index Usage

Two data set options can be used to explicitly control
the use of indexes in WHERE expressions:

- IDXWHERE=YES | NO
- IDXNAME=<*name*> ← Forces usage of a specific named index

These two options are not used in combination. Using
the IDXNAME= option implies IDXWHERE=YES.

21

Controlling Index Usage

Two data set options can be used to explicitly control the use of indexes in WHERE expressions:

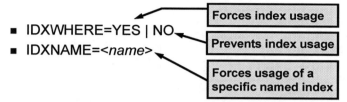

- IDXWHERE=YES | NO
- IDXNAME=<name>

| Forces index usage |
| Prevents index usage |
| Forces usage of a specific named index |

These two options are not used in combination. Using the IDXNAME= option implies IDXWHERE=YES.

22

When the IDXWHERE= option is

YES   SAS uses the best available index to process the WHERE expression, even if SAS estimates that sequential processing is faster.

NO   SAS processes the data sequentially even if SAS estimates that processing with an index is better.

When the IDXNAME= option is <name>, SAS uses the named index regardless of performance estimates.

If you do not use the IDXWHERE= option, the SAS SQL Optimizer chooses whether or not to use an index. You can use either the IDXWHERE= or the IDXNAME= data set option, but not both.

Often, only the first variable of a composite index is used. For example, the following WHERE expression can be resolved using the composite index defined above because **City** is the first key variable in the composite index:

```
where City='Melbourne';
```

However, you can take advantage of all key variables in a composite index by the way you construct the WHERE expression. This technique is referred to as compound optimization. *Compound optimization* is the process of optimizing multiple conditions on multiple variables, which are joined with a logical operator such as AND, using a composite index. If you issue the following WHERE expression, the composite index is used to find all occurrences of **City="San Diego"** and **State="CA"** and **Country="US"**. In this way, all of the conditions are satisfied with a single search of the index:

```
where City="San Diego" and State="CA" and Country="US"
```

  When you decide whether to create a simple index or a composite index, consider how you will access the data. If you often access data for a single variable, a simple index is adequate. If you frequently access data for multiple variables, a composite index could be beneficial.

9.2 Creating Indexes (Self-Study)

Objectives
- Create an index.
- Explain the costs and benefits of indexes.

24

Creating an Index

General form of the CREATE INDEX statement:

```
CREATE <UNIQUE> INDEX index-name
    ON table-name(column-name<, ...column-name>);
```

Precede the INDEX keyword with the UNIQUE keyword to define a unique index. A unique index ensures that no rows have duplicate index values.

25

Use of the optional UNIQUE keyword ensures that values in the row are unique. If a table contains multiple occurrences of the same value, the index will not be created, and an error message is issued in the SAS log. Similarly, if you attempt to add a duplicate value to a table with a unique index applied, the row will be rejected, and an error message is written to the SAS log and indicates that duplicate values are not allowed. Unique indexes are frequently applied to columns containing identifier information, such as driver's license, Social Security, or account numbers to prevent inadvertently adding duplicate records.

Creating an Index

Rules for naming indexes are as follows:

- All indexes must be named.
- Simple index names must match the name of the column being indexed.
- Composite index names cannot be the same as any column name in the table.

26

Index-naming rules are the same as the rules for other SAS data files. Start with a letter or underscore, and continue with a combination of letters, underscores, or numbers, with a 32-character maximum.

- Avoid using the same variable in multiple indexes.
- Index performance is improved if you sort the data before creating the index.

Creating a Unique Simple Index

- Designate the key columns.
- Select a name for the index. Remember that a simple index must have the same name as the column.
- Specify whether the index is to be unique.

```
proc sql;
   create unique index Employee_ID
      on work.Employee_addresses
         (Employee_ID)
;
```

30   s109d01

Creating a Composite Index

- Designate the key columns.
- Select a name for the index. Remember that a composite index cannot have the same name as a table column.
- Specify whether the index is to be unique. (In this case, the index is **not** unique.)

```
proc sql;
   create index Locale
      on work.Employee_addresses
         (State, City)
;
```

34   s109d01

Understanding Variable Order

The order in which the variables are listed when you create a composite index affects when it can be used.

```
proc sql;
   create index Locale
      on work.Employee_Addresses
         (State, City);
```

Sample Query WHERE Clause	LOCALE Index Used?
State="value"	Yes
State="value" and City="value"	Yes
City="value"	No

35

Indexing and Performance

Indexing Guidelines:

- Minimizing the number of indexes reduces disk storage and update costs.
- Indexes perform best when they retrieve 15% or fewer rows in a table.
- Indexes based on uniformly distributed, low cardinality columns, that is, columns with few distinct values, are not usually useful. For example, the `Gender` column values are either `Male` or `Female`, and the population is about 50% male and 50% female. This column is not suitable for a simple index; sequential access is faster.
- Do not create indexes on small tables; sequential access is faster.

36

Indexing and Performance: Tradeoffs

Benefits	Costs
Indexing enables fast access to small (≤15%) subsets of data.	CPU cycles and I/O to create indexes
Equijoins can be performed without sorting.	CPU cycles and I/O to update the index whenever data changes
BY-group processing can be performed without sorting.	Memory to load index pages and code for use
Uniqueness can be enforced.	Disk space to store the index file

37

9.02 Quiz

You frequently need to subset the
`orion.Order_fact` data set, based on
`Order_Type`.

Submit the program **s109a02** and review the output.

Should you index this column to improve query performance?

39

 **Exercises**

Level 1

1. Creating an Index and Using It in a Query

 a. Open and submit the starter program **s109e01** to create a temporary table **work.Products**, which will contain only unique records from **orion.Product_dim**.

 b. Modify the starter program code to create an index on the **work.Products** table based on the column **Product_Name**. Remember to give the simple index the same name as the column on which it is based.

 c. Write a query that returns the rows from **work.Products** where the **Product_Name** column contains the word "T-Shirt." Set **options msglevel=I** before running your report to put notes in the SAS log about index usage. Name your report **T-Shirt list**. Review the SAS log. Were any indexes used to process this query? (Yes or No) _____

  PROC SQL Output

```
                            T-Shirt list

    Product Name                          Supplier Name

    Big Guy Men's T-Shirt                 Eclipse Inc
    Big Guy Men's T-Shirt Dri Fit         Eclipse Inc
    Butch T-Shirt with V-Neck             Luna sastreria S.A.
    Eliza T-Shirt                         Luna sastreria S.A.
    Fred T-Shirt                          Luna sastreria S.A.
    Instyle T-Shirt                       AllSeasons Outdoor Clothing
    Kid Children's T-Shirt                3Top Sports
    Men's T-Shirt Small Logo              A Team Sports
    N.d.gear Basic T-Shirt                Greenline Sports Ltd
    O'my Children's T-Shirt with Logo     Luna sastreria S.A.
    Osprey Men's King T-Shirt w/Small Logo Triple Sportswear Inc
    Roth T-Shirt                          Luna sastreria S.A.
    T-Shirt                               3Top Sports
    T-Shirt, Short-sleeved, Big Logo      A Team Sports
    Toncot Beefy-T Emb T-Shirt            A Team Sports
    Tony's Cut & Sew T-Shirt              Eclipse Inc
    Triffy Logo T-Shirt with V-Neck       Triffy B.V.
    Tyfoon Ketch T-Shirt                  Typhoon Clothing
    Woman's T-Shirt w/Hood                Eclipse Inc
    Wyoming Men's T-Shirt with V-Neck     Luna sastreria S.A.
```

Level 2

2. Creating a Unique Index and Writing a Query Using the Indexed Variable

   a. Using the program **s109e02** as starter code, create a temporary table **work.Products** that contains only unique records from **orion.Product_dim**. Create a unique index on your **work.Products** table based on the column **Product_ID**.

   b. Write a query that joins **work.Products** and **orion.Order_fact** on **Product_ID** and produces a report of the distinct combinations of **Product_Name** and **Supplier_Name** for records where the year of the **Order_Date** is 2007. Name your report as shown in the sample output.

   Partial PROC SQL Output

2007 Products Purchased	
Product Name	Supplier Name
A-team Smoothsport Bra	A Team Sports
A-team Sweat Round Neck, Small Logo	A Team Sports
Abdomen Shaper	TrimSport B.V.
Aim4it 80% Tungsten 22 Gram	Royal Darts Ltd

   c. Name the indexes, if any, selected by the SQL processor to optimize the query:

   _____

   _____

Level 3

3. Creating Indexes and Writing a Query Using the Indexed Variables

   a. Use the program **s109e03** as starter code.

   1) Create temporary tables: **work.Customers**, **work.Orders**, and **work.Products**.

   2) Create a unique index on the **work.Customers** table based on the column **Customer_ID**.

   3) Create an index on the **work.Orders** table based on the column **Customer_ID**.

   4) Create a unique index on the **work.Products** table based on the column **Product_ID**.

b. Write a query that joins **work.Customers**, **work.Orders**, and **work.Products** to produce a report that contains **Product_Name** and **Supplier_Name** for orders placed in 2007 by customers from South Africa (country code ZA). The report should include only one line for each combination of **Product_Name** and **Supplier_Name**. Name your report appropriately.

PROC SQL Output:

```
              Products Ordered by South African Customers in 2007

   Product Name                          Supplier Name
   _____

   A-team Smoothsport Bra                A Team Sports
   Buzz Saw                              CrystalClear Optics Inc
   Children's Roller Skates              Magnifico Sports
   Dartsharpener Key ring                Royal Darts Ltd
   Fred T-Shirt                          Luna sastreria S.A.
   Goodtime Toilet Bag                   Luna sastreria S.A.
   Hot Mini Backboard Bulls              Van Dammeren International
   Pro-roll Hot Rod Roller Skates        Magnifico Sports
   Pro-roll Lazer Roller Skates          Magnifico Sports
   Proskater Kitalpha Gamma Roller Skates Roll-Over Inc
   Proskater Viablade S Roller Skates    Roll-Over Inc
   Rollerskate  Roller Skates            Magnifico Sports
   Ex9 76mm/78a Biofl
```

c. Name the indexes, if any, selected by the SQL processor to optimize the query.

_____

_____

9.3 Maintaining Tables

Objectives

- Update or delete data values in an existing table.
- Add, drop, or alter the attributes of columns in a table.
- Delete tables, views, and indexes.
- Update data values in an existing view. (Self-Study)

44

Maintaining Tables: Overview

You can use PROC SQL to change table data by doing the following:

- adding rows to a table or view
- modifying values of existing rows in a table or view
- deleting rows from a table or view

45

continued...

Maintaining Tables: Overview

You can use PROC SQL to modify table structure
by doing the following:

- altering the column attributes of a table
- adding or dropping columns
- adding or dropping constraints
- completely deleting a table, view, or index

✎ The user must have the necessary permissions
to perform table management actions.

46

Review: Adding Data to a Table

You can add data to a table using the INSERT statement
and one of three methods:

Method	Syntax	Description
A	**INSERT INTO** *table-name* **SET** *column-name=value,* *column-name=value,...;*	One clause per row using column-value pairs
B	**INSERT INTO** *table-name* *<(column list)>* **VALUES** (*value,value,...*);	One clause per row using positional values
C	**INSERT INTO** *table-name* *<(column list)>* **SELECT** *columns* **FROM** *table-name*;	A query returning multiple rows, and based on positional values

47

Modifying Data Values in Existing Rows

Use the UPDATE statement to modify column values in existing rows of a table or SAS/ACCESS view.

General form of the UPDATE statement:

UPDATE *table-name*
    SET *column-name=expression,*
        < , ...column-name=expression>
    WHERE *expression*;

 Omitting the WHERE expression causes **all** rows to be updated.

48

Modifying Data Values in Existing Rows

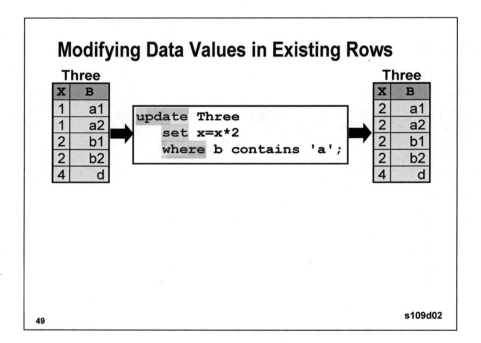

Three	
X	B
1	a1
1	a2
2	b1
2	b2
4	d

```
update Three
    set x=x*2
    where b contains 'a';
```

Three	
X	B
2	a1
2	a2
2	b1
2	b2
4	d

49
s109d02

Modifying Data Values in Existing Rows

Example: Give first-level sales representatives a 5% raise.

```
proc sql;
   update work.Sales
      set Salary=Salary * 1.05
      where Job_Title = 'Sales Rep. I';
quit;
```

50   s109d03

You cannot create additional columns using the UPDATE statement.

A SAS DATA step equivalent is as follows:

```
data work.Sales;
   modify work.Sales;
      if Job_Title='Sales Rep. I' then
         Salary=Salary * 1.05;
run;
```

Conditional Processing (Review)

General form of the CASE expression in the SELECT statement:

```
SELECT column-1<, ...column-n>
    CASE <case-operand>
    WHEN when-condition THEN result-expression
    <WHEN when-condition THEN result-expression>
    <ELSE result-expression>
END <AS column>
FROM table;
```

51

If no ELSE expression is present and every WHEN condition is false, the result of the CASE expression is a missing value.

Business Scenario

The company is reorganizing, and will use new descriptors for a person's job mastery level.

A new column, **Level**, was added to the **work.Staff** table to contain this information.

Your job is to populate the data, based on the following rules:

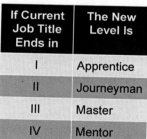

If Current Job Title Ends in	The New Level Is
I	Apprentice
II	Journeyman
III	Master
IV	Mentor

52

Conditional Data Modification

```
proc sql;
   update work.Staff
      set Level=
         case (scan(Job_Title,-1))
            when 'I'    then 'Apprentice'
            when 'II'   then 'Journeyman'
            when 'III'  then 'Master'
            when 'IV'   then 'Mentor'
            else ''
         end;
   select Employee_ID, Job_Title, Level
      from work.Staff;
quit;
```

s109d04

53

Conditional Data Modification

Partial Output

Employee ID	Employee Job Title	Level
120101	Director	
120102	Sales Manager	
120103	Sales Manager	
120104	Administration Manager	
120105	Secretary I	Apprentice
120106	Office Assistant II	Journeyman
120107	Office Assistant III	Master
120108	Warehouse Assistant II	Journeyman
120109	Warehouse Assistant I	Apprentice
120110	Warehouse Assistant III	Master
120111	Security Guard II	Journeyman
120112	Security Guard I	Apprentice
120113	Security Guard II	Journeyman

54

Deleting Rows from a Table or View

Use the DELETE statement to eliminate unwanted rows from a table.

General form of the DELETE statement:

> **DELETE FROM** *table|view*
> **WHERE** *expression*;

 A DELETE statement without a WHERE expression deletes **all** rows, and leaves only the table structure.

55

Deleting Rows from a Table or View

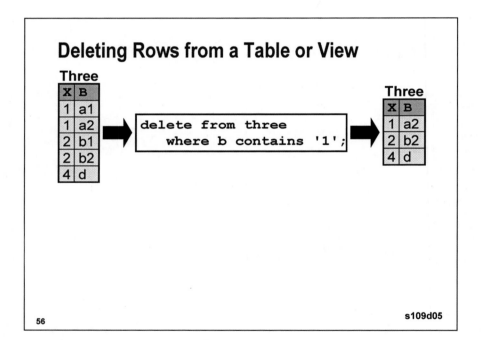

56

s109d05

Deleting Rows from a Table or View

Example: Delete all terminated employees from
the **work.Staff** table.

```
proc sql;
   delete from work.Staff
      where Emp_Term_Date is not missing
;
quit;
```

Partial Log

```
NOTE: 116 rows were deleted from WORK.STAFF.
```

s109d05a

57

9.03 Quiz

Submit the program **s109a03** and review the SAS log.

How many rows were deleted from the temporary
table **work.Staff**?

59

Altering Table Data

Method	Result
INSERT – SET – VALUES	appends new data rows to the end of existing tables.
UPDATE – SET – CASE	modifies values in existing data rows as specified in the WHERE expression.
DELETE	deletes existing rows as specified in the WHERE expression.

61

Altering Table Structure

Use the ALTER statement to manipulate columns in a table three different ways.

General form of the ALTER statement:

```
ALTER TABLE table-name
    ADD column-definition< , ... column-definition>
    DROP column-1<, ...column-2>
    MODIFY column-definition<, ...column-definition>;
```

62

Altering Table Structure

1. Add columns to a table.

```
proc sql;
   alter table orion.Employee_payroll
      add Bonus num format=comma10.2,
         Level char(3)
;
```

You are *enlarging* the table.

63

After adding columns, use the UPDATE statement to assign values to those columns. These added columns initially contain missing values.

Altering Table Structure

2. Drop columns from a table.

```
proc sql;
   alter table orion.Employee_payroll
      drop Birth_Date
;
```

You are *shrinking* the table.

64

Altering Table Structure

3. Modify attributes of existing columns in a table. You can alter a column's length, informat, format, and label.

```
proc sql;
   alter table orion.Employee_payroll
      modify Bonus num format=comma8.2,
             Level char(10)
             label='Employee Level';
quit;
```

✎ PROC SQL cannot modify a column's name or data type.

65

The STRIP Function

The STRIP function returns a character string with all leading and trailing blanks removed.

General form of the STRIP function:

STRIP(*argument*)

argument   A variable name, character constant, or expression that produces a character value

66

Adding and Modifying Columns

Example: Alter the `work.Sales_staff` table as follows:

1. Add new columns named **First** and **Last**.
2. Format the **Birth_Date** column with the **MMDDYY10.** format.

```
proc sql;
   alter table work.Sales_staff
      add First char(10), Last Char(20)
      modify Birth_Date date format=mmddyy10.
   ;
```

s109d06
continued...

67

Populating Newly Added Columns

3. Populate columns **First** and **Last**.

```
proc sql;
   alter table work.Sales_staff
      add First char(10), Last Char(20)
      modify Birth_Date date format=mmddyy10.
   ;
   update work.Sales_staff
      set First=strip(scan(Name,2,',')),
          Last=strip(scan(Name,1,','))
   ;
```

s109d06
continued...

68

Testing Your Work

4. Test the results

```
update work.Sales_staff
   set First=strip(scan(Name,2,',')),
       Last=strip(scan(Name,1,','))
;
select Name, First, Last
   from work.Sales_staff
   where First ne strip(scan(Name,2,','))
         or Last  ne strip(scan(Name,1,','))
;
```

69

s109d06
continued...

Testing Your Work

4. Test the results.

PROC SQL Output

Name	First	Last
Boocks, Michael. R.	Michael. R	Boocks
Plybon, John-Michael	John-Micha	Plybon

⚠ The first name is truncated. The column needs to be wider.

70

continued...

Modifying Columns

5. Increase the length of column **First** to 20 characters.

```
select Name, First, Last
   from work.Sales_staff
   where First ne strip(scan(Name,2,','))
        or Last  ne strip(scan(Name,1,','))
;
alter table work.Sales_staff
   modify First char(20)
;
```

s109d06
continued...

Populating Altered Columns

6. Re-populate the column **First**.

```
alter table work.Sales_staff
   modify First char(20)
;
update work.Sales_staff
   set First=strip(scan(Name,2,','))
;
```

s109d06
continued...

Testing Your Work

7. Re-test the results.

```
update work.Sales_staff
   set First=strip(scan(Name,2,','))
;
select Name, First, Last
   from work.Sales_staff
   where First ne strip(scan(Name,2,','))
         or Last ne strip(scan(Name,1,','))
;
```

Partial SAS Log

```
NOTE: No rows were selected.
```

✎   No output means that the data in columns **First**
    and **Last** is as expected. Problem resolved!

s109d06

73

9.04 Quiz

Both of these code segments change the label for the
Phone_Type column in **orion.Employee_payroll**.
Which is more efficient?

a.
```
create table orion.Employee_phones as
select Employee_ID
     , Phone_Type 'Work, Home, Cell'
     , Phone_Number
   from orion.Employee_phones
;
```

b.
```
alter table orion.Employee_phones
   modify Phone_type 'Work, Home, Cell'
;
```

75

Deleting Tables, Indexes, and Views

Use the DROP statement to delete an entire table, SQL view, or index.

General form of the DROP statement:

DROP TABLE *table-name*<, ...*table-name*>;
DROP VIEW *view-name*<, ...*view-name*>;
DROP INDEX *index-name*<, ...*index-name*>
   FROM *table-name*;

77

Deleting Tables, Indexes, and Views

Example: Delete the index **Locale** from the
      work.Employee_addresses table.

```
proc sql;
   drop index Locale
      from work.Employee_addresses
;
```

Partial Log

```
NOTE: Index Locale has been dropped.
```

78   s109d07

Deleting Tables, Indexes, and Views

Example: Delete the table **work.Employee_addresses**.

```
proc sql;
   drop table work.Employee_addresses
;
```

Partial Log

```
NOTE: Table WORK.EMPLOYEE_ADDRESSES has been dropped.
```

✎ When a table is deleted, all of its associated indexes are automatically deleted as well.

79   s109d07

Maintaining Tables

Method	Result
INSERT – SET – VALUES	appends new data rows to the end of existing tables.
UPDATE – SET – CASE	modifies values in existing data rows as specified in the WHERE expression.
DELETE	deletes existing rows as specified in the WHERE expression.
ALTER – ADD – DROP – MODIFY	modifies table structure by adding columns, dropping columns, or altering column attributes. (You cannot modify name or type.)
DROP	deletes an entire table, view, or index.

80

Updating Views (Self-Study)

You can also update the data underlying PROC SQL views using INSERT, DELETE, and UPDATE statements.

Remember the following:

- You cannot update a view containing an ORDER BY clause.
- You cannot update a table through a summary query.
- You cannot update a derived (calculated) column.
- You can update a column using that column's alias.
- You can only update a single table through a view. Views containing a join, set operator, or subquery cannot be used to update data.

81

Updating Views (Self-Study)

Create some temporary tables that you can use as source tables for views. Then test your assertions about updating views.

```
proc sql;
   create table Address as
      select *
         from orion.Employee_addresses
   ;
   create table Org as
      select *
         from orion.Employee_organization
   ;
   create table Pay as
      select *
         from orion.Employee_payroll
   ;
quit;
```

82   s109d08

Updating Views (Self-Study)

Create a view that includes some table columns and a newly created (calculated) column. Use an alias to modify the name of one of the table's columns.

```
create view Mailing as
   select Employee_ID, Employee_Name as Name,
          catx('',put(Street_Number,12.),Street_Name)
          as Address, City, State, Country
   from work.Address
;
```

83   s109d08

Updating Views (Self-Study)

Update the view.

Change Gabriele Baker's last name to Jones.

```
proc sql;
   update Mailing
      set Name="Jones, Gabriele"
      where Employee_ID=120109
   ;
```

✎   **Name** is an alias for **Employee_Name**.

84   s109d08

9.05 Quiz

Will the query successfully update the data in the underlying table, even though you used an alias for the column name?

○ Yes

○ No

```
proc sql;
   update Mailing
      set Name="Jones, Gabriele"
      where Employee_ID=120109
   ;
   select Employee_Name
      from Address
      where Employee_ID=120109
   ;
quit;
```

86

s109a04

Updating Views (Self-Study)

Attempt to update the derived column by changing Gabriele Jones' address.

```
proc sql;
   update Mailing
      set Address="123 Bland Street"
      where Employee_ID=120109
   ;
```

88

s109d08

Updating Views (Self-Study)

Attempt to update the derived column by changing Gabriele Jones' address.

```
proc sql;
   update Mailing
      set Address="123 Bland Street"
      where Employee_ID=120109
   ;
```

Partial SAS Log

```
WARNING: Cannot provide Address with a value because it
references a non-updatable derived column.
```

Address was created by concatenating Street_Number and Street_Name. Created columns cannot be updated.

89   s109d08

Updating Views (Self-Study)

Re-create the **Mailing** view, and add an ORDER BY clause.

```
create view Mailing as
   select Employee_ID, Employee_Name as Name,
          catx('',put(Street_Number,12.),Street_Name)
          as Address, City, State, Country
      from work.Address
      order by Country, State, City, Name
   ;
```

90   s109d08

Updating Views (Self-Study)

Attempt to change Selina Barcoe's last name to Janes.

```
proc sql;
   update Mailing
      set Name="Janes, Selina"
      where Employee_ID=120168
;
```

91   s109d08

Updating Views (Self-Study)

Attempt to change Selina Barcoe's last name to Janes.

```
proc sql;
   update Mailing
      set Name="Janes, Selina"
      where Employee_ID=120168
;
```

Partial SAS Log

```
ERROR: Update access is not supported for file WORK.MAILING.VIEW.
```

The view **Mailing** cannot be updated
because it contains an ORDER BY clause.

92   s109d08

Updating Views (Self-Study)

Create a summary view.

```
create view Gender_Pay as
   select Gender, sum(Salary) as Total_Pay
      from work.Pay
      group by gender
;
```

s109d08

Updating Views (Self-Study)

Attempt to update a summary view by giving all female workers a 10% raise.

```
proc sql;
   update Gender_pay
      set Total_Pay=Total_pay*1.10
      where Gender="F"
;
```

Partial SAS Log

```
ERROR: Update access is not supported for file WORK.GENDER_PAY.VIEW.
```

**Gender_Pay is a summary view.
Summary views cannot be updated.**

s109d08

Updating Views (Self-Study)

Create a view that joins two tables.

```
create view Skill_level as
   select p.*,
           case (scan(Job_Title,-1))
               when 'I'   then 'Apprentice'
               when 'II'  then 'Journeyman'
               when 'III' then 'Master'
               when 'IV'  then 'Mentor'
               else ''
           end as Level
      from work.Pay as p,
           work.Org as o
      where p.Employee_ID=o.Employee_ID
   ;
```

s109d08

96

Updating Views (Self-Study)

Give all apprentices a 5% raise.

```
proc sql;
   update Skill_level
      set Salary=Salary*1.05
      where Level="Apprentice"
   ;
```

Partial SAS Log

```
ERROR: Update access is not supported for file WORK.SKILL_LEVEL.VIEW.
```

Skill_Level was created using a join.
Views that contain a join cannot be updated.

s109d08

98

Exercises

Level 1

4. Modifying the Table Structure and the Table Data

a. Marketing determined that the reason that product 210200200022 is not selling well is because it is named "Sunfit Slow Swimming Trunks." Change the product name and packaging to **Sunfit Speedy Swimming Trunks**.

The program **s109e04** will create the table **work.Products** for you to use in this exercise.

Write a query to update **work.Products** by setting **Product_Name** to **Sunfit Speedy Swimming Trunks** where **Product_ID=210200200022**.

b. Orion Star wants to add a new line of snorkeling products. Add the following rows to the table **work.Products**. (Before you start typing, see the comments in the program **s109e04**.)

Product Information					Supplier Information		
ID	Line	Category	Group	Name	Country	Name	ID
240600100202	Sports	Swim Sports	Snorkel Gear	Coral Dive Mask - Med	AU	Dingo Divers	21001
240600100203	Sports	Swim Sports	Snorkel Gear	Coral Dive Mask - Large	AU	Dingo Divers	21001
240600100212	Sports	Swim Sports	Snorkel Gear	Coral Dive Fins - Med	AU	Dingo Divers	21001
240600100213	Sports	Swim Sports	Snorkel Gear	Coral Dive Fins - Large	AU	Dingo Divers	21001
240600100222	Sports	Swim Sports	Snorkel Gear	Coral Advanced Snorkel	AU	Dingo Divers	21001
240600100223	Sports	Swim Sports	Snorkel Gear	Coral Pro Snorkel	AU	Dingo Divers	21001

c. Drop the table **work.Products**. (Delete the entire table.)

Level 2

5. Modifying the Table Structure and the Table Data

a. Orion Star will drop the entire group of Kid's Eclipse products from the catalog. The starter program **s109e05** will create the tables **work.Products** and **New_Products** to use in this exercise. Delete the rows containing information for these products from the table **work.Products**. A list of the discontinued products is shown below:

\multicolumn{5}{c}{Product Information}				
ID	**Line**	**Category**	**Group**	**Name**
210200300006	Children	Children Sports	Eclipse, Kid's Clothes	Fleece Cuff Pant Kid's
210200300007	Children	Children Sports	Eclipse, Kid's Clothes	Hsc Dutch Player Shirt Junior
210200300052	Children	Children Sports	Eclipse, Kid's Clothes	Tony's Cut & Sew T-Shirt
210200400020	Children	Children Sports	Eclipse, Kid's Shoes	Kids Baby Edge Max Shoes
210200400029	Children	Children Sports	Eclipse, Kid's Shoes	Toddle Children's Air Terra Grande Shoes
210200400070	Children	Children Sports	Eclipse, Kid's Shoes	Tony's Children's Deschutz (Bg) Shoes

b. Add the products in the **work.New_Products** table to the **work.Products** table.

c. Top Sports (**Supplier_ID**=755) experienced delays of one week in shipping all sleeping bags (**Product_Group="Sleepingbags"**) from the factory. Modify **work.Products** to add a numeric **Shipping_Delay** column. Update the column **Shipping_Delay** in the **work.Products** table to show a delay of seven days in shipping Top Sports sleeping bags.

d. Write a query to display the **Supplier_Name**, **Product_Group**, **Product_Name**, and **Shipping_Delay** for all rows in **work.Products** where **Shipping_Delay** is not missing. Title the report as shown in the sample output.

PROC SQL Output

```
                            Product Shipping Delays

                                                                 Shipping_
     Product Name                          Supplier Name            Delay
     ────────────────────────────────────────────────────────────────────
     Basic 10, Left , Yellow/Black         Top Sports                   7
     Expedition Zero,Medium,Left,Charcoal  Top Sports                   7
     Expedition Zero,Medium,Right,Charcoal Top Sports                   7
     Expedition Zero,Small,Left,Charcoal   Top Sports                   7
     Expedition Zero,Small,Right,Charcoal  Top Sports                   7
     Expedition10,Medium,Right,Blue Ribbon Top Sports                   7
     Expedition 10,Small,Left,Blue Ribbon  Top Sports                   7
     Expedition 10,Small,Right,Blue Ribbon Top Sports                   7
     Expedition 20,Large,Right,Forestgreen Top Sports                   7
     Expedition 20,Medium,Right,Forestgreen Top Sports                  7
     Outback Sleeping Bag, Large,Left,Blue/Black  Top Sports            7
     Outback Sleeping Bag, Large,Right, Blue/Black Top Sports           7
```

e. Remove the column **Shipping_Delay** from the **work.Products** table. Write a query that describes the **work.Products** table structure in the log, and review the SAS log to make sure that the column was actually dropped.

f. Delete both the **work.Products** and **work.NewProducts** tables.

Level 3

6. **Maintaining Tables**

a. The program **s109e06** will create the **work.Products**, **work.New_Products**, and **work.Supplier** tables for you to use in this exercise. Information about new products is in the **work.NewProducts** table. Information about the supplier of these new products is in the **work.Supplier** table. Add all of the products in the **work.New_Products** table to the **work.Products** table, including the appropriate supplier information for each row.

Hint: There might be data type mismatches between some of the columns in the **work.Products** and **work.New_Products** tables.

b. When the data is successfully added to **work.Products**, delete the **work.New_Products** and **work.Supplier** tables.

c. For products in the category Swim Products, query **work.Products** to display **Supplier_Country** and the percentage of swim products supplied by each country. The percentage should be calculated as follows:

number of swim products supplied by this country / total number of swim products

Give the report a title as shown in the sample output.

PROC SQL Output

```
                        Swim Product Sourcing

                            Supplier
                            Country
                            ─────────────────
                            AU          67%
                            US          19%
                            ES          14%
```

9.4 Chapter Review

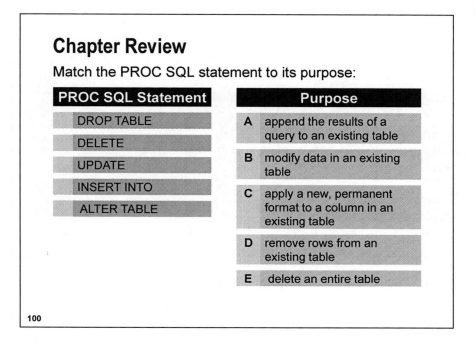

Chapter Review

Match the PROC SQL statement to its purpose:

PROC SQL Statement		Purpose
DROP TABLE	A	append the results of a query to an existing table
DELETE	B	modify data in an existing table
UPDATE	C	apply a new, permanent format to a column in an existing table
INSERT INTO	D	remove rows from an existing table
ALTER TABLE	E	delete an entire table

100

9.5 Solutions

Solutions to Exercises

1. **Creating an Index and Using It in a Query**

    a.

    ```
    *** s109s01 ***;
    proc sql;
       create table work.Products as
           select distinct *
               from orion.Product_DIM
       ;
       create index Product_Name
           on Products (Product_Name)
    ;
    quit;
    ```

    b.

    ```
    options msglevel=i;
    proc sql;
    title "T-Shirt list";
       select distinct Product_Name format=$45.,
                        Supplier_Name format=$30.
           from Products
           where Product_Name like '%T-Shirt%'
       ;
    quit;
    ```

    Yes, the **Product_Name** index was used to optimize the query.

    Partial SAS Log

    ```
    INFO: Index Product_Name selected for WHERE clause optimization.
    ```

2. **Creating a Unique Index and Writing a Query Using the Indexed Variable**

    a.

    ```
    *** s109s02 ***;
    proc sql;
       create table work.Products as
           select distinct *
               from orion.Product_DIM
       ;
    proc sql;
       create unique index Product_ID
           on Products (Product_ID)
       ;
    quit;
    ```

b.

```
options msglevel=i;
proc sql;
title "2007 Products Purchased";
   select distinct Product_Name, Supplier_Name
      from Products as p, orion.Order_fact as o
      where o.product_id=p.product_id
         and year(Order_Date)=2007
   ;
quit;
```

c. Name the indexes, if any, selected by the SQL processor to optimize the query:

Product_ID on work.Products

3. Creating Indexes and Writing a Query Using the Indexed Variables

a.

```
*** s109s03 ***;
proc sql;
   create table work.Customers as
      select distinct *
         from orion.Customer
   ;
   create table work.Orders as
      select *
         from orion.Order_Fact
   ;
   create table work.Products as
      select distinct *
         from orion.Product_DIM
   ;
quit;

proc sql;
   create unique index Customer_ID
      on Customers (Customer_ID)
   ;
   create index Customer_ID
      on Orders (Customer_ID)
   ;
   create unique index Product_ID
      on Products (Product_ID)
   ;
quit;
```

b.

```
options msglevel=i;
proc sql flow=15 40;
title "Products Ordered by South African Customers in 2007";
    select distinct p.Product_Name, p.Supplier_Name
        from Customers as c,
             Orders as o ,
             Products as p
        where o.product_id=p.product_id
          and c.Customer_ID=o.Customer_id
          and c.Country="ZA"
          and year(o.Order_Date)=2007
    ;
quit;
```

c. Name the indexes, if any, selected by the SQL processor to optimize the query:

Customer_ID on **work.Orders** and **Product_ID** on **work.Products**

---

4. Modifying the Table Structure and the Table Data

a.

```
*** s109s04 ***;
proc sql;
    update work.Products
        set Product_Name ="Sunfit Speedy Swimming Trunks"
        where Product_ID=210200200022
    ;
quit;
```

b.

```
/* Method 1 */
proc sql;
    insert into work.Products(Product_ID,Product_Line,
                Product_Category, Product_Group,
                Product_Name ,Supplier_Country,
                Supplier_Name, Supplier_ID)
        values(240600100202,"Sports","Swim Sports","Snorkel Gear",
            "Coral Dive Mask - Med","AU","Dingo Divers",21001)
        values(240600100203,"Sports","Swim Sports","Snorkel Gear",
            "Coral Dive Mask - Large","AU","Dingo Divers",21001)
        values(240600100212,"Sports","Swim Sports","Snorkel Gear",
            "Coral Dive Fins - Med","AU","Dingo Divers",21001)
        values(240600100213,"Sports","Swim Sports","Snorkel Gear",
            "Coral Dive Fins - Large","AU","Dingo Divers",21001)
        values(240600100222,"Sports","Swim Sports","Snorkel Gear",
            "Coral Advanced Snorkel","AU","Dingo Divers",21001)
        values(240600100223,"Sports","Swim Sports","Snorkel Gear",
            "Coral Pro Snorkel","AU","Dingo Divers",21001)
    ;
quit;
```

(Continued on the next page.)

```
  /* Method 2 */
proc sql;
   insert into work.Products
      set Product_ID=240600100202,Product_Line="Sports",
         Product_Category="Swim Sports",Product_Group="Snorkel
         Gear",Product_Name="Coral Dive Mask - Med",
         Supplier_Country="AU", Supplier_Name="Dingo
         Divers",Supplier_ID=21001
      set Product_ID=240600100203,Product_Line="Sports",
         Product_Category="Swim Sports",Product_Group="Snorkel
         Gear",Product_Name="Coral Dive Mask - Large",
         Supplier_Country="AU",Supplier_Name="Dingo
         Divers",Supplier_ID=21001
      set Product_ID=240600100212,Product_Line="Sports",
         Product_Category="Swim Sports",Product_Group="Snorkel
         Gear", Product_Name="Coral Dive Fins - Med",
         Supplier_Country="AU",Supplier_Name="Dingo
         Divers",Supplier_ID=21001
      set Product_ID=240600100213,Product_Line="Sports",
         Product_Category="Swim Sports",Product_Group="Snorkel
         Gear",Product_Name="Coral Dive Fins - Large",
         Supplier_Country="AU",
         Supplier_Name="Dingo Divers",Supplier_ID=21001
      set Product_ID=240600100222,Product_Line="Sports",
         Product_Category="Swim Sports",Product_Group="Snorkel
         Gear", Product_Name="Coral Advanced
         Snorkel",Supplier_Country="AU",
         Supplier_Name="Dingo Divers",Supplier_ID=21001
      set Product_ID=240600100223,Product_Line="Sports",
         Product_Category="Swim Sports",Product_Group="Snorkel
          Gear", Product_Name="Coral Pro Snorkel",
          Supplier_Country="AU",
          Supplier_Name="Dingo Divers",Supplier_ID=21001
   ;
quit;
```

c.

```
proc sql;
   drop table work.Products;
quit;
```

5. **Modifying the Table Structure and the Table Data**

a.

```
*** s109s05 ***;
proc sql;
   delete from work.Products
      where Product_Group like '%Eclipse, Kid%'
;
quit;
```

b.

```
proc sql;
   insert into work.Products
      select *
         from work.NewProducts
   ;

   select Product_Name, Supplier_Name, Supplier_Country
      from work.Products
      where Product_Category="Swim Sports"
   ;
quit;
```

c.

```
proc sql;
   alter table work.Products
      add Shipping_Delay num
   ;
   update work.Products
      set Shipping_Delay=7
      where Supplier_ID=755
         and Product_Group="Sleepingbags"
   ;

title "Product Shipping Delays";
   select Product_Name, Supplier_Name, Shipping_Delay
      from work.Products
      where not Shipping_Delay is missing
   ;
quit;
title;
```

d.

```
proc sql;
title "Product Shipping Delays";
   select Product_Name, Supplier_Name, Shipping_Delay
      from work.Products
      where not Shipping_Delay is missing
   ;
quit;
title;
```

e.

```
proc sql;
   alter table work.Products
      drop Shipping_Delay
   ;
   describe table work.Products;
quit;
```

f.

```
proc sql;
   drop table work.Products;
   drop table work.NewProducts;
quit;
```

6. Maintaining Tables

a.

```
*** s109s06 ***;
proc sql;
   insert into work.Products
      (Product_ID,Product_Line, Product_Category, Product_Group,
       Product_Name ,Supplier_Country, Supplier_Name, Supplier_ID)
      select input(Product_ID,12.),Product_Line, Product_Category,
             Product_Group, Product_Name ,Country,
             Name, ID
        from work.NewProducts as p,
             work.Supplier as s
   ;
quit;
```

b.

```
proc sql;
   drop table work.NewProducts;
   drop table work.Supplier;
quit;
```

c.

```
proc sql;
title "Swim Product Sourcing";
   select Supplier_Country,
          Product_Count/SUM(Product_Count) format=percent6.1
      from (select Supplier_Country, Count(*) as Product_Count
               from work.Products
               where Product_Category="Swim Sports"
               group by Supplier_Country)
      order by 2 desc
   ;
quit;
```

Solutions to Student Activities (Polls\Quizzes)

9.01 Multiple Choice Poll – Correct Answer

Which query (or queries) used the **Locale** index?

a. Query 1 (State)
b. Query 2 (State and City)
c. Query 3 (City)
d. Queries 1 and 2
e. Queries 1 and 3
f. All queries used the index
g. None of the above

17

9.02 Quiz – Correct Answer

Should you index this column to improve query performance?

No, Order_Type is a low-cardinality column, and none of the values returns a subset less than 15%. A full-table scan yields better performance without the overhead required to maintain an index.

Order_Type	Frequency	Percent
1	324	52.51
2	170	27.55
3	123	19.94

40

9.03 Quiz – Correct Answer

How many rows were deleted from the temporary table `work.Staff`? **424 (All of them)**

```
proc sql;
   delete from work.Staff;
      where Emp_Term_Date is not missing
;
quit;
```

This semicolon ends this statement.

SQL cannot interpret the stand-alone WHERE clause.

```
   delete from work.Staff;
NOTE: 424 rows were deleted from WORK.STAFF.
   where Emp_Term_Date
WARNING: This SAS global statement is not supported in PROC
         SQL. It has been ignored.
```

Remember that PROC SQL queries execute immediately.

60

9.04 Quiz – Correct Answer

Both of these code segments change the label for the `Phone_Type` column in `orion.Employee_payroll`. Which is more efficient?

a.
```
create table orion.Employee_phones as
select Employee_ID
     , Phone_Type 'Work, Home, Cell'
     , Phone_Number
   from orion.Employee_phones
;
```

This query reads and writes all the data rows in the table to effect the changes.

b.
```
alter table orion.Employee_phones
   modify Phone_type 'Work, Home, Cell'
;
```

This query modifies only the table metadata.

76

9.05 Quiz – Correct Answer

Will the query successfully update the data in the
underlying table, even though you used an alias
for the column name?

(◉) Yes

( ) No

```
proc sql;
    select Employee_Name
        from Address
        where Employee_ID=120109
    ;
```

Output

Employee_Name
Jones, Gabriele

The update writes to the underlying
table even though Name is the view's
alias for Employee_Name.

87

s109a04

Solutions to Chapter Review

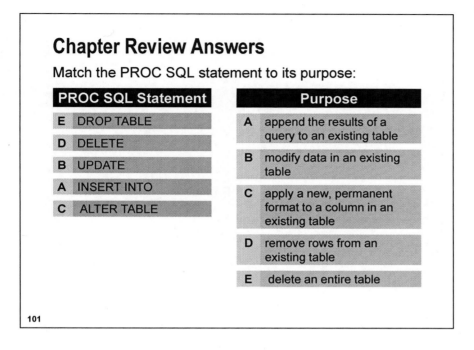

Chapter Review Answers

Match the PROC SQL statement to its purpose:

PROC SQL Statement		Purpose	
E	DROP TABLE	A	append the results of a query to an existing table
D	DELETE	B	modify data in an existing table
B	UPDATE	C	apply a new, permanent format to a column in an existing table
A	INSERT INTO	D	remove rows from an existing table
C	ALTER TABLE	E	delete an entire table

101

Chapter 10   Accessing Relational Databases (Self-Study)

10.1 LIBNAME Access to DBMS Data

Objectives

- Connect to a database management system (DBMS) using the LIBNAME statement.
- Use DBMS tables in PROC SQL statements.
- Disconnect from the DBMS.

3

The LIBNAME Statement (Review)

The LIBNAME statement can do the following:

- establish a libref that acts as a nickname pointing to a collection of data sets (SAS data library)
- enable referencing of data sets by a two-level name
- make operating environment-specific references in the remaining program code unnecessary

Accessing a SAS library via a libref does not override authentication/permissions restrictions set by the operating system.

4

The LIBNAME Statement (Review)

General form of the LIBNAME statement:

> **LIBNAME** *libref* *'SAS-data-library location'* *<options>*;

5   ...

The LIBNAME Statement (Review)

General form of the LIBNAME statement:

> **LIBNAME** *libref* *'SAS-data-library location'* *<options>*;

Example (Windows operating system):

```
libname orion 's:\workshop';
```

O/S-specific information

```
proc sql;
select *
    from orion.customer;
quit;
```

Portable code:
No O/S-specific information

s:\workshop

```
customer.sas7bdat
employee_addresses.sas7bdat
employee_data.sas7bdat
employee_donations.sas7bdat
...
```

11

LIBNAME Statements Using Access Engines

- Syntax is modified to provide information required by the DBMS and SAS/ACCESS engine.
- The assigned libref acts as a nickname for the DBMS.
- DBMS tables are referenced using two-level names, in the same manner as native SAS data sets.
- Read access and Write access are controlled by the DBMS authentication/authorization system.

✎ SAS/ACCESS engines can be licensed separately from Base SAS.

Check with your SAS Administrator for details specific to your site.

12

The LIBNAME Statement (Review)

General form of the LIBNAME statement using a SAS/ACCESS engine:

```
LIBNAME libref <engine> <engine-specific-options>;
```

13   ...

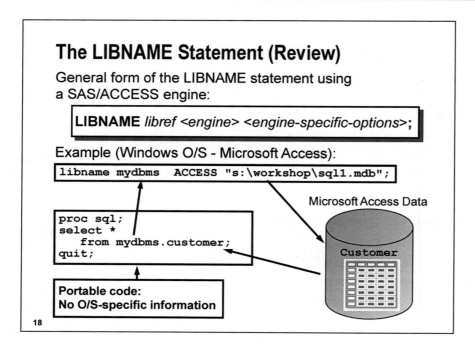

The LIBNAME Statement (Review)

General form of the LIBNAME statement using
a SAS/ACCESS engine:

> **LIBNAME** *libref <engine> <engine-specific-options>*;

Example (Windows O/S - Microsoft Access):

```
libname mydbms   ACCESS "s:\workshop\sql1.mdb";
```

Microsoft Access Data

```
proc sql;
select *
   from mydbms.customer;
quit;
```

Customer

Portable code:
No O/S-specific information

18

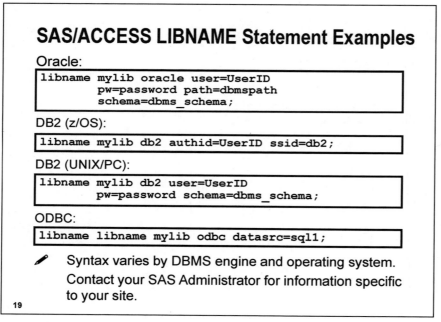

SAS/ACCESS LIBNAME Statement Examples

Oracle:

```
libname mylib oracle user=UserID
       pw=password path=dbmspath
       schema=dbms_schema;
```

DB2 (z/OS):

```
libname mylib db2 authid=UserID ssid=db2;
```

DB2 (UNIX/PC):

```
libname mylib db2 user=UserID
       pw=password schema=dbms_schema;
```

ODBC:

```
libname libname mylib odbc datasrc=sql1;
```

🖉   Syntax varies by DBMS engine and operating system.
Contact your SAS Administrator for information specific
to your site.

19

🖉   SAS/ACCESS syntax varies with the DBMS used and the operating system. Review the
documentation for your DMBS engine and operating system for more detail.

The LIBNAME Statement – Disconnecting

General form of the LIBNAME statement when de-allocating a SAS library or disconnecting from a DBMS:

```
LIBNAME libref CLEAR;
```

Example:

```
libname mydbms clear;
```

20

Accessing DBMS Data with the LIBNAME Statement

s110d01

🖊 This demonstration code only works in a Microsoft Windows environment with Microsoft Access and SAS/ACCESS Interface to PC Files installed.

1. Retrieve the program **s110d01**.

2. Highlight and submit the LIBNAME statement.

```
libname MyDBMS ACCESS "./sql1.mdb";
```

3. In the SAS Explorer pane, notice that the icon for **Mydbms** includes the world symbol, which indicates that a SAS library is not in native SAS format.

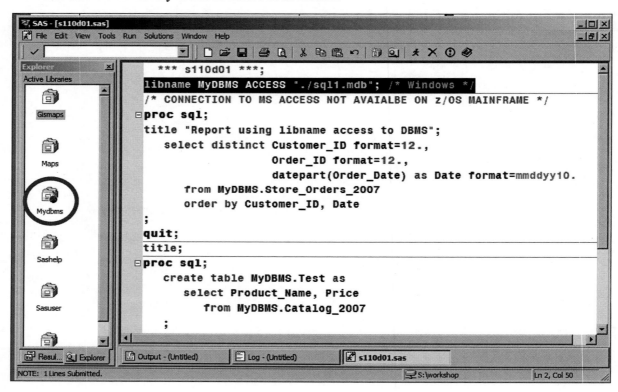

4. Double-click the **Mydbms** library icon to reveal the tables inside the library.

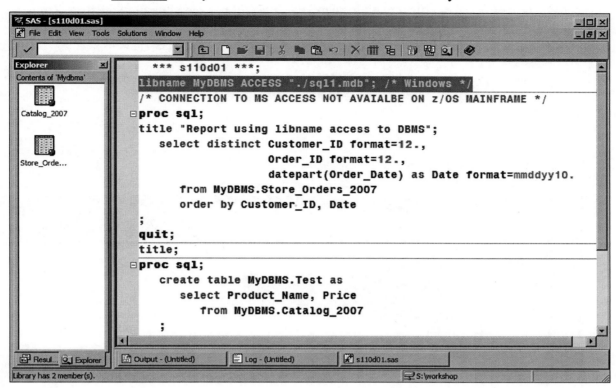

5. Highlight and submit the first PROC SQL step to produce a report for the table
MyDBMS.Store_Orders_2007.

```
proc sql;
title "Report using libname access to DBMS";
   select distinct Customer_ID format=12.,
           Order_ID format=12.,
           datepart(Order_Date) as Date format=mmddyy10.
      from MyDBMS.Store_Orders_2007
      order by Customer_ID, Date
;
quit;
title;
```

Partial PROC SQL Output

Report using libname access to DBMS		
Customer_ID	Order_ID	Date
5	1242493791	06/10/2007
5	1243315613	09/09/2007
5	1244296274	12/26/2007
10	1241686210	03/13/2007
10	1242012259	04/18/2007
10	1242265757	05/16/2007

6. Highlight and submit the next PROC SQL statement to create a new Microsoft Access DBMS table
    named **MyDBMS.Test**. After creation, your new table will be accessible from the SAS Explorer
    window in the same way as a SAS data set.

```
proc sql;
   create table MyDBMS.Test as
       select Product_Name, Price
       from MyDBMS.Catalog_2007
;

   select *
       from MyDBMS.Test
       order by Price desc;
;
```

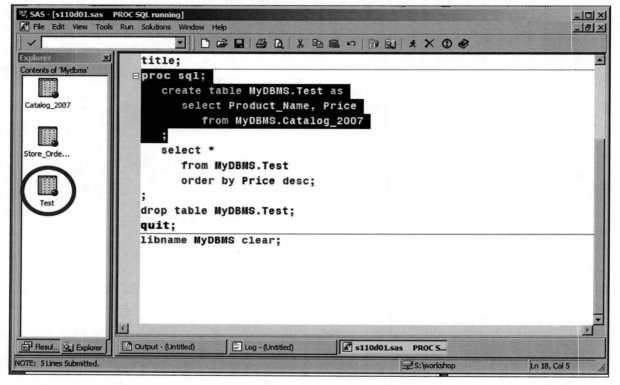

7. Highlight and submit the next PROC SQL statement to generate a report from your new table.

```
proc sql;
   create table MyDBMS.Test as
      select Product_Name, Price
         from MyDBMS.Catalog_2007
;
   select *
      from MyDBMS.Test
      order by Price desc;
;
```

Partial PROC SQL Output

Product_Name	Price
Letour Trimag Bike	$630.40
Family Holiday 6	$568.10
Top R&D Long Jacket	$541.66
Letour Heart Bike	$533.20
Family Holiday 4	$519.30
Top Men's R&D Ultimate Jacket	$509.80
Proplay Executive Bi-Metal Graphite	$484.30

8. Highlight and submit the last PROC SQL statement that deletes the Microsoft Access DBMS table that you created (**MyDBMS.Test**). The table **MyDBMS.Test** should no longer appear in the SAS Explorer window.

```
drop table MyDBMS.Test;
quit;
```

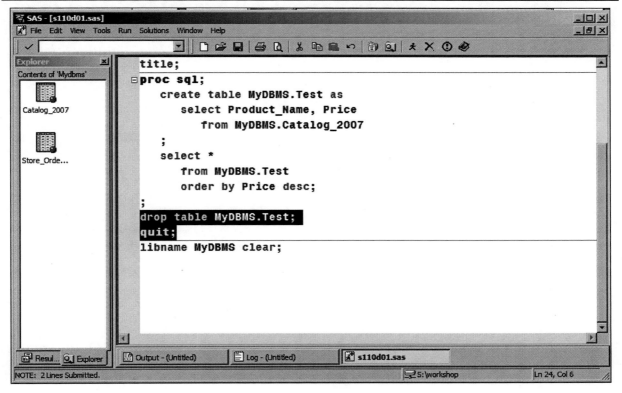

9. Highlight and submit the last LIBNAME statement in the program to disconnect from the Microsoft Access DBMS. Click on the SAS Explorer pane, and select ![UP button] (the UP button) to return to the list of available SAS libraries. The library **Mydbms** should no longer appear.

```
libname MyDBMS clear;
```

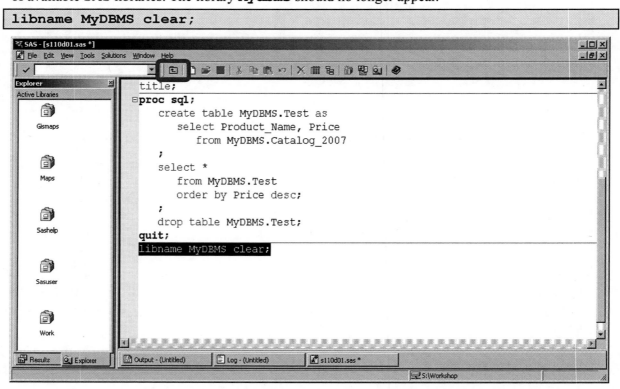

10.2 Executing DBMS-Specific SQL Using the SQL Pass-Through Facility

Objectives

- Connect to a DBMS using the CONNECT statement.
- Issue native SQL statements to the DBMS for execution.
- Disconnect from the DBMS.

23

Overview

The SQL Procedure Pass-Through Facility communicates with the DBMS through the SAS/ACCESS engine.

The facility enables you to do the following:

- pass native DBMS SQL statements to a DBMS
- display query results formatted by PROC SQL
- save query results as SAS data files
- create SAS data views containing pass-through queries

24

Overview

SQL statements you can submit to the DBMS include these statements:

- SELECT statements (pass-through queries), which return output to SAS in a manner similar to in-line views
- EXECUTE statements, which include SQL statements that do not produce output (for example, CREATE TABLE, UPDATE, and DELETE)

25

SQL Procedure Pass-Through Queries

An SQL pass-through query consists of the statements listed below:

- a CONNECT statement
- a SELECT expression
- a DISCONNECT statement

26

Connecting to the DBMS

The CONNECT statement can do the following:

- specify the DBMS name
- provide other DBMS-specific connection information (optional for some databases)
- establish the connection to the DBMS
- specify an alias for the connection (optional)

27

Connecting to the DBMS

General form of the CONNECT statement:

> **CONNECT TO** *dbms-engine* *<AS alias>* *(options)*;

28

Connecting to Microsoft Access

Example: Connect to a Microsoft Access table.

```
proc sql;
   connect to ACCESS as mydbms
       (path="./sql1.mdb");
```

29   s110d02

The SELECT Expression

The PROC SQL SELECT expression for SQL pass-through consists of these elements:

- a PROC SQL SELECT expression
- a FROM CONNECTION TO component
- the SQL code to be passed to the DBMS
- other PROC SQL clauses necessary to finish processing the data returned by the pass-through query

30

The SELECT Expression

The query passed to the DBMS

- uses DBMS-specific SQL syntax that will be processed inside the DBMS and not by SAS
- must reference only DBMS table column names
- is enclosed in matching parentheses.

🖉   A pass-through query must have valid DBMS SQL syntax. PROC SQL does not evaluate the syntax of pass-through queries.

31

SELECT from Microsoft Access

Example: Select from pass-through to Microsoft Access.

```
proc sql;
   connect to ACCESS as mydbms
      (path="./sql1.mdb");

title "Report using SQL Passthrough";
   select *
      from connection to mydbms
         (select Product_Name, Price
            from Catalog_2007
            order by Product_Name)
;
```

The SELECT statement containing the FROM
CONNECTION TO clause uses the data returned
by the pass-through query in a manner similar to
an in-line view.

32   s110d02

SELECT from Microsoft Access

Example: Combine a pass-through and SAS data.

```
proc sql;
   connect to ACCESS as mydbms
      (path="./sql1.mdb");
title "SQL Passthrough and SAS Tables";
   select of.Product_ID, Product_Name,
          Price, count(*) as Number_Sold
      from connection to mydbms
         (select Product_ID, Product_Name,
            Price
            from Catalog_2007
            order by Product_Name) as pt,
      orion.Order_Fact as of
   where of.Product_ID=pt.Product_ID
   group by of.Product_ID
;
```

33   s110d02

Closing the DBMS Connection

You can close the connection to the DBMS by either of these methods:

- submitting a DISCONNECT statement
- terminating the SQL procedure, for example, with a QUIT statement

General form of the DISCONNECT statement:

DISCONNECT FROM *dbms-engine* | *alias*;

34

Closing the Connection to Microsoft Access

Example: Disconnect from Microsoft Excel or Access.

```
proc sql;
   connect to ACCESS as mydbms
      (path="./sql1.mdb");

title "Report using SQL Passthrough";
   select *
      from connection to mydbms
         (select Product_Name, Price
             from Catalog_2007
             order by Product_Name)
;
   disconnect from mydbms;
quit;
```

35   s110d02

Accessing DBMS Data with the LIBNAME Statement

s110d02

✎   This demonstration code only works in a Microsoft Windows environment with Microsoft Access and SAS/ACCESS Interface to PC Files installed.

1. Retrieve the program **s110d02**.

2. Highlight and submit the first PROC SQL step. SAS passes the SQL in parentheses directly to the DBMS for execution, without syntax checking or validation.

```
proc sql;
   connect to ACCESS as MyDBMS
      (path="./sql1.mdb");
title "Report using SQL Passthrough";
   select *
      from connection to MyDBMS
         (select Product_Name, Price
             from Catalog_2007
             order by Product_Name)
   ;
   disconnect from MyDBMS;
quit;
```

Partial PROC SQL Output

```
                       Report using SQL Passthrough

        Product_Name                                    Price

        2bwet 3 Cb Swimming Trunks                     $32.40
        2bwet 3 Solid Bikini                           $51.00
        Aim4it 16 Gram Softtip Pil                     $16.00
        Aim4it 80% Tungsten 22 Gram                    $35.20
        Alexis Women's Classic Shoes                   $56.90
        Amber Cc                                       $87.20
```

3. The results from the SQL pass-through are returned to PROC SQL for processing, and can be used in a manner similar to an in-line view. Highlight and submit the second PROC SQL step. Again, SAS passes the SQL in parentheses directly to the DBMS for execution, but this time joins the results with **orion.Order_Fact** to produce a report with elements from both the DBMS table and the SAS table.

```
proc sql;
   connect to ACCESS as MyDBMS
       (path="./sql1.mdb");
title "SQL Passthrough Results Joined With SAS Table";
   select of.Product_ID, Product_Name,
          Price, count(*) as Number_Sold
      from connection to MyDBMS
        (select Product_ID, Product_Name,
               Price
           from Catalog_2007
           order by Product_Name) as pt,
        orion.Order_Fact as of
      where of.Product_ID=pt.Product_ID
      group by of.Product_ID
;
   disconnect from MyDBMS;
quit;
```

Partial PROC SQL Output

```
                  SQL Passthrough Results Joined With SAS Table

   Product ID  Product_Name                                  Price  Number_Sold

   210200100009  Kids Sweat Round Neck,Large Logo           $34.70            1
   210200100017  Sweatshirt Children's O-Neck               $40.00            1
   210200200023  Sunfit Stockton Swimming Trunks Jr.        $19.80            1
   210200600067  Children's Knit Sweater                    $67.00            2
   210200600067  Children's Knit Sweater                    $67.00            2
   210200600085  Gordon Children's Tracking Pants           $39.40            1
```

4. Because SAS passes the SQL in parentheses directly to the DBMS for execution, without syntax checking or validation, you can even execute Data Definition Language (DDL) SQL statements in the DBMS, if you have proper authorization.

    a. Submit the LIBNAME statement to provide access to the DBMS via the SAS Explorer:

```
libname MyDBMS ACCESS "./sql1.mdb";
```

b. In the SAS Explorer, open the **MyDBMS** library and right-click on the icon for the **Catalog_2007** table. Select **View Columns** and examine the structure of this table.

Column Name	Type	Length	Format	Informat	Label
Product_ID	Number	8			Product_ID
Product_Line	Text	20	$20.	$20.	Product_Line
Product_Categ...	Text	25	$25.	$25.	Product_Category
Product_Group	Text	25	$25.	$25.	Product_Group
Product_Name	Text	45	$45.	$45.	Product_Name
Supplier_Country	Text	2	$2.	$2.	Supplier_Country
Supplier_Name	Text	30	$30.	$30.	Supplier_Name
Supplier_ID	Number	8			Supplier_ID
Price	Number	8	DOLLAR21.2	DOLLAR21.2	Price

Mydbms.Catalog_2007 Properties — tabs: General | Details | Columns | Indexes | Integrity — Find column name:

c. Highlight and submit the third PROC SQL step to add a **Comments** column to **Catalog_2007** and populate it with values. Create a view named **Test** in the DBMS, and then generate a report using the newly created view.

```
proc sql;
   connect to ACCESS as MyDBMS
      (path="./sql1.mdb");
   execute (alter table Catalog_2007
               add column Comments TEXT(10))
      by MyDBMS;
   execute (update Catalog_2007
               set Comments='Pricey!'
               where Price > 100)
      by MyDBMS;
   execute (create view Test AS
               select Product_Name, Price, Comments
                  from Catalog_2007)
      by MyDBMS;
   disconnect from MyDBMS;
title "Report using the view 'MyDBMS.Test'";
   select *
      from MyDBMS.Test
      where Comments ne "";
quit;
```

Partial SQL Output

```
                        Report using the view 'MyDBMS.Test'

                                                              Price   Comments
   Product_Name

   Truls Polar Fleece Cardigan                              $208.60  Pricey!
   Dmx 10 Women's Aerobic Shoes                             $188.60  Pricey!
   Armadillo Road Dmx Women's Running Shoes                 $104.60  Pricey!
   Tcp 6 Men's Running Shoes                                $155.94  Pricey!
   Trooper Ii Dmx-2x Men's Walking Shoes                    $122.82  Pricey!
```

d. In the SAS Explorer, open the **MyDBMS** library and right-click on the icon for the **Catalog_2007** table. Select **<u>View Columns</u>** and notice that the structure of this table was modified.

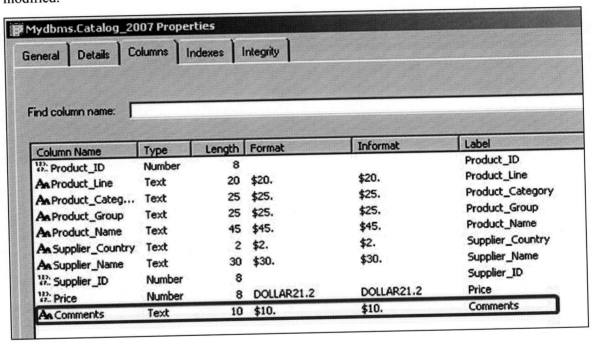

e. Highlight and submit the fourth PROC SQL step to delete the view **Test** and restore the **Catalog_2007** table to its original condition in the DBMS.

```
proc sql;
    connect to ACCESS as MyDBMS
        (path="./sql1.mdb");
    execute (alter table Catalog_2007
                drop column Comments)
        by MyDBMS;
    execute (drop view Test)
        by MyDBMS;
    disconnect from MyDBMS;
quit;
```

Chapter 11   Learning More

11.1 SAS Resources

Objectives

- Identify areas of support that SAS offers.

3

Education

Comprehensive training to deliver greater value to your organization

- More than 200 course offerings
- World-class instructors
- Multiple delivery methods: instructor-led and self-paced
- Training centers around the world

http://support.sas.com/training/

4

SAS Publishing

SAS offers a complete selection of publications to help customers use SAS software to its fullest potential:

- Multiple delivery methods: e-books, CD-ROM, and hard-copy books
- Wide spectrum of topics
- Partnerships with outside authors, other publishers, and distributors

http://support.sas.com/publishing/

5

SAS Global Certification Program

SAS offers several globally recognized certifications.

- Computer-based certification exams – typically 60-70 questions and 2-3 hours in length
- Preparation materials and practice exams available
- Worldwide directory of SAS Certified Professionals

http://support.sas.com/certify/

6

Support

SAS provides a variety of self-help and assisted-help resources.

- SAS Knowledge Base
- Downloads and hot fixes
- License assistance
- SAS discussion forums
- SAS Technical Support

http://support.sas.com/techsup/

7

User Groups

SAS supports many local, regional, international, and special-interest SAS user groups.

- SAS Global Forum

- Online SAS Community: www.sasCommunity.org

http://support.sas.com/usergroups/

8

11.2 Beyond This Course

Objectives

- Identify training opportunities to build on the skills you learned in this course.

10

Next Steps

SAS® SQL 1: Essentials provides portable skills that are useful in most of the focus areas shown below.

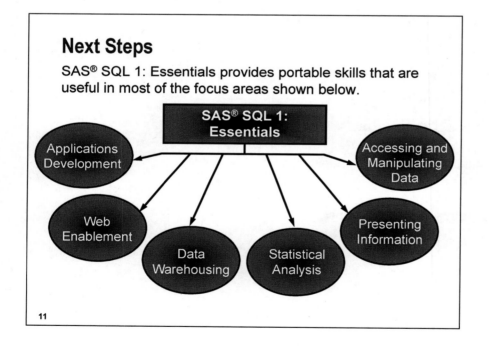

11

Next Steps

To learn more about this:

Enroll in the following:

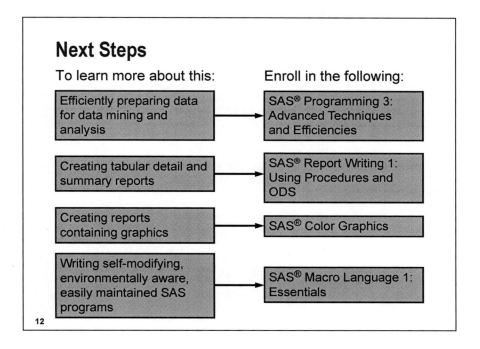

To learn more about this:	Enroll in the following:
Efficiently preparing data for data mining and analysis	SAS® Programming 3: Advanced Techniques and Efficiencies
Creating tabular detail and summary reports	SAS® Report Writing 1: Using Procedures and ODS
Creating reports containing graphics	SAS® Color Graphics
Writing self-modifying, environmentally aware, easily maintained SAS programs	SAS® Macro Language 1: Essentials

12

Next Steps

In addition, there are prerecorded short technical discussions and demonstrations called e-lectures.

http://support.sas.com/training/

13

Appendix A Overview of Table and Column Names

A.1 Table and Column Names Sorted by Column Names

Column Name	Table Names
Birth_Date	CUSTOMER
	EMPLOYEE_PAYROLL
	SALES
	SALESSTAFF
	STAFF
City	EMPLOYEE_ADDRESSES
CostPrice_Per_Unit	ORDER_FACT
Country	CUSTOMER
	EMPLOYEE_ADDRESSES
	SALES
Customer_Address	CUSTOMER
Customer_FirstName	CUSTOMER
Customer_ID	CUSTOMER
	ORDER_FACT
	QTR1_2007
	QTR2_2007
Customer_LastName	CUSTOMER
Customer_Name	CUSTOMER
Customer_Type_ID	CUSTOMER
Delivery_Date	ORDER_FACT
	QTR1_2007
	QTR2_2007
Department	EMPLOYEE_ORGANIZATION
Dependents	EMPLOYEE_PAYROLL
Discount	ORDER_FACT
Emp_Hire_Date	SALESSTAFF
	STAFF
Emp_Term_Date	SALESSTAFF
	STAFF

(Continued on the next page.)

Column Name	Table Names
Employee_Gender	EMPLOYEE_PAYROLL
Employee_Hire_Date	EMPLOYEE_PAYROLL
Employee_ID	EMPLOYEE_ADDRESSES
	EMPLOYEE_DONATIONS
	EMPLOYEE_ORGANIZATION
	EMPLOYEE_PAYROLL
	EMPLOYEE_PHONES
	ORDER_FACT
	QTR2_2007
	SALES
	SALESSTAFF
	STAFF
Employee_Name	EMPLOYEE_ADDRESSES
	SALESSTAFF
Employee_Term_Date	EMPLOYEE_PAYROLL
End_Date	PRICE_LIST
	STAFF
Factor	PRICE_LIST
First_Name	SALES
Gender	CUSTOMER
	SALES
	SALESSTAFF
	STAFF
Hire_Date	SALES
Job_Title	EMPLOYEE_ORGANIZATION
	SALES
	SALESSTAFF
	STAFF

(Continued on the next page.)

Column Name	Table Names
Last_Name	SALES
Manager_ID	EMPLOYEE_ORGANIZATION
	SALESSTAFF
	STAFF
Marital_Status	EMPLOYEE_PAYROLL
Order_Date	ORDER_FACT
	QTR1_2007
	QTR2_2007
Order_ID	ORDER_FACT
	QTR1_2007
	QTR2_2007
Order_Type	ORDER_FACT
	QTR1_2007
	QTR2_2007
Paid_By	EMPLOYEE_DONATIONS
Personal_ID	CUSTOMER
Phone_Number	EMPLOYEE_PHONES
Phone_Type	EMPLOYEE_PHONES
Postal_Code	EMPLOYEE_ADDRESSES
Product_Category	PRODUCT_DIM
Product_Group	PRODUCT_DIM
Product_ID	ORDER_FACT
	PRICE_LIST
	PRODUCT_DIM
Product_Line	PRODUCT_DIM
Product_Name	PRODUCT_DIM
Qtr1	EMPLOYEE_DONATIONS
Qtr2	EMPLOYEE_DONATIONS
Qtr3	EMPLOYEE_DONATIONS
Qtr4	EMPLOYEE_DONATIONS

(Continued on the next page.)

Column Name	Table Names
Quantity	ORDER_FACT
Recipients	EMPLOYEE_DONATIONS
SSN	SALESSTAFF
Salary	EMPLOYEE_PAYROLL
	SALES
	SALESSTAFF
	STAFF
Start_Date	PRICE_LIST
	STAFF
State	EMPLOYEE_ADDRESSES
Street_ID	CUSTOMER
	EMPLOYEE_ADDRESSES
	ORDER_FACT
Street_Name	EMPLOYEE_ADDRESSES
Street_Number	CUSTOMER
	EMPLOYEE_ADDRESSES
Supplier_Country	PRODUCT_DIM
Supplier_ID	PRODUCT_DIM
Supplier_Name	PRODUCT_DIM
Total_Retail_Price	ORDER_FACT
Unit_Cost_Price	PRICE_LIST
Unit_Sales_Price	PRICE_LIST

A.2 Table and Column Names Sorted by Table Name

Table Name	Column Name	Column Type	Column Length	Column Label
CUSTOMER	Customer_Type_ID	num	8	Customer Type ID
	Customer_Address	char	45	Customer Address
	Customer_Name	char	40	Customer Name
	Personal_ID	char	15	Personal ID
	Customer_ID	num	8	Customer ID
	Gender	char	1	Customer Gender
	Street_Number	char	8	Street Number
	Country	char	2	Customer Country
	Customer_FirstName	char	20	Customer First Name
	Street_ID	num	8	Street ID
	Customer_LastName	char	30	Customer Last Name
	Birth_Date	num	8	Customer Birth Date
EMPLOYEE_ADDRESSES	Street_ID	num	8	
	Employee_Name	char	40	
	Employee_ID	num	8	
	Country	char	2	
	Postal_Code	char	10	
	State	char	2	
	City	char	30	
	Street_Name	char	40	
	Street_Number	num	8	
EMPLOYEE_DONATIONS	Paid_By	char	17	
	Recipients	char	65	
	Qtr4	num	8	
	Qtr3	num	8	
	Qtr2	num	8	
	Qtr1	num	8	
	Employee_ID	num	8	Employee ID
EMPLOYEE_ORGANIZATION	Department	char	40	
	Job_Title	char	25	
	Employee_ID	num	8	
	Manager_ID	num	8	

(Continued on the next page.)

Table Name	Column Name	Column Type	Column Length	Column Label
EMPLOYEE_PAYROLL	Employee_Term_Date	num	8	
	Employee_Hire_Date	num	8	
	Birth_Date	num	8	
	Salary	num	8	
	Employee_Gender	char	1	
	Employee_ID	num	8	
	Dependents	num	8	
	Marital_Status	char	1	
EMPLOYEE_PHONES	Phone_Number	char	200	
	Phone_Type	char	4	
	Employee_ID	num	8	
ORDER_FACT	Quantity	num	8	Quantity Ordered
	Customer_ID	num	8	Customer ID
	Order_Type	num	8	Order Type
	Employee_ID	num	8	Employee ID
	Product_ID	num	8	Product ID
	Total_Retail_Price	num	8	Total Retail Price for This Product
	Order_ID	num	8	Order ID
	Delivery_Date	num	8	Date Order was Delivered
	Order_Date	num	8	Date Order was placed by Customer
	Discount	num	8	Discount in percent of Normal Total Retail Price
	Street_ID	num	8	Street ID
	CostPrice_Per_Unit	num	8	Cost Price Per Unit
PRICE_LIST	Unit_Sales_Price	num	8	Unit Sales Price
	Factor	num	8	Yearly increase in Price
	Unit_Cost_Price	num	8	Unit Cost Price
	End_Date	num	8	End Date
	Start_Date	num	8	Start Date
	Product_ID	num	8	Product ID

(Continued on the next page.)

Table Name	Column Name	Column Type	Column Length	Column Label
PRODUCT_DIM	Supplier_Name	char	30	Supplier Name
	Supplier_Country	char	2	Supplier Country
	Product_Name	char	45	Product Name
	Supplier_ID	num	8	Supplier ID
	Product_Group	char	25	Product Group
	Product_Category	char	25	Product Category
	Product_Line	char	20	Product Line
	Product_ID	num	8	Product ID
QTR1_2007	Delivery_Date	num	8	Date Order was Delivered
	Order_Date	num	8	Date Order was placed by Customer
	Customer_ID	num	8	Customer ID
	Order_Type	num	8	Order Type
	Order_ID	num	8	Order ID
QTR2_2007	Order_Type	num	8	Order Type
	Order_ID	num	8	Order ID
	Employee_ID	num	8	Employee ID
	Order_Date	num	8	Date Order was placed by Customer
	Customer_ID	num	8	Customer ID
	Delivery_Date	num	8	Date Order was Delivered
SALES	Last_Name	char	18	
	First_Name	char	12	
	Birth_Date	num	8	
	Country	char	2	
	Job_Title	char	25	
	Hire_Date	num	8	
	Salary	num	8	
	Employee_ID	num	8	
	Gender	char	1	

(Continued on the next page.)

Table Name	Column Name	Column Type	Column Length	Column Label
SALESSTAFF	Employee_ID	num	8	Employee ID
	Job_Title	char	25	Employee Job Title
	SSN	char	16	
	Manager_ID	num	8	Manager for Employee
	Emp_Term_Date	num	8	Employee Termination Date
	Employee_Name	char	40	
	Emp_Hire_Date	num	8	Employee Hire Date
	Birth_Date	num	8	Employee Birth Date
	Gender	char	1	Employee Gender
	Salary	num	8	Employee Annual Salary
STAFF	Birth_Date	num	8	Employee Birth Date
	Gender	char	1	Employee Gender
	Salary	num	8	Employee Annual Salary
	Emp_Hire_Date	num	8	Employee Hire Date
	Job_Title	char	25	Employee Job Title
	End_Date	num	8	End Date
	Start_Date	num	8	Start Date
	Employee_ID	num	8	Employee ID
	Manager_ID	num	8	Manager for Employee
	Emp_Term_Date	num	8	Employee Termination Date

A.3 Partial Table Listings

```
                            ORION.CUSTOMER Table


                               Personal_                    Customer_    Customer_
Customer_ID    Country   Gender    ID      Customer_Name    FirstName    LastName

          4      US        M              James Kvarniq      James       Kvarniq
          5      US        F              Sandrina Stephano  Sandrina    Stephano
          9      DE        F              Cornelia Krahl     Cornelia    Krahl
         10      US        F              Karen Ballinger    Karen       Ballinger
         11      DE        F              Elke Wallstab      Elke        Wallstab


   Birth_                                      Street_    Customer_
    Date     Customer_Address     Street_ID    Number     Type_ID

27JUN1974    4382 Gralyn Rd       9260106519    4382        1020
09JUL1979    6468 Cog Hill Ct     9260114570    6468        2020
27FEB1974    Kallstadterstr. 9    3940106659    9           2020
18OCT1984    425 Bryant Estates Dr 9260129395   425         1040
16AUG1974    Carl-Zeiss-Str. 15   3940108592    15          1040
```

```
                        ORION.EMPLOYEE_ADDRESSES Table
```

Employee_ID	Employee_Name	Street_ID	Street_Number	Street_Name	City	State	Postal_Code	Country
121044	Abbott, Ray	9260116912	2267	Edwards Mill Rd	Miami-Dade	FL	33135	US
120145	Aisbitt, Sandy	1600101803	30	Bingera Street	Melbourne		2001	AU
120761	Akinfolarin, Tameaka	9260121030	5	Donnybrook Rd	Philadelphia	PA	19145	US
120656	Amos, Salley	9260123736	3524	Calico Ct	San Diego	CA	92116	US
121107	Anger, Rose	9260120989	744	Chapwith Rd	Philadelphia	PA	19142	US

```
                        ORION.EMPLOYEE_DONATIONS Table

        E
        m
        p                                           R
        l                                           e
        o                                           c
        y                                           i                               P
        e                                           p                               a
        e   Q  Q  Q  Q                              i                               i
        _   t  t  t  t                              e                               d
        I   r  r  r  r                              n                               _
        D   1  2  3  4                              t                               B
                                                    s                               y

      120265  .  .  . 25 Mitleid International 90%, Save the Baby Animals 10% Cash or Check
      120267 15 15 15 15 Disaster Assist, Inc. 80%, Cancer Cures, Inc. 20%    Payroll Deduction
      120269 20 20 20 20 Cancer Cures, Inc. 10%, Cuidadores Ltd. 90%          Payroll Deduction
      120270 20 10  5  . AquaMissions International 10%, Child Survivors 90%  Cash or Check
      120271 20 20 20 20 Cuidadores Ltd. 80%, Mitleid International 20%        Payroll Deduction
```

```
                    ORION.EMPLOYEE_ORGANIZATION Table

        Employee_                                       Manager_
            ID      Job_Title            Department         ID

        120101    Director              Sales Management  120261
        120102    Sales Manager         Sales Management  120101
        120103    Sales Manager         Sales Management  120101
        120104    Administration Manager Administration    120101
        120105    Secretary I           Administration    120101
```

```
                        ORION.EMPLOYEE_PAYROLL Table

                  Employee_           Birth_   Employee_  Employee_  Marital_
    Employee_ID    Gender   Salary     Date    Hire_Date  Term_Date   Status   Dependents

        120101       M      163040     6074     15887        .          S          0
        120102       M      108255     3510     10744        .          O          2
        120103       M       87975    -3996      5114        .          M          1
        120104       F       46230    -2061      7671        .          M          1
        120105       F       27110     5468     14365        .          S          0
```

ORION.EMPLOYEE_PHONES Table

Employee_ID	Phone_Type	Phone_Number
120101	Home	+61(2)5555-1849
120101	Work	+61(2)5551-0001
120102	Home	+61(3)5555-9700
120102	Work	+61(3)5551-0002
120103	Home	+61(2)5555-3998

ORION.ORDER_FACT Table

Customer_ID	Employee_ID	Street_ID	Order_Date	Delivery_Date	Order_ID
63	121039	9260125492	11JAN2003	11JAN2003	1230058123
5	99999999	9260114570	15JAN2003	19JAN2003	1230080101
45	99999999	9260104847	20JAN2003	22JAN2003	1230106883
41	120174	1600101527	28JAN2003	28JAN2003	1230147441
183	120134	1600100760	27FEB2003	27FEB2003	1230315085

Order_Type	Product_ID	Quantity	Total_Retail_Price	CostPrice_Per_Unit	Discount
1	220101300017	1	$16.50	$7.45	.
2	230100500026	1	$247.50	$109.55	.
2	240600100080	1	$28.30	$8.55	.
1	240600100010	2	$32.00	$6.50	.
1	240200200039	3	$63.60	$8.80	.

ORION.PRICE_LIST Table

Product_ID	Start_Date	End_Date	Unit_Cost_Price	Unit_Sales_Price	Factor
210200100009	09JUN2007	31DEC9999	$15.50	$34.70	1.00
210200100017	24JAN2007	31DEC9999	$17.80	$40.00	1.00
210200200023	04JUL2007	31DEC9999	$8.25	$19.80	1.00
210200600067	27OCT2007	31DEC9999	$28.90	$67.00	1.00
210200600085	28AUG2007	31DEC9999	$17.85	$39.40	1.00

```
                              ORION.PRODUCT_DIM Table

                           Product_
   Product_ID   Product_Line      Category      Product_Group    Product_Name

   220101300017  Clothes & Shoes  Clothes       T-Shirts         Toncot Beefy-T Emb T-Shirt
   230100500026  Outdoors         Outdoors      Outdoor Gear     Trekking Tent
   220200300082  Clothes & Shoes  Shoes         Tracker Shoes    Indoor Handbold Special Shoes
   240600100080  Sports           Swim Sports   Bathing Suits    Sharky Swimming Trunks
   240600100010  Sports           Swim Sports   Bathing Suits    Goggles, Assorted Colours

   Supplier_
   Country      Supplier_Name            Supplier_ID

     US         A Team Sports                3298
     GB         Prime Sports Ltd              316
     US         3Top Sports                  2963
     US         Dolphin Sportswear Inc      16292
     US         Nautlius SportsWear Inc      6153
```

```
                              ORION.QTR1_2007 Table

                     Order_                        Order_     Delivery_
            Order_ID  Type    Customer_ID           Date       Date

            1241054779   3            24         02JAN2007   05JAN2007
            1241063739   1            89         03JAN2007   04JAN2007
            1241066216   1           171         04JAN2007   04JAN2007
            1241086052   3            53         06JAN2007   09JAN2007
            1241147641   1            53         13JAN2007   13JAN2007
```

```
                              ORION.QTR2_2007 Table

                   Order_                                Order_      Delivery_
          Order_ID  Type   Employee_ID   Customer_ID      Date        Date

         1241895594   1       121051           56       05APR2007   09APR2007
         1241909303   0     99999999        46966       07APR2007   08APR2007
         1241930625   3     99999999           27       09APR2007   14APR2007
         1241977403   1       120152          171       15APR2007   15APR2007
         1242012259   1       121040           10       18APR2007   12APR2007
```

```
                            ORION.SALES Table

              First_     Last_                                    Birth_  Hire_
Employee_ID   Name       Name      Gender  Salary  Job_Title   Country  Date    Date

   120102     Tom        Zhou        M     108255  Sales Manager   AU    3510   10744
   120103     Wilson     Dawes       M      87975  Sales Manager   AU   -3996    5114
   120121     Irenie     Elvish      F      26600  Sales Rep. II   AU   -5630    5114
   120122     Christina  Ngan        F      27475  Sales Rep. II   AU   -1984    6756
   120123     Kimiko     Hotstone    F      26190  Sales Rep. I    AU    1732    9405
```

```
                          ORION.SALESSTAFF Table

                                                        Birth_     Emp_Hire_
   Employee_ID    Job_Title          Salary   Gender    Date        Date

      120121      Sales Rep. II     $26,600     F     02AUG1944   01JAN1974
      120134      Sales Rep. II     $28,015     M     06JUN1949   01JAN1974
      120151      Sales Rep. II     $26,520     F     21NOV1944   01JAN1974
      120154      Sales Rep. III    $30,490     F     20JUL1944   01JAN1974
      120166      Sales Rep. IV     $30,660     M     14JUN1944   01JAN1974

   Emp_Term_
     Date       Manager_ID     SSN           Employee_Name

        .         120102     42-8321-982    Elvish, Irenie
   30JUN2006      120102     905-76-7767    Shannan, Sian
        .         120103     798-16-4924    Phaiyakounh, Julianna
        .         120102     534-14-1428    Hayawardhana, Caterina
   31AUG2006      120102     878-79-9390    Nowd, Fadi
```

```
                            ORION.STAFF Table

                   Start_
   Employee_ID     Date      End_Date   Job_Title               Salary

      120101     01JUL2003   31DEC9999  Director                $163,040
      120102     01JUN1989   31DEC9999  Sales Manager           $108,255
      120103     01JAN1974   31DEC9999  Sales Manager            $87,975
      120104     01JAN1981   31DEC9999  Administration Manager   $46,230
      120105     01MAY1999   31DEC9999  Secretary I              $27,110

              Birth_     Emp_Hire_    Emp_Term_
   Gender     Date        Date         Date       Manager_ID

     M      18AUG1976   01JUL2003         .          120261
     M      11AUG1969   01JUN1989         .          120101
     M      22JAN1949   01JAN1974         .          120101
     F      11MAY1954   01JAN1981         .          120101
     F      21DEC1974   01MAY1999         .          120101
```

Appendix B Index

NOSTIMER option, 8-4
NOT EXISTS condition, 4-33
NOT NULL integrity constraint, 7-53
NUMBER option, 8-5
numeric functions, 2-25–2-26
   CEIL, 3-19
   FLOOR, 3-19
   FREQ, 3-19
   INT, 3-19
   MAX, 3-19
   MEAN, 3-19
   MIN, 3-19
   NMISS, 3-19
   ROUND, 3-19
   STD, 3-19
   SUM, 3-15–3-17, 3-19
   VAR, 3-19

O

ON clause, 5-18, 5-21
operators, 2-38–2-39
   CONTAINS, 9-4
   JOIN, 5-21
   LIKE, 9-4
options
   DOUBLE, 8-5
   DQUOTE=, 3-10
   ERRORSTOP, 8-58
   FEEDBACK, 2-13, 2-15, 8-59
   FLOW=, 8-5, 8-7–8-10
   FORMAT=, 3-7
   FULLSTIMER, 8-60
   FULLSTIMER system, 8-58
   IDXNAME=, 9-11
   IDXWHERE=, 9-11
   INOBS=, 8-4, 8-11, 8-58
   LABEL=, 3-7
   MSGLEVEL=, 9-5
   NOEXEC, 8-58
   NOPRINT, 8-37
   NOREMERGE, 3-21
   NOSTIMER, 8-4
   NUMBER, 8-5
   OUTOBS=, 8-4, 8-12, 8-58
   PRESERVE_COL_NAMES, 8-20
   PRESERVE_TAB_NAMES, 8-20
   PRINT, 8-5
   SQLREMERGE, 3-21
   STIMER, 8-4, 8-60
   STIMER SQL, 8-58

   SYMBOLGEN, 8-35
   testing and performance, 8-58–8-63
ORDER BY clause, 3-4–3-6, 5-26
   DESC keyword, 3-4
Orion Star Sports & Outdoors, 1-4–1-5
outer joins, 5-5, 5-19–5-23, 5-25
   comparing with inner joins, 5-20
   determining left and right table, 5-22
   full, 5-6, 5-20, 5-23
   left, 5-6, 5-20–5-22
   right, 5-6, 5-20, 5-23
OUTER UNION operator, 6-6
OUTOBS= option, 8-4, 8-12, 8-58
Output Delivery System (ODS), 2-3

P

performance
   benchmarking, 8-60
performance statistics
   benchmarking, 8-62
   macros, 8-62
populating a table, 7-41–7-42
PRESERVE_COL_NAMES option, 8-20
PRESERVE_TAB_NAMES option, 8-20
PRIMARY KEY integrity constraint, 7-53
PRINT option, 8-5
PRINT procedure, 3-27
PUT function, 8-45

Q

queries, 4-3–4-5
   complex, 5-41–5-48
query expression, 7-46
query output
   enhancing, 3-7–3-10

R

RESET statement, 2-10–2-11, 8-6
   SQL procedure, 2-10
right joins, 5-20, 5-23
ROLLBACK statement, 7-57
ROUND function, 3-19

S

SAS data sets, 1-14
SAS date values, 2-24
SAS Help facility, 1-5–1-6
SAS macro language
   overview, 8-29–8-30